Midnight Marquee's HORROR MOVIE SCRAPBOOK

1930s

Vol. 1

Copyright © 2017 Gary J. and Susan Svehla
Interior layout: Susan Svehla
Cover design: A. Susan Svehla

Midnight Marquee Press, Inc., Gary J. Svehla and A. Susan Svehla do not assume any responsibility for the accuracy, completeness, topicality or quality of the information in this book. All views expressed or material contained within are the sole responsibility of the author.

Without limiting the rights under copyright reserved above, no part of this publication may be reproduced, stored in or introduced into a retrieval system, or transmitted, in any form, or by any means (electronic, mechanical, photocopying, recording or otherwise), without the prior written permission of the copyright owner or the publishers of the book.

ISBN 13: 978-1-936168-74-3
Library of Congress Catalog Card Number 2017908616
Manufactured in the United States of America

First Printing by Midnight Marquee Press, Inc., June 2017

To the past, current and future lovers of
the true golden oldies,
the horror films of the 1930s

A Word from the Publishers

Midnight Marquee Press, Inc. has published over 120 books, most on classic movies and moviemakers. Over the years we have spent many hours doing research for many of those titles. We are fascinated by the way these films were seen at the time. So, since you can only do so many articles or chapters on *Frankenstein*, we can do something new—based on something old. We hope movie fans will be as intrigued as we were by the original newspaper clippings, ads, photos and just strange items found in the 1930s newspapers, magazines, and pressbooks. We wish some of the images were easier to read, but we did our best to clean them up as much as possible.

This volume took much longer to do than we had anticipated. And we had too much material for just one volume. So we plan to do a 1930s Volume 2 before moving on to the 1940s.

1931

Genre films released in 1931

Dracula
Spanish Dracula
Svengali (in Vol. 2)
Frankenstein
Dr. Jekyll and Mr. Hyde

Dracula

Released Feb. 12, 1931
(New York)
Wide Feb. 14, 1931

THE air at Universal City is thick with rumors about the contemplated productions of "Frankenstein" and Poe's "Murders in the Rue Morgue." The real news, though, is limited to the announcement that Bela Lugosi, who played the title rôle in "Dracula," will have the lead in Mary Shelley's macabre story and probably also in the Poe mystery.

From Two Wide-Apart Rialtos

BOSTON, Jan. 22.

FOR the moment the theatrical wonder in this town is "Dracula." Of course, New York will not understand, and explanations are in order. In the first place, "Dracula" is housed in the Lyric, which shelter passes locally for death warrant to any play consigned to it. The warrant merely waits the signature of the public, heretofore quickly added. But "Dracula" is now running out a second week with a well-developed seat sale for two more. Better still, at week-ends it is selling out the Lyric to the last seat, while the nightly box office sheet keeps the Messrs. Shuberts' accountants wide-eyed.

As Boston usually takes mystery or "horror" plays, they depart after a first stay, never to return. "Dracula," however, is making its fourth visit in three seasons and rounding out a grand total of twelve weeks as though as it were the regular thing in the regular way. There are habitués who have seen it almost as many times and still get their goose-flesh. They say, also, that the present were-wolf baron, Courtney White, outdoes his predecessors. All of which is respectfully submitted as a note on the habits and customs of this hinterland with the theatre. Generally it is catching up with the theatrical times. This week the "resident company" at the Copley is giving it "The Racket" and there are discovering audiences.

An ancient superstition, which claims that "undead" persons, hovering strangely between life and death, leave their graves on a certain night of each year, forms the basis of "Dracula," the hair-raising Universal drama which will continue thru Tuesday at the Cecil theater. This old belief still persists in certain parts of Europe, and as the fateful night approaches abject terror seizes the peasants of the district, who cease all activities at sundown and securely bolt all doors and windows. Wolves howl in the hills—and it is claimed that these animals are in reality vampires who are able to change themselves at will into either wolves or bats, and thus gain access to places where a human being could not penetrate. Count Dracula is the strange vampire of this startling story, and a trail of terror and death results from his horrible influence. The picture has been produced with such sincerity and such artistry that the spectator is apt to forget for the presented for the last time Monday evening at the Iowa theater.

HOLLYWOOD, Jan. 13 (AP).— Word goes around in film circles that there are probably some 500 players, writers, technical advisers and members of production staffs that may be subjects of investigation in the Federal drive against illegal entry of persons from foreign lands.

However, no concern is expressed by the film executives and the foreign stars here. It was explained that the foreign stars being featured in Hollywood-made films are all under contract, such contracts being known by the Immigrant Service and permission legally provided for these foreign stars to remain in America for the term of such contracts.

Among such players are those from England including George Arliss, Clive Brooks, Ronald Colman, Colin Clive, Leslie Howard and Elissa Landi. France is represented by Maurice Chevalier, Ireland by Maureen O'Sullivan and Una O'Connor, Germany by Marlene Dietrich, Sweden by Nils Asther and Hungary by Bela Lugosi.

It is in the ranks of minor players, those not under contract, and the multitude of individuals attracted by the industry, some as writers, some technical advisers, some on production staffs, and the great majority waiting for the crumbs of an occasional share in the industry's activities, in which the Federal investigators may find a field for inquiry.

"DRACULA" AT RIALTO

HELEN CHANDLER, BELA LUGOSI
in a scene from "Dracula," strange drama that is the current attraction at the Fox Rialto.

Brooklyn

ALBEE Albee Sq. TRi.5-2000 — NOW

"3 Star picture—we enjoyed it."—News.

DRACULA

"CAN BOAST OF BEING THE BEST OF MYSTERY FILMS."—N. Y. Times.
and 5 STAR RKO Vaudeville Show
Vivacious Star of "No, No, Nanette"
BERNICE CLAIRE
IN PERSON
COUNT BERNIVICI
& 14 SYMPHONIC GIRLS
EDDIE PARDO
PILETTO—AL NORMAN & RIO

EINSTEINS SEE HOW MOVIES ARE MADE

Hollywood, Calif.— (AP)—Leaving the problems of relativity in their Pasadena bungalow, Dr. and Frau Albert Einstein came here yesterday to see how motion pictures are made.

They saw a talkie in the making and viewed the picture "All Quiet on the Western Front," which was barred in Germany.

The Einsteins were guests of Carl Laemmle, president of Universal Pictures, also a native of Germany.

BETTER MOVIES MOVEMENT SPONSORED BY CLUB WOMEN

"Making 1931 a year of good movies." This was the New Year message dispatched today by Mrs. Thomas G. Winter, spokesman between all the organized women of the United States and the motion picture industry, to millions of organized women in all parts of the nation.

"When we say 'good' we do not mean merely innocuous," said Mrs. Winter. "Let's take a dictionary definition of 'good'—having kindly social qualities.' To those of us who are in ruts, dull; to those of us who feel shut in; to those of us who are having a hard time, give pictures that have colorful, human qualities, and a bit of thrill, and above all, clean, spontaneous laughter. Entertainment is what pictures are for. There are a good many movies that have one of those qualities. Once in a while, one comes along that has all of them. It is up to us in our home town to make these the pictures that succeed."

Mrs. W. W. Green, Los Angeles, motion picture advisor for the California Federation of Women's Clubs said, "Better movies is one of the direct challenges to organized womenhood today. Are we going to accept or disregard it?

"Organized groups are apt to get into ruts in their work by continually following a stereotyped program. Not only does the challenge of better movies face organized women, but also that of our present economic problem. Such an economic condition as now exists should never be permitted to occur again and much can be done by organized women toward its prevention."

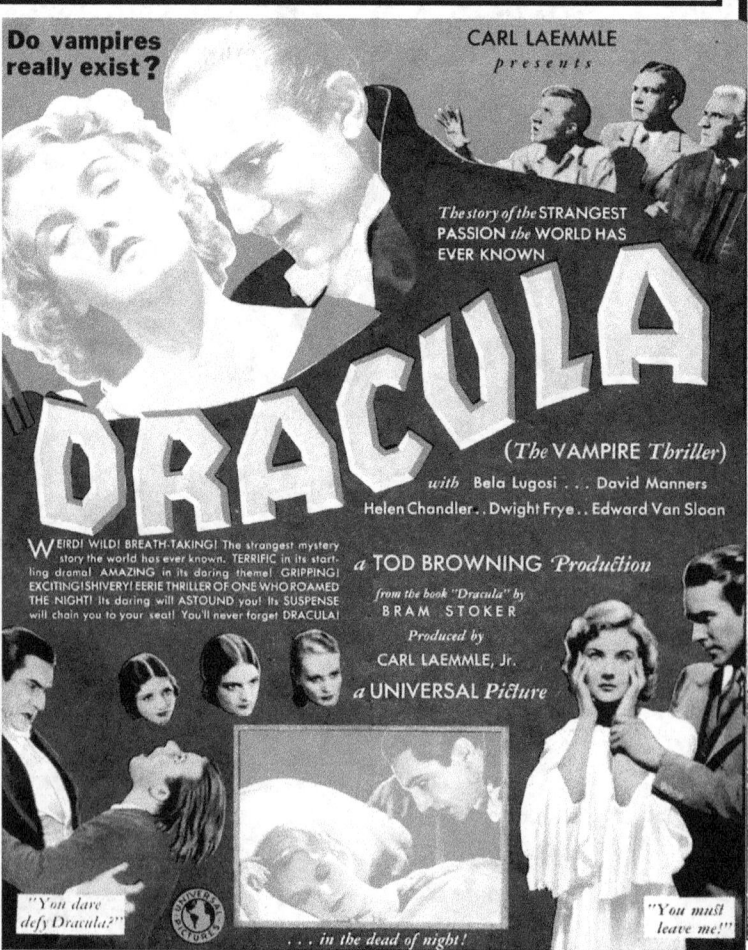

You'll Never Know
You'll Never Believe It

? READ BELOW

UNTIL You Join the THRIFTY SHOW-WISE CROWDS That Now Have the FAUROT HABIT

Here's Why The Faurot Is Now Lima's Busy Theatre

1. QUALITY TALKIES
2. MANY GOOD COMEDIES & NOVELTIES.
3. PATHE NEWS
4. PERFECT SOUND.
5. FAUROT COMFORT
6. VALUE YOU'VE NEVER IMAGINED POSSIBLE.

START TODAY !
LEARN WHY !

Everybody Is Now Going to the Home-Like HOME OF SOUND

FAUROT

EVERY DAY Including Sunday
1-6 P. M. **10c**
6-7..15c 7-10..20c
Extra! Extra!
EVERY MON.-FRI. SAT.
—at—
9 O'CLOCK
Stage Shows You'll Like—

Children and the Movies

By GARRY C. MYERS, PH. D.
Head Division Parental Education, Cleveland College, Western Reserve University.

PARENTS BURN up a lot of energy condemning movies in general, and a few in particular. In the meanwhile most of them let their children go without much restraint, and slip to the theater themselves about as often as they find it convenient to do so.

I have a notion that most parental heat about movies has been expended off the vital factor.

Dr. Myers

No doubt some pictures are entirely harmful for children, through unwholesome suggestions which lead to undesirable conduct. Nevertheless, this aspect of the movies has perhaps been exaggerated. Children, particularly adolescents, pretty generally take the attitude: "Well, that's just a movie stunt!" They come to expect certain performances which they consider as unreal, and accept them more or less as mere jokes. Even the bizarre and impossible so frequently presented are no doubt interpreted by them as mere movie tricks.

Suggestions of relaxing marital relationship clearly appear to be harmful when exposed forever to the adolescent. But the greatest harm is not to them, I do believe, but to the young and middle-aged married couples, an item which seems to have been wholly overlooked by critics. Wives and husbands who live pretty closely in accordance with convention and standard of marital fidelity get a lot of suggestions from the movies which had never occurred to them before.

For the young child under ten or twelve the movies may be overexciting, contributing to disturbing dreams and general nervousness. The sleep he loses while attending, the habits of neglecting school work, and the habit of going, and seeking canned excitement, in addition to exposure to communicable diseases, are all indescribable. Wise parents set definite age limits for first attending movies in the public theaters. Most children go much too young and far too often.

How absurd that school children should be allowed to frequent the moving picture theaters on evenings before school days. Parents who are concerned about the school success of their children are strict about these matters.

Parents find it easy to limit attendance by their children at the movies by naming definite nights and a definite number limit per month or school term.

Schools and churches are in places doing a good deal to encourage better movies, some by showing good pictures in the church or school; others by directing children to those that are best and keeping them away from the less desirable ones. Too bad it is, that groups of children attending shows in schools and churches so often have little supervision. Sometimes bedlam reigns when the noise proves exceedingly nerve racking. We will have better movies when we really want them, when we and our children attend only those most wholesome and avoid the poorer ones. The trouble is that we parents often get a sneaking satisfaction from those we would not like our children to observe. We enjoy the risque more than we are willing to admit. Although we can easily fool ourselves that we are safe in any situation, there doubtless are a number of movies not so wholesome for us as we think. Maybe I am wrong. Surely we need recreation, and for many parents the movies, most of them, are very wholesome. There are times when for us to see one brings more happiness indirectly to our children than for them to see it themselves.

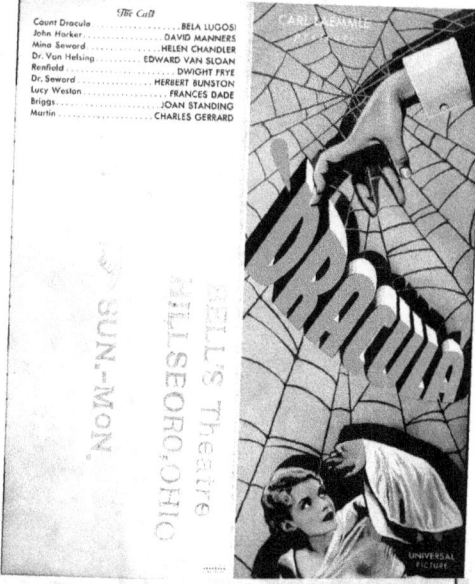

MYSTERY STORY AT FOX-RIALTO IS UNCANNY ONE

'Dracula,' Current Feature, Built Around Strange Human Vampires.

Uncanny mystery—the most unusual probably ever recorded on the screen—greeted large audiences at the Fox-Rialto yesterday when "Dracula" opened a four-day engagement.

Those audiences found "Dracula" a sensationally different, weird and startling story of life after death, of strange human vampires of legend, who rise from their graves at night and bring terror to the hours of darkness.

Count Dracula, the main character in the strange drama, apparently is a polished gentleman, but in reality is a vampire whose horrible attacks reduce his victims to madness or death.

The action action takes place in an ancient castle in Transylvania and in England with the series of hair-raising events reaching an amazing climax.

The title role is portrayed in stirring fashion by Bela Lugosi, famous European stage star. David Manners, Helen Chandler and others appear in the cast.

"Dracula" is a play that is so different that some of the biggest crowds of weeks will probably see its amazing ramifications.

The program includes several short features, among them another Johnny Farrell golf demonstration.

SUPER-SHOWMANSHIP POSTERS TO PUT OVER THE GREATEST THRILLER OF THE CENTURY IN A RECORD-SMASHING WAY!

PRINTED IN COLOR COMBINATIONS THAT THROW AN EERIE SPELL!

PAPER THAT LURES LIKE THE VAMPIRE HIMSELF --IT WILL GET 'EM!

TWENTY FOUR SHEET

MIRACULOUS!

MYSTERIOUS!

ONE SHEET "A" ONE SHEET "B" ONE SHEET "C"

SEE INSIDE BACK COVER FOR OTHER STYLES POSTERS AND CARDS!

THREE-SHEET "D" SIX SHEET THREE-SHEET "E"

 TWO STYLES OF WINDOW CARDS! SEE INSIDE BACK COVER!

50 Enormous Bats in New Mystery Film

Fifty enormous bats, those strange flapping creatures of the night, were recently taken to Universal City for use in a number of scenes of "Dracula," the amazing drama which comes to the Fox theatre on Tuesday and Wednesday, with a cast which includes the famous Bela Lugosi, the original Dracula of the stage play.

The bats were captured in a great cave in Nevada by three residents of Las Vegas, who made an expedition into the nearby hill region when an emissary of Universal arrived in town with the strangest order ever delivered into the dessert country.

It is interesting to note that for two months Universay City qualified as the only place in the world where a large number of giant bats were being maintained in captivity.

In addition to Lugosi, the cast of "Dracula" includes Helen Chandler, David Manners, Edward Van

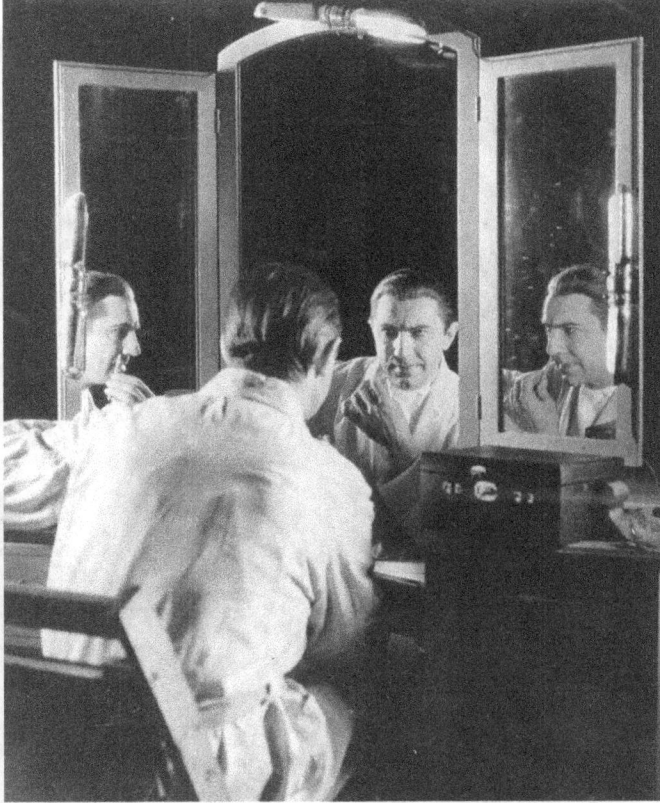

LADIES—

SPECIAL GUEST MATINEE MONDAY AT 2:30

ANN HARDING in "EAST LYNNE"

Clip the coupon appearing elsewhere in today's Chronicle and bring a guest FREE by paying one admission.

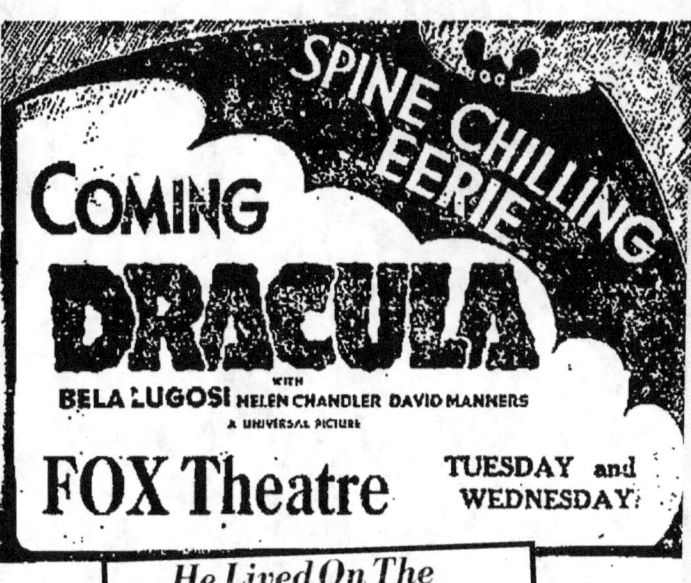

EXHIBITORS' CAMPAIGN

'HUNCHBACK' AS TALKER WITH BELA LUGOSI

Universal is giving serious consideration to making the "Hunchback" into a talker special. Bela Lugosi is chiefly responsible, that actor being figured the next best to Lon Chaney who played the title role in the silent version. The picture was U's greatest money maker.

"Notre Dame" as a talker will probably be at least 50% new and more than that unless a continuity can be devised which would lend itself to proper editing.

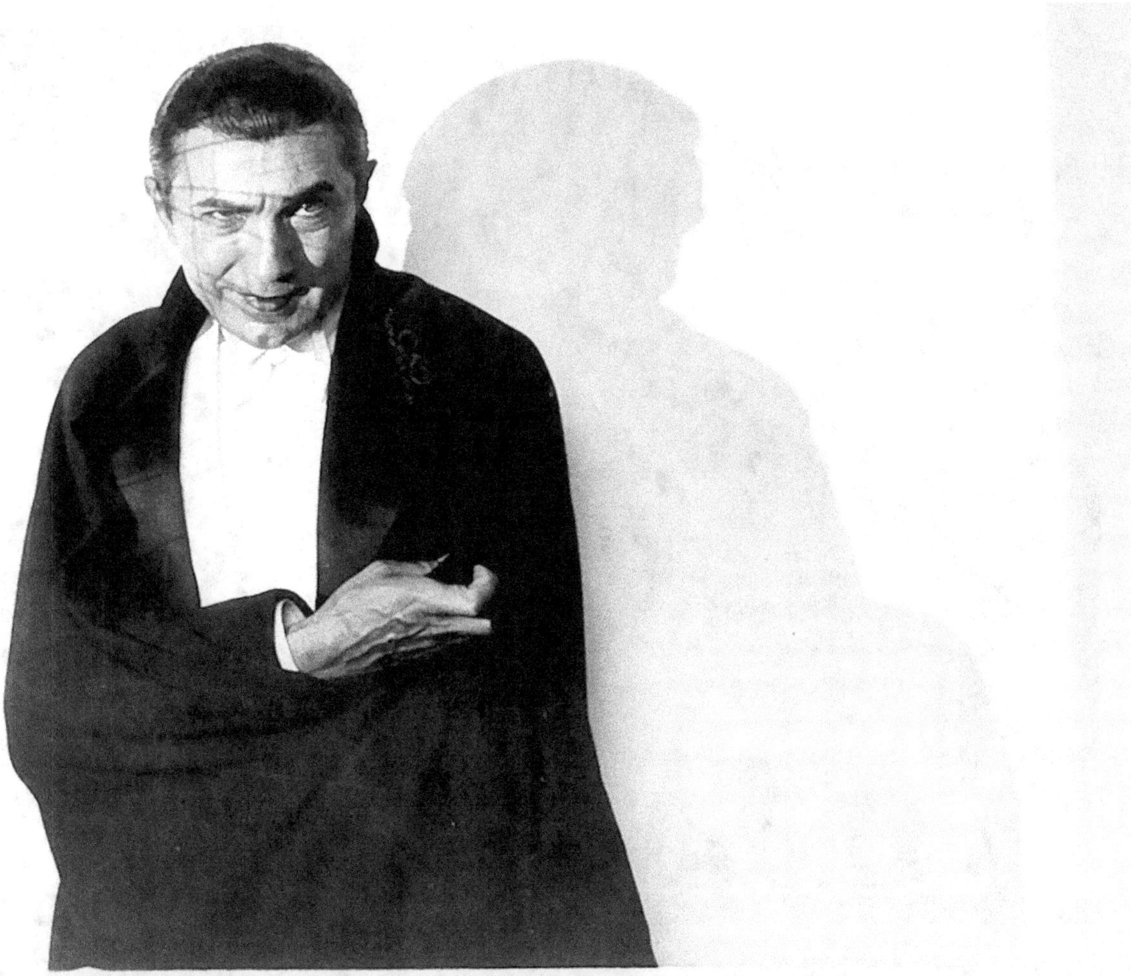

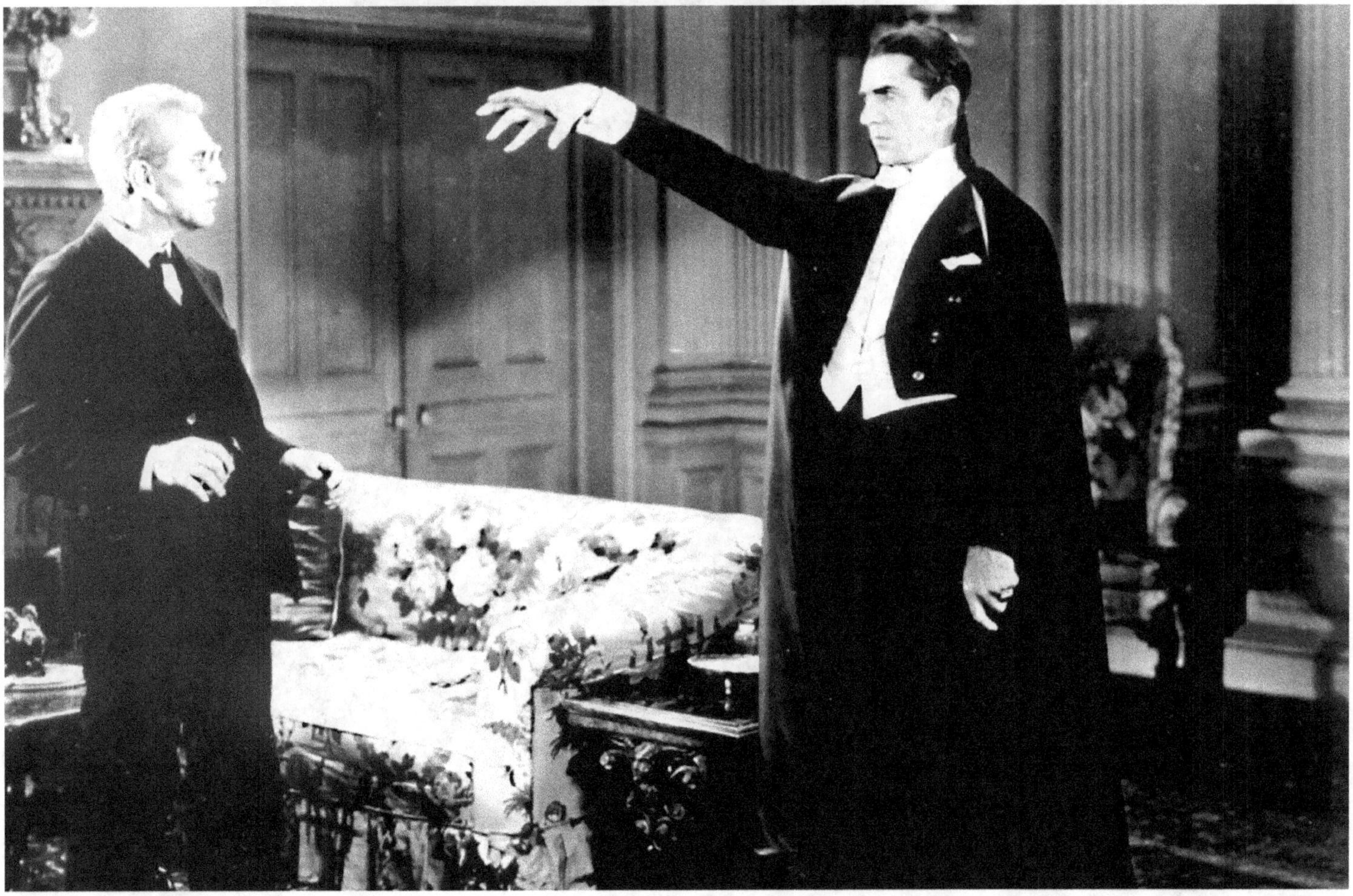

CARL LAEMMLE presents DRACULA the vampire thriller

...Out of the Cobwebby Darkness
of an age-old castle heavy with the dust of centuries, comes DRACULA, the terrible, the fascinator, the destroyer... to roam the night for his weird, wild, breath-taking adventures!

"You dare defy Dracula?"

Without fear of contradiction —the most gripping, exciting, amazing, spine-creeping THING ever to reach the screen! "DRACULA" has held two generations in fascination and terror! Its daring will ASTOUND you! Its SUSPENSE will chain you to your seat! You'll never forget DRACULA!

Do Vampires Really Exist?
Do they leave their prisons in the dark hours, reaching out with their fiery fingers to find new victims—MEN, who seek beautiful girls—WOMEN, who drive men to madness and worse...?

It will haunt you!
It will chill you!
It will thrill you!
YOU WILL LOVE "DRACULA"

TERRIFIC IN THRILLS AND BREATH-TAKING DRAMA   WEIRD—SHIVERY—SHADOWY—EERIE SENSATION!

at the Biltmore, next week, with the advance sale reported as encouraging. The other is a mystery play announced as "Murdered Alive," with Bela Lugosi, who has come to be a great local favorite, doing the murdering. On close inspection the play gives evidence of being "Black Tower" under a slightly more chilling title. The theatre is the Carthay Circle, which has shifted from pictures to plays several times this season, and which has been dark since an ill-fated attempt was made to put on "Sons o' Guns" there.

STATE BLUE LAWS UNDER FIRE

SHEBOYGAN APPROVES---

BETTER SHOWS!
GREATER VARIETY!
LOWER PRICES!

NOW IN EFFECT!

15c 12 to 1 P. M. Daily, including Sunday.

25c 1 to closing.

35c 1 to Closing Sunday.

Kiddies, A Dime Any Time.

Midnight Pre-View every Saturday of Sunday's feature — 2 shows for the price of one.

Five New Shows Weekly—A new show on Sunday, Monday, Wednesday, Friday and Saturday.

Perfect Sound   *Perfect Pictures*

Today Only!
MARILYN MILLER "SUNNY"

Majestic

U HAS HORROR CYCLE ALL TO SELF

Hollywood, April 7.

With "Dracula" making money at the box office for Universal, other studios are looking for horror tales —but very squeamishly. Producers are not certain whether nightmare pictures have a box office pull, or whether "Dracula" is just a freak.

To date, no other studio has tried to follow in U's steps, one of the few occasions when a hit wasn't followed by a cycle of similar pictures.

Following "Dracula," U will make "Murders in the Rue Morgue"; then "Frankenstein," mid-Victorian melo of a medical student who finds the secret of life and chemically creates a man. Bela Lugosi goes into the latter.

Universal has gone for the horror thing in the past, Carl Laemmle being one of the few to spend money on such stories.

THE CAST

Edward Van Sloan as DR. VAN HELSING | Herbert Bunston as DR. SEWARD | Helen Chandler as MINA SEWARD | Bela Lugosi as COUNT DRACULA | Dwight Frye as RENFIELD | Frances Dade as LUCY WESTON | David Manners as JOHN HARKER

FIRST—a best selling book!

THEN—a stage sensation!

NOW—one of the truly important achievements of the talking screen!

Coming to the

ROXY

Thursday Lincoln's Birthday Feb. 12

"DRACULA"

A UNIVERSAL PICTURE

A TOD BROWNING PRODUCTION   PRODUCED BY CARL LAEMMLE, JR.

Ride with a Winner

--- the only company in the business that is giving you Hit after HIT!

Take a look at these!

SEED now in its third big week at Rivoli, N. Y. and held over at Boyd Theatre, Philadelphia... held over at Paramount... held over at Keith Theatre, Boston... held over at State-Lake Theatre, Chicago... held over at Downtown Theatre, Detroit... held over in Indianapolis and just starting to go...

BAD SISTER better than average business all over the land

FATE first romantic story from the pen of Eric Maria Remarque, author of "All Quiet on the Western Front", "Wait for Fate Be Great".

UP FOR MURDER the best Lew Ayres picture since "All Quiet on the Western Front" now standing them up at the GLOBE, N. Y.

STRICTLY DISHONORABLE starring John Boles of "Seed" and Sidney Fox of "Bad Sister"... it set New York athrill with excitement and laughter for 65 weeks.

EX-BAD BOY starring Robert Armstrong... the fight manager of "Iron Man", beautiful Jean Arthur and Lola Lane.

LEW AYRES - IRON MAN top-notcher hitting the high spots getting the big money.

DRACULA world's greatest hold over picture still grabbing all the coin in sight wherever it plays.

The SHE WOLF now playing Broadway's ace house the RIALTO, the STANLEY, Philadelphia and WARNER'S, Pittsburgh.

Ride with UNIVERSAL and you ride with a winner!

HELD OVER EVERYWHERE

at RKO'S **GRANADA**
South Bend, Indiana

at **FOX ECKEL**
Syracuse, New York

at **ALHAMBRA**
Milwaukee, Wisconsin

at **RIALTO**
Washington, D.C.

...and look at this from Jack Alicoate's column in "Film Daily"

"Peeking out of our window we see <u>a line a mile long</u> waiting to see 'DRACULA' at the Roxy."

TOD BROWNING'S greatest production Presented by CARL LAEMMLE
Based on the stage play—adapted by Hamilton Deane and John Balderston from Bram Stoker's novel of the same name.

DRACULA

Bela Lugosi,
(of the original stage cast)
David Manners,
Helen Chandler,
(and the following players also of the original stage cast)
Dwight Frye
Edward Van Sloan
Herbert Bunston
and other well-known players

Produced by Carl Laemmle Jr

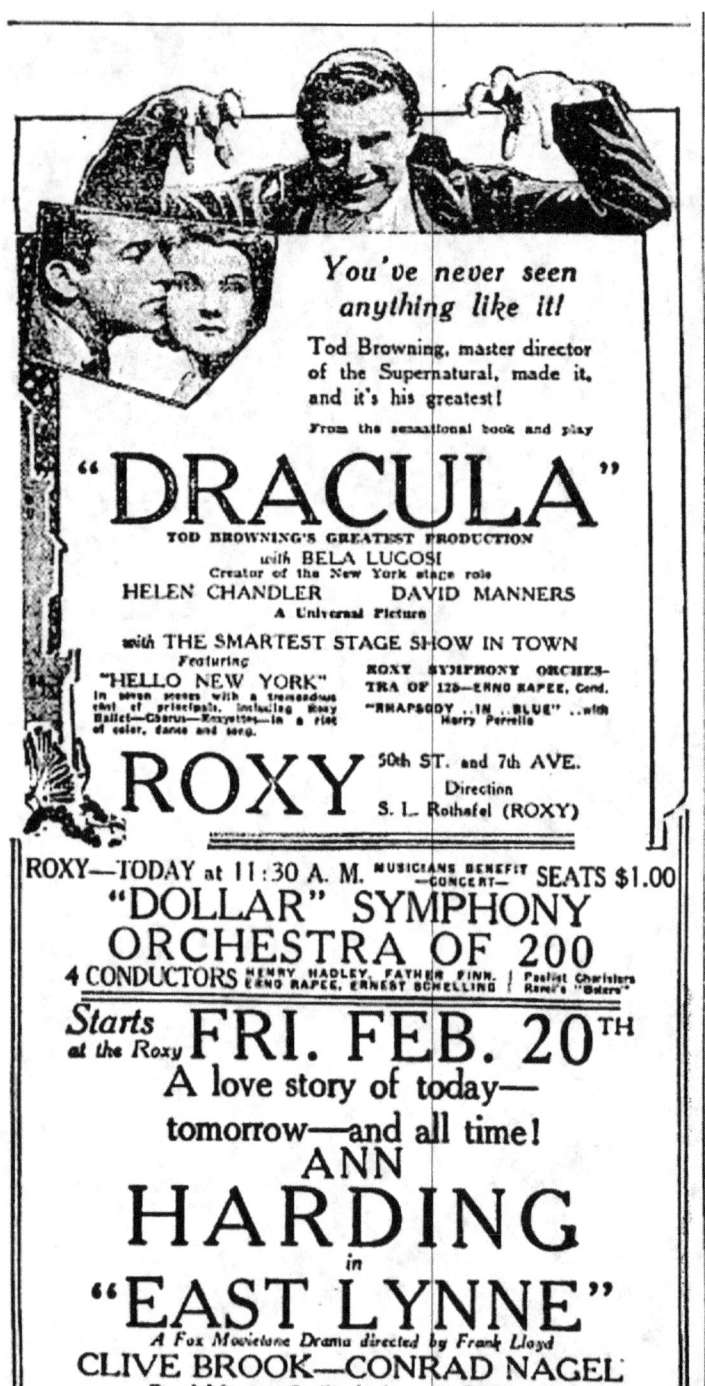

... and the story is the same country over .. DRACULA packs 'em in at ORPHEUM, PORTLAND .. DRACULA packs 'em in at MAJESTIC, DALLAS .. DRACULA packs 'em in at ORPHEUM, ST. LOUIS .. at the HENNEGIN, MEMPHIS .. held over at SOUTH BEND .. held over at SIOUX FALLS and doubles preceding week box-office receipts .. held over at WASHINGTON .. capacity business in ALBANY .. hold over in BALTIMORE .. in BROOKLYN .. in CLEVELAND .. in MILWAUKEE .. in MINNEAPOLIS .. in PHILADELPHIA .. in ROCHESTER .. in ST. PAUL .. breaks all house records at EMBOYD, FORT WAYNE .. at CAPITOL, MADISON .. at FOX COLLEGE, NEW HAVEN .. capacity in PITTSBURGH and PROVIDENCE .. "DRACULA" -- THE WORLD'S GREATEST HOLD OVER PICTURE!!

LUGOSI'S PASHY FAN MAIL

Male Vamp of "Dracula" Attracts Femmes

Hollywood, July 20.

That women as well as men fall for screen vampires, the femmes liking the type of vamp played by Bela Lugosi in "Dracula," is shown in the amount and kind of fan mail reaching Lugosi.

Actor's mail is from women who were intrigued by the romantic side of being kissed by a male vamp. Nearly all asked the question: "How does it feel to be kissed by a vampire?" Some gave their own opinions, most thinking it packed more thrill.

Many of the femme fans wanted to know what kind of a girl a he-vamp would like.

BECOME A VAMPIRE

ORDER YOUR EXCLUSIVE DO-IT-YOURSELF VAMPIRE KIT AND JOIN THE RANKS OF THE UNDEAD

HERE IS WHAT YOU GET:

- **CURSE OF THE UNDEAD**
  Horrifying secret instructions and incantations for changing a human into a VAMPIRE!
- **THE ORIGIN AND HISTORY OF VAMPIRES**
  A darkly enlightening theme by the world's leading authority on Vampirism — Prof. Raoul Kosatravich!
- **VAMPIRE FANGS**
  Realistic and frightening — They glow in the dark to help you track down victims at night!
- **YOUR OWN PERSONAL PET VAMPIRE BAT**
  Jet black, rubbery and life-like! No true Vampire should be without one!
- **SIX WALLET-SIZE PHOTOS OF THE MOST BLOOD-CURDLING VAMPIRES OF ALL TIME**
  as portrayed by
  BELA LUGOSI   CHRISTOPHER LEE
  DAVID PEEL   JOHN VAN EYSSEN

Only $1.00 ppd.

YOU CAN DO IT! You can drive everybody bats! YOU can become a Vampire! All you need is a little imagination, a little belief, and . . . our How-To-Do-It Vampire Kit! Then you, too, can become a horrible, foul, monstrous spawn of the Undead . . . a real Vampire, you lucky devil, you. The stakes are high, so don't let this rare opportunity to BE somebody slip away from you! Don't be a bloody fool . . . be a bloody Vampire and learn how to neck the easy way! Send now for your Easy-To-Do-It Vampire Kit! It can change your whole life . . . heh, heh, heh, heh, heh, heh, heh, heh, heh!

RUSH YOUR ORDER TODAY!

VICTOR SPECIALTIES, DEPT. mu-10
P.O. BOX 151, DERBY, CONN.   (No C.O.D.)

Enclosed is $1.00 (cash, check, money order)
Please rush me my DO-IT-YOURSELF VAMPIRE KIT

Name _____
Address _____
City _____ Zone ___ State _____

U's Full Program Set; Surprise of "Dracula"

Final approval of the Universal '31-'32 program, soon to be officially announced to the field, is 36 features, 50 two-reel subjects, 65 one-reelers, four serials, and 104 issues of the Talking Reporter.

On the strength of the reception of "Dracula" generally over the country, U will make sufficient provision of mystery specials on the coming season's program, planning three or four, of which a Frankenstein idea and "Waterloo Bridge" will be two.

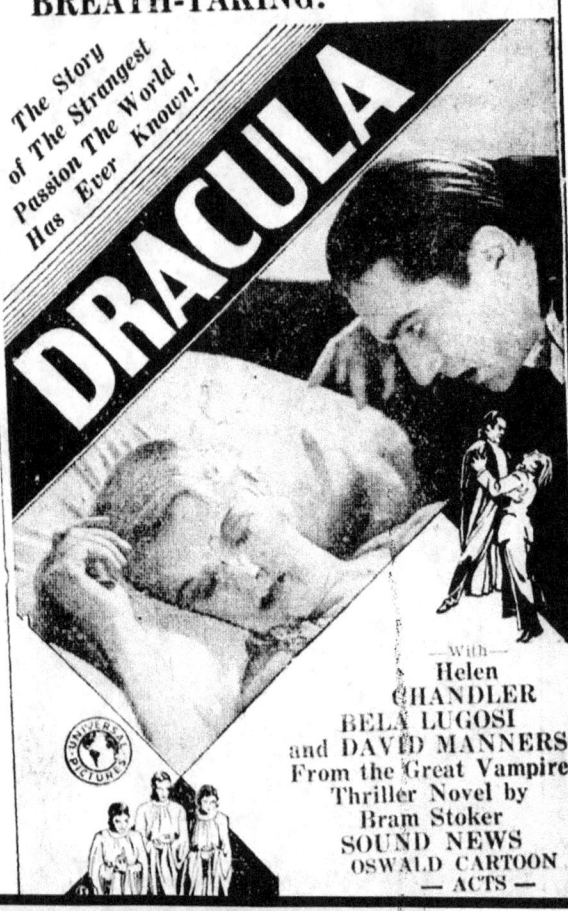

PICTURING "DRACULA"

It has long been the ambition of Tod Browning to produce "Dracula" on the screen, and but for the untimely death of Lon Chaney it is likely that Mr. Browning's ambition would have been realized, with Mr. Chaney in the rôle of Count Dracula, the "human vampire."

Mr. Browning is known as the creator of weird screen characters in fiction, and nearly all of them were brought to life by Mr. Chaney. "The Unholy Three," that strange story of thieves, was one of them; "The Unknown," dealing with the adventures of an armless man in a traveling gypsy circus, was another; and still another was "London After Midnight," in which, curiously, Chaney did appear in a story of human vampires impersonated by members of a vaudeville act.

This handling of the vampire legend was, of course, utterly dissimilar from that of "Dracula," which does not involve impersonation of the "undead" creatures, but depicts the "undead" themselves. Nevertheless, it is a curious coincidence that Browning and Chaney seemed to be preparing for what both intended should be the masterpiece of Chaney's career by this approach to the vampire legend.

Mr. Chaney was himself greatly interested in this strange superstition, and had read and re-read several times Bram Stoker's "Dracula." Both he and the director felt, however, that the picturization should be done in dialogue form. At this time, Mr. Chaney had never made a talking picture, and was reluctant to undertake one. It was Browning's hope that Mr. Chaney could be persuaded to play Count Dracula as a talker, but before the plan could be fully developed Chaney passed away.

Browning, however, did not give up his plan to bring "Dracula" to the screen. He suggested to Carl Laemmle Jr. that the picture be made, and then followed a long period of deliberation and consideration. Mr. Laemmle Jr. had his doubts about the wisdom of producing it.

It was Mr. Browning's view, nevertheless, that the conveying of the sense of terror to the audience could be done very largely through creation of atmosphere of the eerie. The stage production was limited in its locale to the London sequences, but the screen offers wider scope. The result is that Count Dracula's castle in Transylvania, the scene of the opening sequences of the picture, is shown on a large scale. The impression of the supernatural is conveyed by photography and staging.

Mr. Browning chose the talented German cameraman, Karl Freund, who was one of the first foreigners who started to perambulate the camera around the set to obtain effects. With the huge traveling crane which Carl Laemmle Jr. bought for the filming of "Broadway," Mr. Browning has, through the camera, essayed to disclose all kinds of disquieting vistas in the huge ruined castle of Count Dracula and the vast dark caverns of Carfax Abbey.

A great deal of work was necessary to make the sets have the appearance of age, desolation and ruin which Mr. Browning wanted. The monumental front of the castle was a combination of the expensive permanent sets which Universal already had standing.

The forbidding effect of the dungeons of Carfax Abbey is heightened by a staircase of 129 steps, built flush against the dungeon wall and without a balustrade. On this staircase much of the concluding action of the picture takes place, and in addition to disclosing the unusual proportions of the dungeon, it also serves a dramatic purpose in providing a fall for Renfield as the climax of his mad career. One of the most difficult things here was achieving the proper sound values, as Bela Lugosi, Dwight Frye and Helen Chandler walked or raced up and down this stairway.

Bela becomes a U.S. citizen!

Returns To Local Screen

'Dracula,' With Bela Lugosi In Starring Role, Shows At Capitol

A STRANGE, weird motion picture that outdoes all previous mysteries of the screen is "Dracula," the startling Universal production which opens an engagement at the Capitol theater today.

It may safely be said that this story is distinctly in a class by itself, and that its subject matter is absolutely unique among film productions. For "Dracula," which was adapted from Bram Stoker's famous novel of the same name, deals with human vampires, which ancient superstition describes as horrible "undead" creatures who rise from their graves at night.

Whether or not you believe in this major premise of the story, you will be enthralled by its presentation on the screen. The entire picture is done with such artistry and such compelling sincerity that while the story is unfolding on the screen one can hardly fail to regard its incidents as true representations of actual occurrences. It is as powerful in its effect on the emotions of the audience as any picture we can recall.

Great is the power of illusion. This was never better illustrated than in "Dracula."

On leaving the theater the audience knows that it cannot be true, and yet while the story is unfolding on the screen the spectators sit enthralled by its gruesome horrors. Their belief, temporary though it may be, is indicated by the powerful manner in which the picture affects them. Indeed, it is stated that no other motion picture ever made equals this in its hold on the emotions of the audience —which, perhaps, is a compliment to the artistry with which the film was produced.

Scenically, "Dracula" is magnificent, and its settings fully preserve the thrillingly uncanny atmosphere of the story.

The title role of Count Dracula is played with remarkable effect by Bela Lugosi, who created the same part in the stage play, and who delivers an arresting performance as the sinister vampire who is the central character of the story. Helen Chandler is altogether charming and capable in the principal feminine part, and David Manners, as her fiance, does the type of work which has made him one of the most popular of leading men.

AT THE PARAMOUNT

TODAY—Norma Shearer and Tyrone Power in "Marie Antoinette," with John Barrymore, Robert Morley, Anita Louise, Joseph Schildkraut, Gladys George and Henry Stephenson.

MONDAY AND TUESDAY—Janet Gaynor and Robert Montgomery in "Three Loves Has Nancy," with Franchot Tone, Guy Kibbee, Claire Dodd, Reginald Owen and Cora Witherspoon.

WEDNESDAY AND THURSDAY—The "Dead End" Kids in "Little Tough Guy," with Helen Parish, Robert Wilcox, Jackie Searle and Marjorie Main.

FRIDAY, SATURDAY AND SUNDAY—Sonja Henie in "My Lucky Star," with Richard Greene, Joan Davis, Cesar Romero, Buddy Ebsen, Arthur Treacher, George Barbier, Louise Hovick, Billy Gilbert and Patricia Wilder.

AT THE CAPITOL

TODAY AND MONDAY—Bela Lugosi in "Dracula," with David Manners, Helen Chandler, Dwight Frye, Edward Van Sloan and Herbert Bunston.

TUESDAY—"Mystery House," with Dick Purcell, Ann Sheridan, Anne Nagel and Anthony Averill.

WEDNESDAY—Joan Bennett and Randolph Scott in "The Texans," with May Robson, Walter Brennan, Robert Cummings, Raymond Hatton, Robert Barrat and Harvey Stephens.

THURSDAY—Warren William and Gail Patrick in "Wives Under Suspicion," with Constance Moore, William Lundigan and Ralph Morgan.

FRIDAY AND SATURDAY—Gene Autry in "Prairie Moon," with Smiley Burnette, Shirley Deane and Tommy Ryan.

Spanish Dracula

Released U.S. April 24, 1931

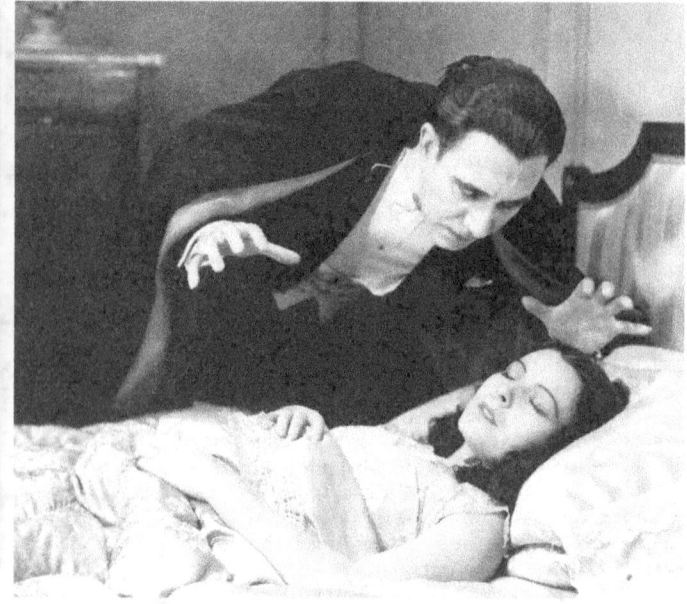

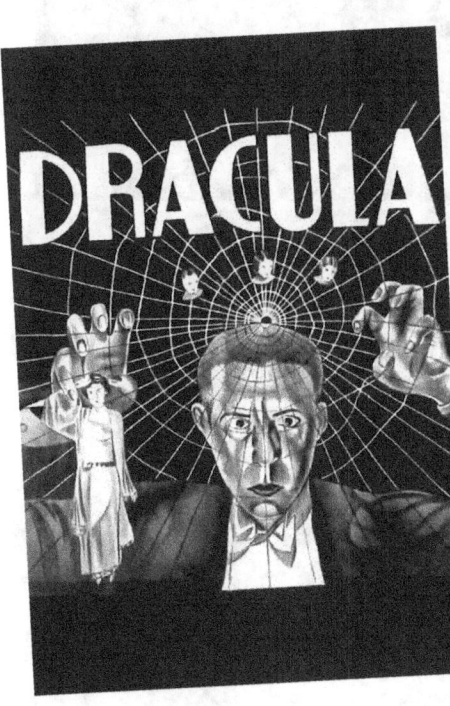

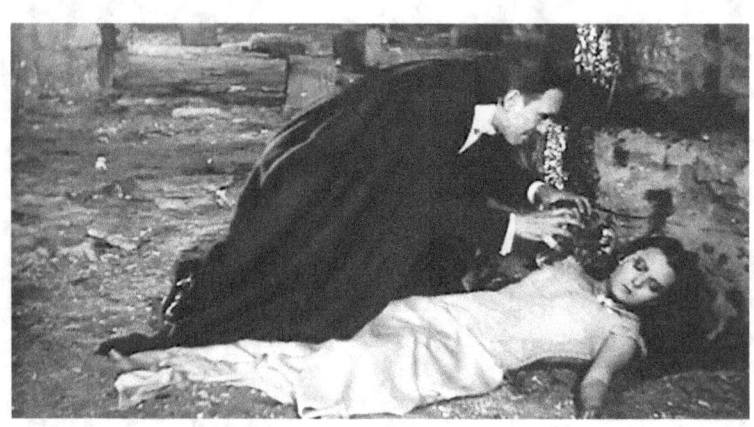

Buenos Aires, April 7.

With only one day to go before the Argentine film shop is closed down as a whole, the tax situation remains uncertain. No news has come from the government, which evidently isn't very much frightened over the closing threat. Film men are meeting daily in an effort to iron out the situation without too many headaches all around.

United Artists is releasing "Hell's Angels" here today (Tuesday); Fox is turning loose "The Big Trail" (Spanish), and U is also putting out a Spanish version of "Dracula." These are the last releases under the agreement passed by Argentine film men a week ago to completely close shop unless the government rebates the recent film tax bill.

Meantime an unusual situation has arisen, in that practically all newspaper advertising has stopped, with the papers retorting by stopping use of any text matter about pictures.

During the present week and the closing down, results of one kind or another are assured, with the next move necessarily coming from the government.

Lupita Tovar, la popularísima actriz mejicana, que aparece como dama joven en la cinta hispanoparlante "Carne de Cabaret", de Columbia Pictures.

Frankenstein

Released U.S. Nov. 21, 1931

The Woman's Angle

'**Frankenstein**' (Universal). Hoping to be horrified, adventuresome ladies will be lured to this picture by the tradition of its title plus its eerie exploitation. Expert dealings with the macabre will give them an even more thrilling time than they were hoping for.

U HAS HORROR CYCLE ALL TO SELF

Hollywood, April 7.

With "Dracula" making money at the box office for Universal, other studios are looking for horror tales—but very squeamishly. Producers are not certain whether nightmare pictures have a box office pull, or whether "Dracula" is just a freak.

To date, no other studio has tried to follow in U's steps, one of the few occasions when a hit wasn't followed by a cycle of similar pictures.

Following "Dracula," U will make "Murders in the Rue Morgue"; then "Frankenstein," mid-Victorian melo of a medical student who finds the secret of life and chemically creates a man. Bela Lugosi goes into the latter.

Universal has gone for the horror thing in the past, Carl Laemmle being one of the few to spend money on such stories.

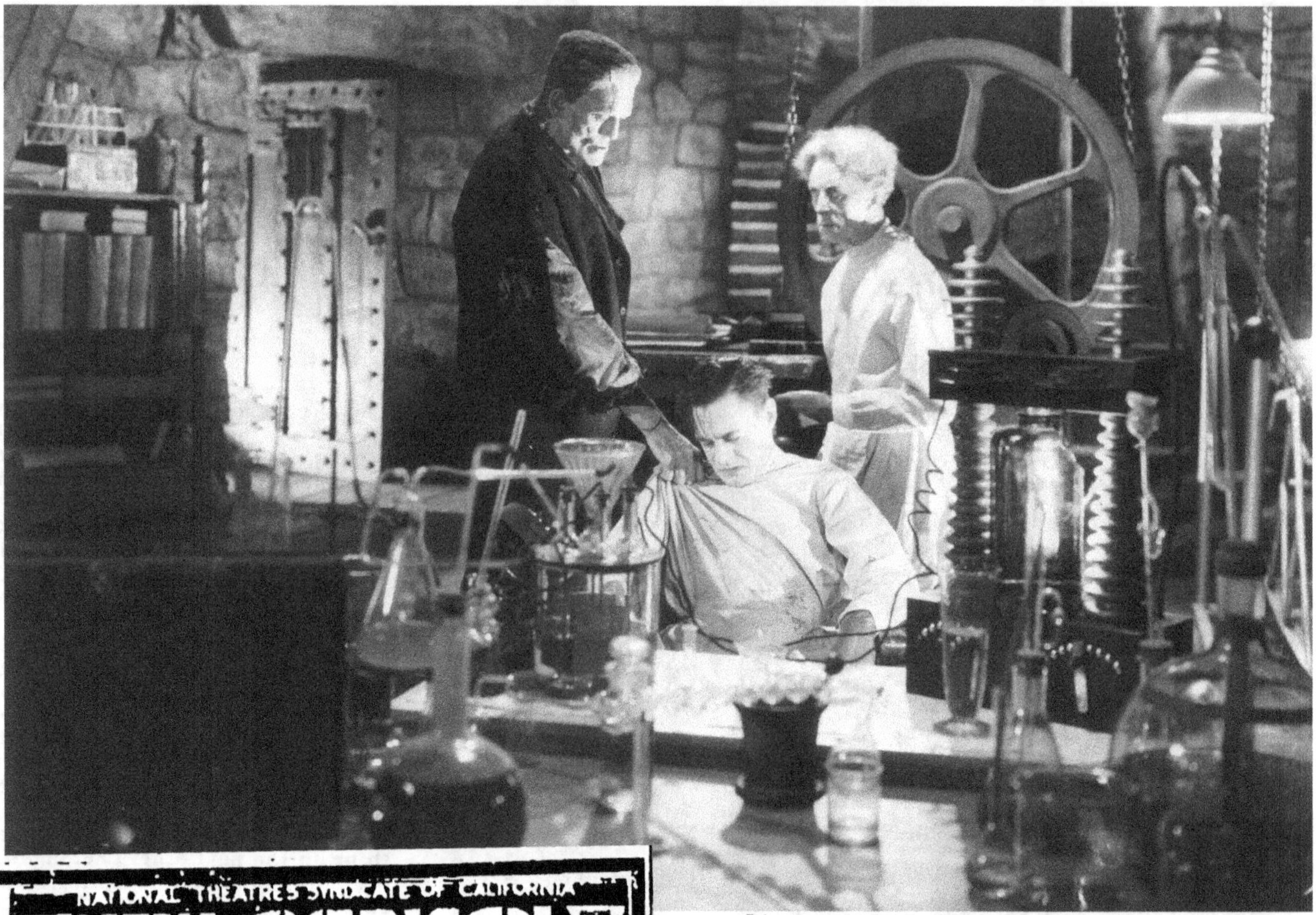

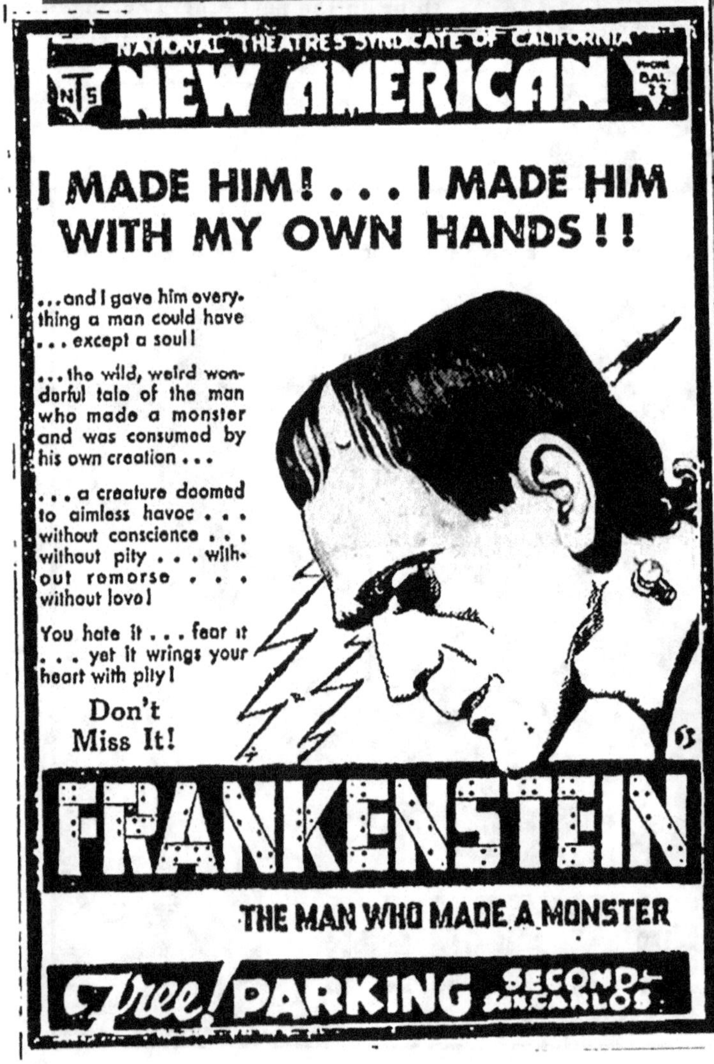

NATIONAL THEATRES SYNDICATE OF CALIFORNIA
NTS NEW AMERICAN PHONE BAL. 32
I MADE HIM! . . . I MADE HIM WITH MY OWN HANDS!!
. . . and I gave him everything a man could have . . . except a soul!
. . . the wild, weird wonderful tale of the man who made a monster and was consumed by his own creation . . .
. . . a creature doomed to aimless havoc . . . without conscience . . . without pity . . . without remorse . . . without love!
You hate it . . . fear it . . . yet it wrings your heart with pity!
Don't Miss It!
FRANKENSTEIN
THE MAN WHO MADE A MONSTER
Free! PARKING SECOND-SAN CARLOS

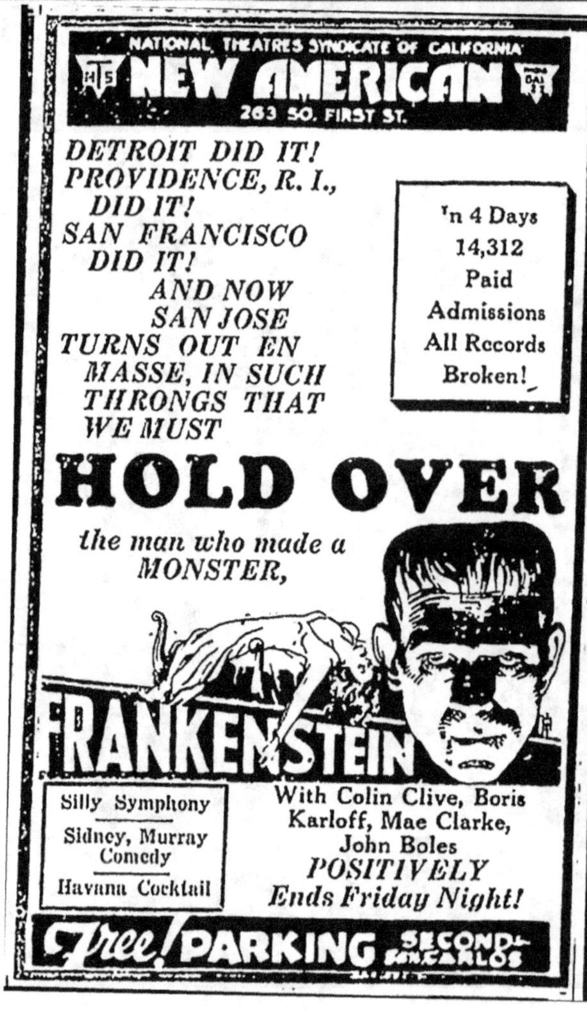

NATIONAL THEATRES SYNDICATE OF CALIFORNIA
NTS NEW AMERICAN PHONE BAL. 32
263 SO. FIRST ST.
DETROIT DID IT! PROVIDENCE, R. I., DID IT! SAN FRANCISCO DID IT! AND NOW SAN JOSE TURNS OUT EN MASSE, IN SUCH THRONGS THAT WE MUST
In 4 Days 14,312 Paid Admissions All Records Broken!
HOLD OVER
the man who made a MONSTER,
FRANKENSTEIN
Silly Symphony
Sidney, Murray Comedy
Havana Cocktail
With Colin Clive, Boris Karloff, Mae Clarke, John Boles
POSITIVELY Ends Friday Night!
Free! PARKING SECOND-SAN CARLOS

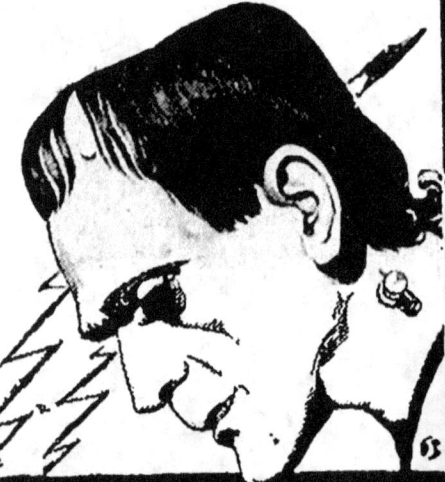

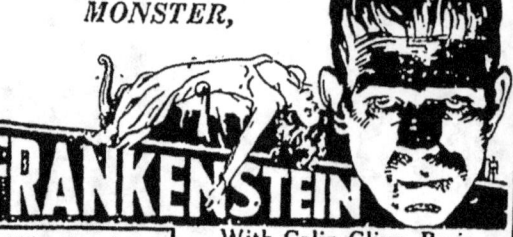

FAMOUS MYSTERY THRILLER COMING

"Frankenstein"—to Play at Warner's Appleton Theatre

"Frankenstein," the man who made a monster, is coming to Warner's Appleton Theatre for four days starting with the Midnite Pre-view to-nite. If on the other hand you like an unusual thrill, you are certain to find it in "Frankenstein."

The story of this picture was written as a result of a contest held over 100 years ago among three writers which could write the most fantastic story. Mary Shelley, P. B. Shelley, her poet husband, and Lord Byron were the three contestants. Mary Shelley won with her "Frankenstein." Ever since its original publication this book has been a best seller. The story tells of a half-man scientist who constructs a mechanical giant and gives him a brain—and life!

The cast in "Frankenstein" is one that is hard to equal. Each player was especially selected for their part. Colin Clive, who made such a hit in "Journey's End" has the leading role. Supporting him are Mae Clarke of "Waterloo Bridge" and John Boles, and not forgetting Boris Karloff who plays the monster.

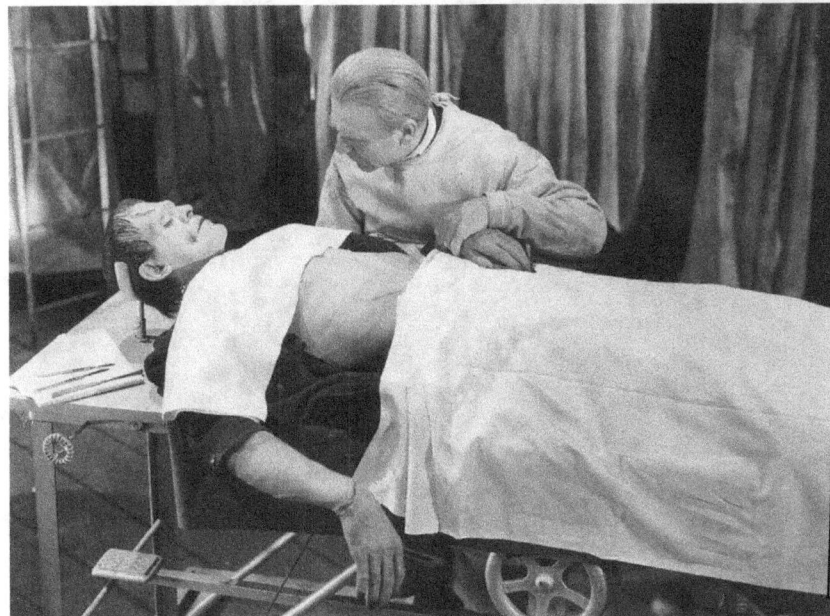

Whoopsie!

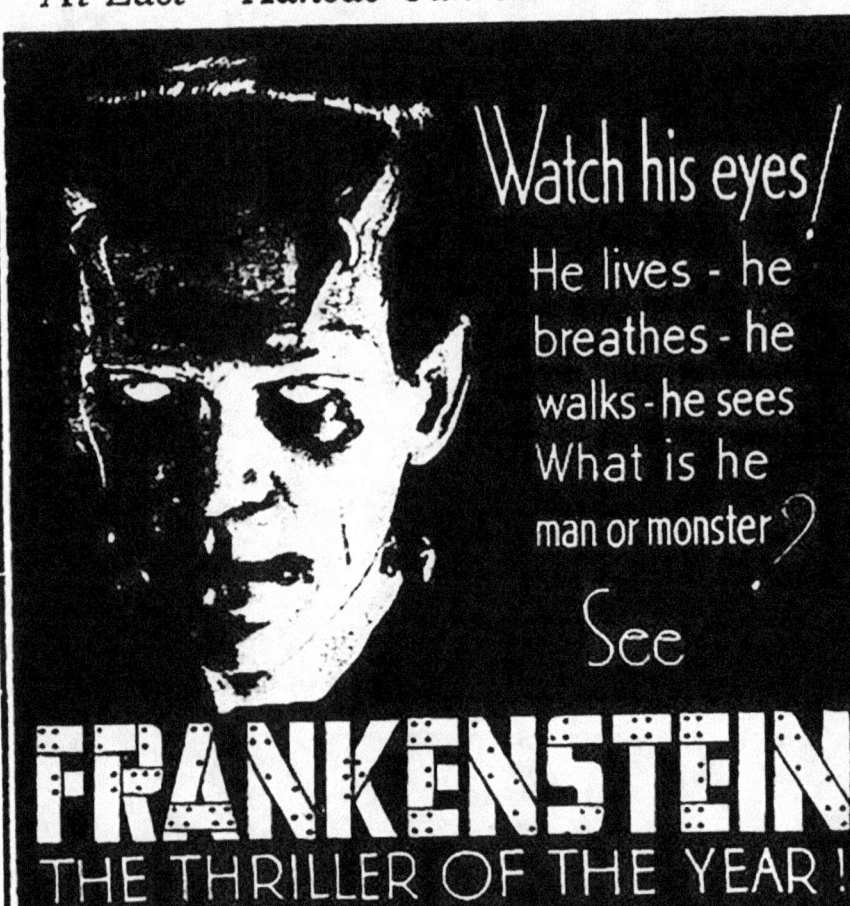

KANS. WOMEN CENSORS RUIN 'FRANKENSTEIN'

Kansas City, Dec. 14.

'Frankenstein,' Universal's thriller, may be kept out of Kansas by the state's board of picture censors through 34 cuts made in the talker, which practically destroys it as a picture.

The entire eighth reel, with the exception of a short interior in the home of Baron Frankenstein, is ruined. This reel shows the destruction of the man-made creature on the roof of a mill, by fire, set by an angry mob. The board's report says the film shows cruelty and tends to debase morals.

Action of the censors will hold out the film from some 400 picture theatres in Kansas, including cities of Topeka, Wichita, Leavenworth and Kansas City, Kans.

The Kansas censor board consists of Hazel Myers, Kansas City, Kans.; Mrs. Edward Redmond, Kansas City, Kans.; Jessie Hodges, Olathe.

The picture 'Frankenstein' was shown at the Mainstreet, here (Kansas City, Mo.), last week to capacity business.

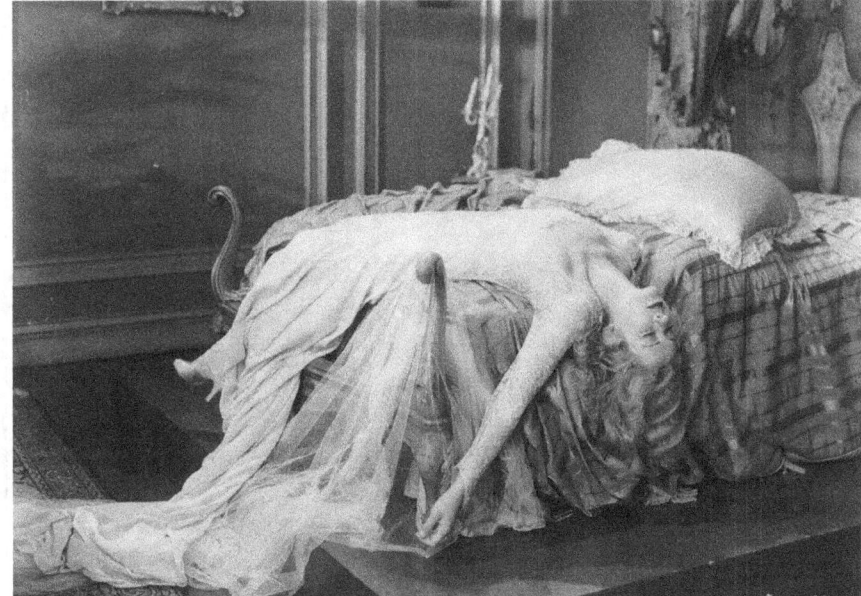

"Frankenstein" is taking shape under the knowing guidance of James Whale. Boris Karloff and not Bela Lugosi is the final choice to play the monster. Colin Clive has been imported from England to play the rôle of Frankenstein, the student who builds the semblance of a man out of bits of human wreckage and then, by an extraordinary light ray, endows the creature with life. This was the rôle which Lon Chaney all his life was anxious to play. Mae Clarke is the tentative choice for the rôle of Elizabeth. Frederick Kerr will appear as the Baron, Edward Van Sloan as the Professor and Dwight Frye as the Dwarf. John Boles, now recovered from the mishap which kept him out of "Strictly Dishonorable," has been assigned the rôle of Victor.

When "Frankenstein," Universal's horror picture, was previewed at Santa Barbara, women screamed, strong men cowered and little children fainted. The theatre was in the grip of terror.

One man telephoned the theater later and said he was going to file suit because of injuries to his wife, his child and himself. He claimed their nerves were shattered.

Another man called the manager regularly every five minutes, to say "I can't sleep because of that picture and you aren't going to either. You showed it and I am going to see that you are as restless as I am."

CLEVER WIDOW!

A really clever and weirdly horrifying window effect has been worked out by the Lyric theater staff and is now on display in the window of the Lindelow drug store. The scene representing the monster that "Frankenstein" made has been cleverly arranged, showing the monster, a horrible creature, lying in a state just before being brought to life by special electrical and laboratory equipment which have also been faithfully reproduced with the addition of special and appropriate lighting effects, lends to the scene as stated a most weird ghostly effect. Take a "peep" when you go by Lindelow's but beware! Copies of the "Frankenstein" book may be obtained at that store.

Happy Birthday Carl Laemmle, some guest list!!!

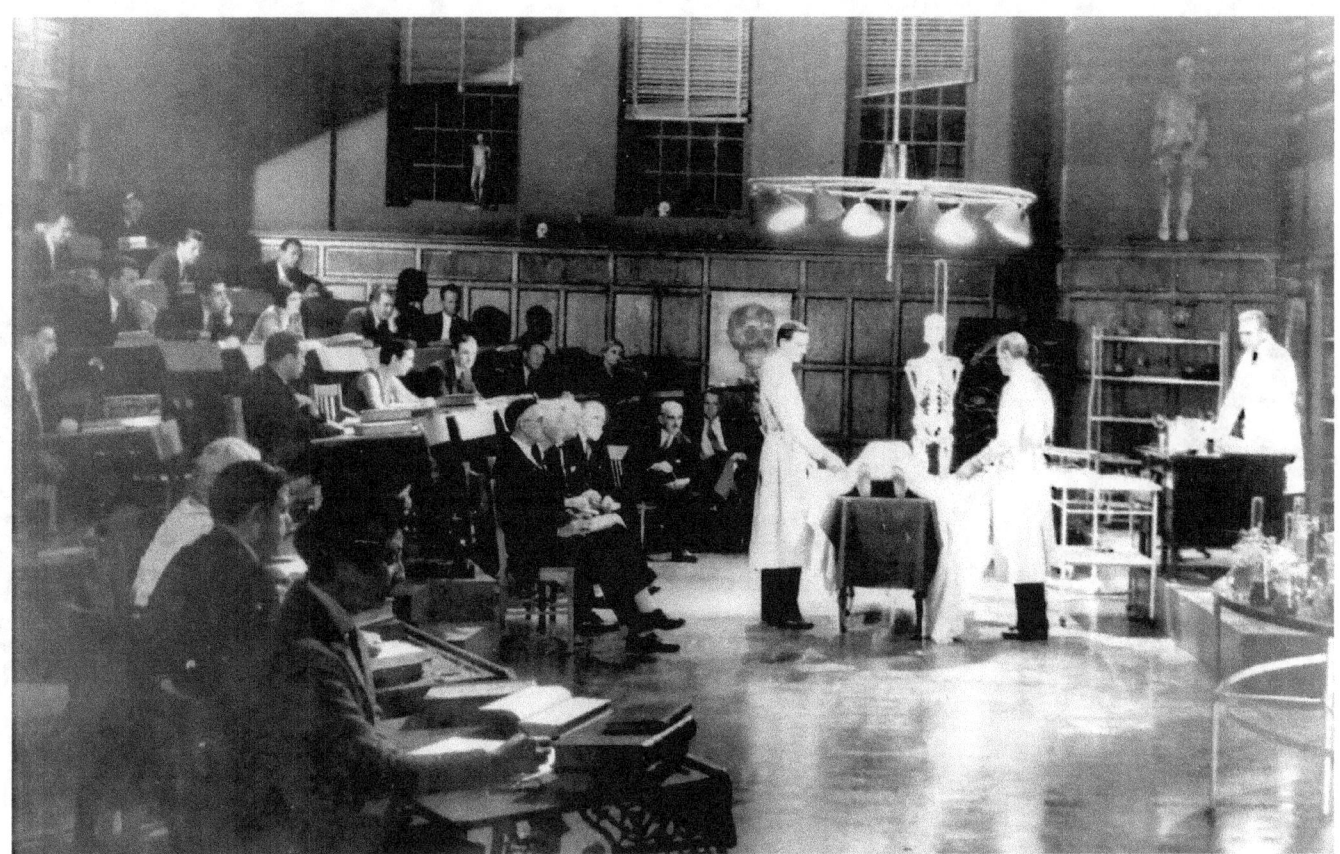

BORIS KARLOFF DWIGHT FRYE COLIN CLIVE MAE CLARKE JOHN BOLES EDWARD VAN SLOAN FREDERIC KERR

"FRANKENSTEIN"
TO PLAY AT THE
CAPITOL THEATRE
From Friday 24th June for four nights only.

A WARNING!

The management of the Capitol theatre is hereby issuing a warning That:

If you are of a soft mind

or

If you have a weak brain

or

If you are inclined more towards sentiment than facts

or

If you cannot stand terrible excitement

PLEASE
Keep away from "FRANKENSTEIN."

We will not be responsible for any reactionary effects which the picture may have upon you!

IT IS ONE OF THE MOST ASTOUNDINGLY TERRIFYING TALKING PICTURE STORY THAT HAS EVER REACHED THE SCREEN!

Printed in the U.S.A.

WE DARE YOU TO SEE IT!

The chilling horror... The icy mystery of a hundred thrilling tales frozen into a superb epic of terror!

FRANKENSTEIN
—THE MAN WHO MADE A MONSTER

Will Be Shown
TONIGHT
THANKSGIVING EVE
Midnite Show 11 P. M.

—Also—

ALL NEW, STELLAR
RKO
VAUDEVILLE
Reserved Seats Now on Sale at Box Office

"FRANKENSTEIN"

—This most horrible and Electrifying Picture is Coming to the Lyric Next Thurs.-Fri.-Sat.

WARNING

HERE COMES the world's most famous shocker. Just a word of friendly warning: If you have a weak heart and cannot stand excitement or gruesomeness, we advise you NOT to see this production. Take our word for it, it will thrill, it will shock, it may even horrify you. But if your nerves can stand electrifying drama, you will find it in our next picture, "Frankenstein" which plays at the Lyric theatre next Thursday, Friday and Saturday.

You may have seen a production called "Dracula." If you did, take our tip: "Frankenstein" far out-Draculas "Dracula." If you didn't it may interest you to know that it was one of the most exciting and popular pictures of last year. You missed something that everybody was talking about. But don't miss "Frankenstein." It will be talked about plenty.

James Whale directed it with a cast including Colin Clive, Mae Clarke, John Boles, Boris Karloff, Edward Van Sloan, Dwight Frye and Frederick Kerr. It is the boldest thing he or any other director ever attempted. It is all about a man who made a monster. Bones and bits of human bodies from graveyards and gallows and trees went into the making of this eight foot caricature of humanity. But alas, he had the brain of a criminal and the fiendish fury of twenty maniacs.

Don't fail to see what happened when this terrific monster escaped to prey upon terrified men and women.

Most Unusual Picture Ever Filmed!

PACKED to the brim with thrills, and called by experts the most original film ever to reach the screen, Universal's eerie "Frankenstein," will make its debut at the Lyric Theatre next Thursday, Friday and Saturday, with Colin Clive, Mae Clarke, John Boles and Boris Karloff in the featured roles.

The extraordinary story of a young scientist who brought a human monster to life through weird electrical mechanisms and surgery is based upon the fantastic eighteenth century narrative of the same name written by Mary Shelley, wife of the poet.

Karloff, in his characterization of the man monster, is reported to wear a makeup weighing 48 pounds in itself. Colvin Clive, of "Journey's End" fame, was brought expressly from London to enact the scientist, and Dwight Frye, of "Dracula" plays the important Dwarf of the picture. Edward Van Sloan and Frederick Kerr complete the cast.

James Whale, the famous Englishman, directed "Frankenstein," and John Balderston, Garret Fort and Francis Faragoh prepared the screen adaption. Arthur Edeson, the well known cinematographer of "All Quiet on the Western Front" and "Waterloo Bridge," photographed the picture and Danny Hall, the equally distinguished artist, designed the unusual settings of the film. Don't forget the date, next Thursday, Friday and Saturday.

When "Frankenstein," Universal's horror picture, was previewed at Santa Barbara, women screamed, strong men cowered and little children fainted. The theatre was in the grip of terror. One man telephoned the theater later and said he was going to file

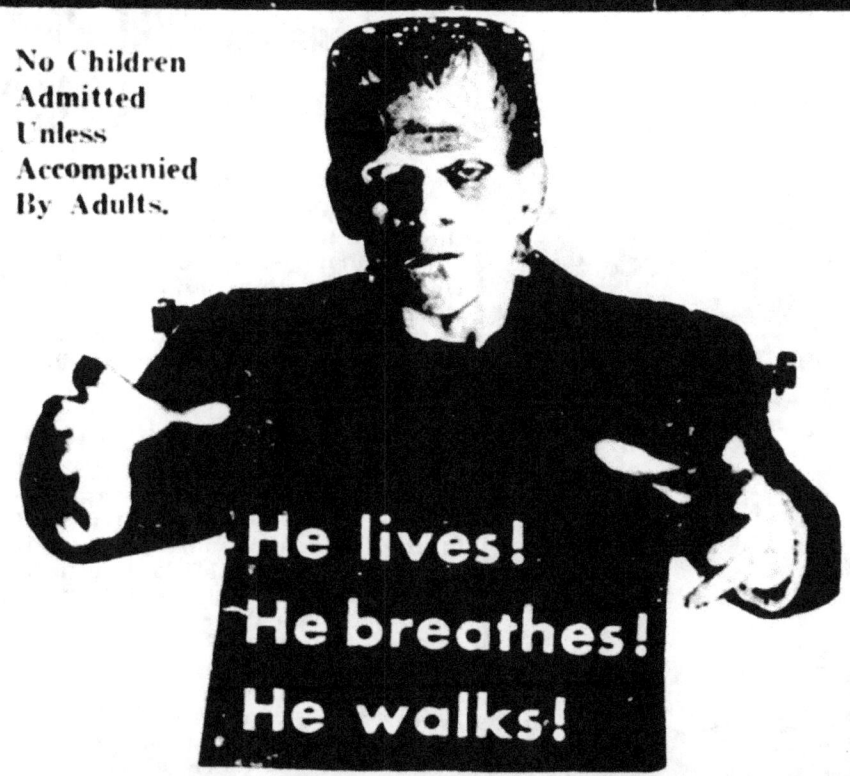

No Children Admitted Unless Accompanied By Adults.

He lives! He breathes! He walks!

The chilling horror of the infinite and the immortal... the icy mystery of a hundred thrilling tales... frozen into a superb epic of terror... an undying story that ravels the emotions into knots of fear.

WARNING!

If your heart is weak, or nerves bad, do not see this picture.

A NURSE, however, in attendance at all performances.

FRANKENSTEIN

John Boles, Mae Clark, Colin Clive, Boris Karloff

TO HAVE SEEN "FRANKENSTEIN" IS TO WEAR A BADGE OF COURAGE!

Mystery, darkness, death... which sane men shun... these madmen sought when they made from stolen bodies the monster who never knew a woman's kiss... to make the "thing" they pried into tombs and then their misfit, snarling, creation escaped and roamed the world dripping terror and death.

—Added—
RUDY VALLEE
"Musical Justice"
Paramount News

—Extra—
Just For Fun
"All American"
"Kick Back"

PALACE

Positively Ends
TUESDAY

'Frank' Smothering All Pitt This Week On $32,000, Stanley

Pittsburgh, Dec. 14.
(Drawing Population, 1,000,000)

It's the Stanley's week to cop. 'Frankenstein' is the film and heading for a sensational $32,000, several grand better than anything has done here since straight picture policy went into effect. House had standees all day Saturday.

Everything else is off as a result of the Stanley trade. Penn and 'His Woman' will be lucky to get $15,000, while 'Girls About Town,' at the Fulton, likewise feeling the pinch.

The Davis inaugurated a two-for-one ticket policy with 'Age for Love' but stunt didn't help any and may not be felt for a time yet. 'Our Children,' plugged for months by the Warner, got opening break from Xmas shopping crowds Saturday and may better $10,000 if it can hold up.

'Frankenstein' B'klyn's Bright Spot on $34,000

Brooklyn, Dec. 14.

'Frankenstein,' at the Albee, has them all licked for attendance, and should bring in at least $34,000 this week. The Paramount, with 'The Cheat,' took a lacing from the critics but Russ Columbo and Mills Brothers may save for $43,000. Fox is very quiet with 'Cuban Love Song.'

Estimates for This Week

Paramount—'The Cheat' (Par) (4,000; 25-35-50-75) and stage show. Business can be attributed to Columbo, who has won the women in this staid town; Mills Brothers in their second week and likely to go another seven days; in the vicinity of fair enough $43,000. Last week 'His Woman' (Par), $44,300.

Fox—'Cuban' (M-G) (4,000; 25-35-50-75) and stage show. Weak picture, and very bad $21,000. Last week 'Surrender' (Fox), $21,100.

Albee—'Frankenstein' (U) (3,800; 25-35-50-75) and vaude. Steady flow figures at $34,000, big. Last week 'Secret Service' (Radio) and Lou Holtz, $24,700, all right.

Loew's Met—'Corsair' (UA) (3,000; 25-35-50-75) and vaude. Total of around $17,000. Last week $17,900.

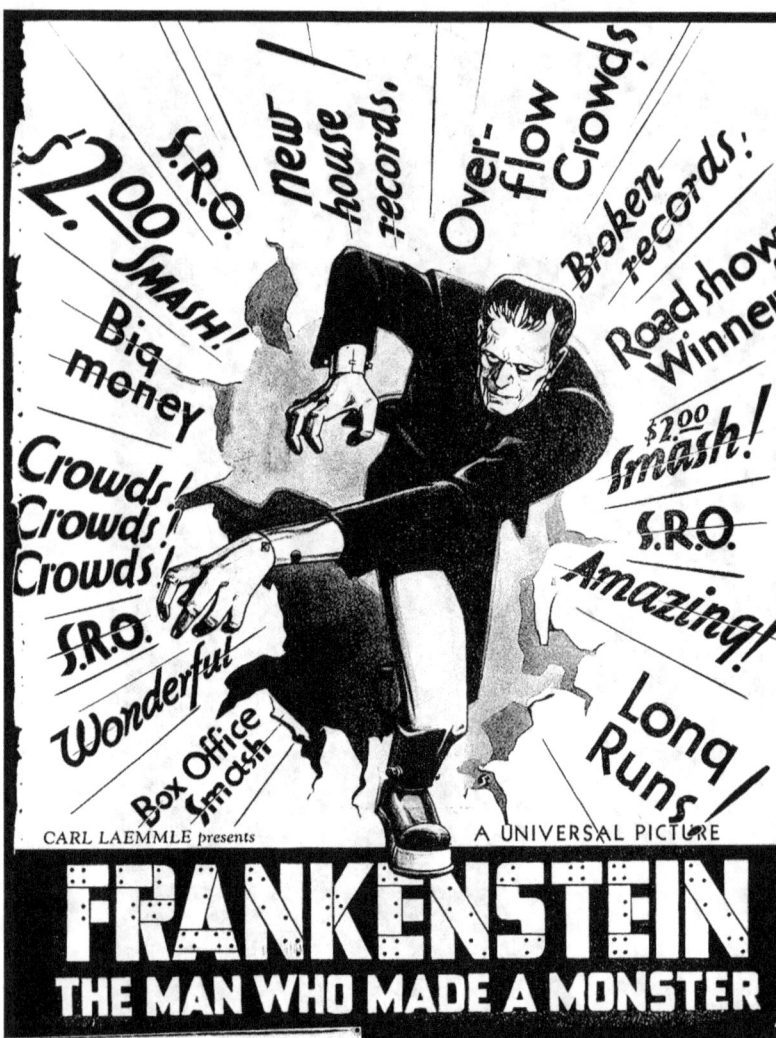

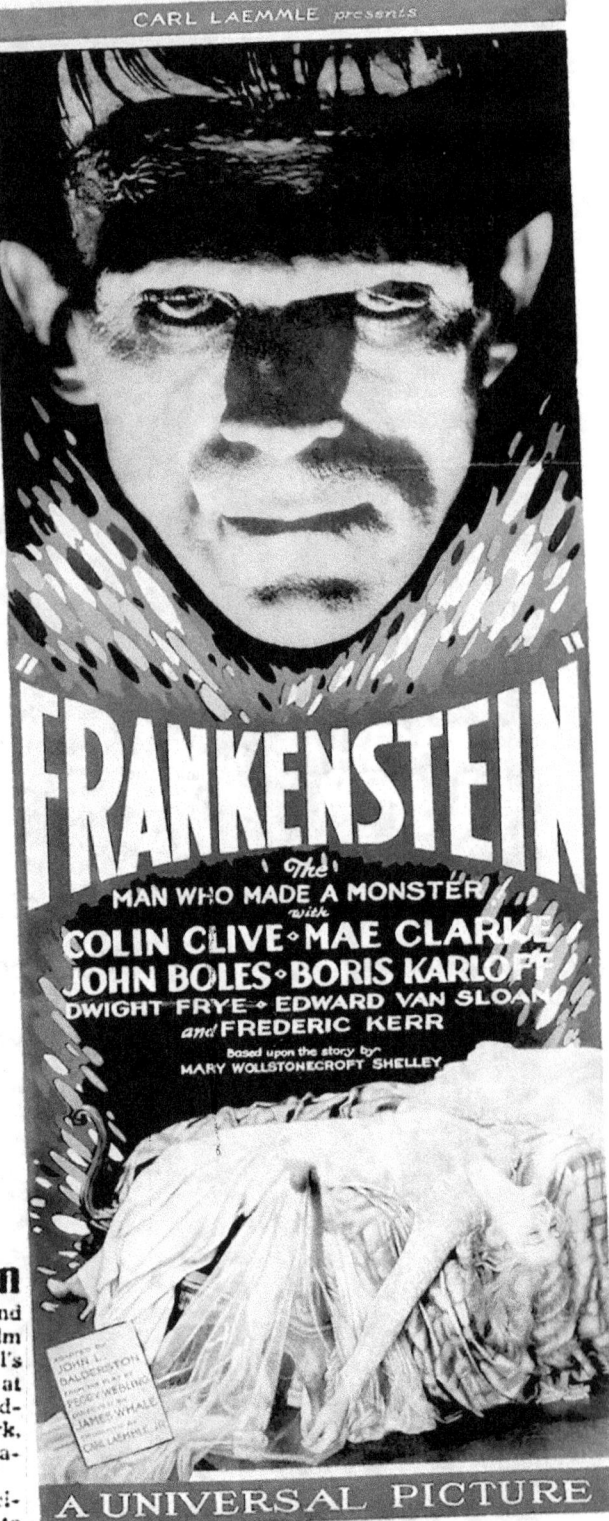

VIRGINIAN FILM TO BE "FRANKENSTEIN"

Colin Clive, Mae Clarke Stars of Picture; Wheeler and Woolsey Coming

"Frankenstein," based on the famous story by Mary Wollstoncroft Shelley, opens Sunday at the Virginian theater to remain through Thursday. The cast includes Colin Clive, Mae Clarke, John Boles, and Boris Karloff as the monster.

This is the story of a young scientist, intent on recreating life through an electrical process. He fashions a human form, but the brain which he places in it is the brain of a criminal. When at last he brings his monster to life, it embarks on a career of crime which ends only after it has destroyed the scientist's assistant, an aged doctor, and nearly destroyed the scientist himself.

"Peach O'Reno," a comedy, with Bert Wheeler, Robert Woolsey, Dorothy Lee, Zelma O'Nea and Joseph Cawthorn, will open at the Virginian with a special midnight show on New Year's eve to continue through Saturday.

This is the story of Wheeler and Woolsey as bargain divorce lawyers in the famous divorce center at Reno.

As an added attraction at the New Year's eve midnight show only, there will be at the Virginian an amateur contest of 12 selected acts with 30 entertainers.

"Frankenstein" Will Be Run Here Again

Packed to the brim with thrills, and called by experts the most original film ever to reach the screen, Universal's eerie "Frankenstein" will be shown at the State theatre next Tuesday and Wednesday with Colin Clive, Mae Clark, John Boles and Boris Karloff in the featured roles.

The extraordinary story of a young scientist who brought a human monster to life through weird electrical mechanisms and surgery is based upon the fantastic eighteenth century narrative of the same name written by Mary Shelley, wife of the poet.

Karloff, in his characterization of the man monster, is reported to wear make-up weighing 48 pounds in itself. Colin Clive, of "Journey's End" fame, was brought expressly from London to enact the scientist, and Dwight Fyre, of "Dracula," plays the important dwarf of the picture. Edward Van Sloan and Frederick Kerr complete the cast.

'FRANKENSTEIN' OPENS, PALACE

Ghouls and Eerie Adventure Add to Breath-Taking Talkie of Thrills

Arch man-made fields, life-breathing electrical machines, dangling bodies, human skeletons, ghouls, and wicked hunchbacks all have their sinister places in shivery, eerie and ghostly, daddy of all the thrill-films, "Frankenstein," that opened to a half-scared, half-fascinated, packed house at the Palace yesterday for four days. The weak-nerved patrons had been warned to stay home. So they were there to a man.

The producer has taken the most daring story in all literature—the eighteenth-century Mary Shelley tale of a man who created a monster—has added the ingredients of a superb cast, truly marvelous photography, fascinating sets, and has duly presented the screen with its greatest film-fantasy.

There are many scenes in the film that will both literally and figuratively prompt you to clutch at your neighbor's closest arm as the screen very nearly devours you, but there is one in particular that the most blase will never be able to resist. The excited young Dr. Frankenstein, played brilliantly by Colin Clive, and his devilish little dwarf-assistant, Dwight Frye, complete the last surgical operation on their home-made man. They dash to their shrieking electrical inventions and test the life-giving ray . . . then. . . .! But it is entirely too precious to give away! Of course you will see "Frankenstein," and anyone who takes the least bit of thrill away from it for you should most certainly be relegated to the basement.

Mae Clarke, the talented little actress who is taking the world's film fans by storm; John Boles of the golden voice, charming manner, and excellent acting ability; sagacious-looking Edward Van Sloan; and chattering Frederick Kerr and Dwight Frye, have many honors to divide in "Frankenstein," but the screen has never seen anything quite like Clive and Karloff in their characterizations. Karloff, wearing the most hideously fascinating make-up in creation, and in their extraordinary performances the brilliant Englishman give you something that you will, in all probability, remember for many a day.

IT'S HERE! GIGANTIC FRANKENSTEIN

AURORA'S ALL PLASTIC ASSEMBLY KIT

"BIG FRANKIE" IS ALMOST 2 FEET HIGH—COMPLETE WITH PAINTS AND BRUSHES!

EASY TO ASSEMBLE • COMES COMPLETE WITH PAINTS & BRUSH

ARMS MOVE UP AND DOWN

GIGANTIC FRANKENSTEIN STANDS ALMOST 2 FEET HIGH

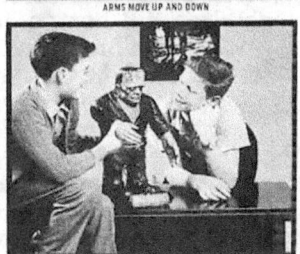
GREAT FUN AS A SHOW PIECE

See "Big Frankie" at any store carrying Aurora's Monster Movie Model Kits—or you can order your Aurora "Big Frankie" by mail; see coupon on page 97

AURORA PLASTICS CORP.
WEST HEMPSTEAD, L.I., N.Y.

CHILDREN AND MOVIES

Women of Nineteenth Century Club Hear Discussion by Alice Miller Mitchell, Who Has Studied Film Theater

Alice Miller Mitchell, pioneer in movie research, addressed the Nineteenth Century club Monday afternoon on "Children and the Movies." Since 1923 Mrs. Mitchell has been making an intensive study of the movies for a well-known foundation. She has served on boards of censorship, questioned children in various organizations such as boy and girl scouts, discussed movies with those in institutions for delinquents, and inquired into methods of the industry. The results of her findings have recently been published in a book, "Children and the Movies."

"Censorship is obviously not the solution for movie problems," said Mrs. Mitchell, who knows whereof she speaks, having struggled with the inadequacies of such attempts. "We have no Federal board of censorship, only a National board which almost automatically puts its stamp on all films and is no more national than the National Biscuit Company. A movie already made can not be cut down to a child's standards and when the attempt is made gaps are left which the imagination fills in with mental pictures worse than the original. The only thing to do is to have some method of censorship before pictures are made; a set of standards which producers will be required to meet might serve."

However, the real solution, Mrs. Mitchell believes, is in having children's movies just as we have a children's department in public libraries. Harmful material finds no place there and it is the constant aim of librarians to cultivate the taste to even higher standards. This could be done with movies but won't until there is a strong demand. Leaders in the industry are always responsive to an overwhelming expression of public opinion. At present it is uncertain whether the movies are forcing objectionable pictures on the public or the public is demanding them.

When the children's special matinees were tried a few years ago they were not a success, "not," said Mrs. Mitchell, "because the children did not go but because out of date, revamped films were shown and the youngsters would have none of them."

The speaker referred to this great industry as a modern piper piping all the children away not because they really wanted to go but because modern conditions lead them to. Seventy-five per cent of the youngsters questioned preferred games, hikes, and other play to attending movies but too often in our cities such pleasures are not available and the movies profit because "there is nothing else to do." In addition parents use the theater as a kind of nursery where their offspring may be left in safety, seventy per cent of the children attending going without parents. Moreover, only one and a half per cent of parents select movies for their children. More should follow the example of the old negress who, when asked if her little ones attended the movies, answered, "No ma'am, my chillen don't go to no movies, 'cause de movies makes bandages out o' 'em."

Questions have been raised as to the effect of movies on health, morals, nervous systems, eye-sight, etc. As yet no accurate surveys have been made, but doctors say the new ventilating systems in the best theaters prevent general health impairment. Another says while children may not understand things they see those images are made to return later with fuller comprehension. Nervous systems undoubtedly are affected by thrillers as they cause nightmares, hysterics, and even violent illness. As to eye-sight one doctor says the flicker of the film exercises a muscle not ordinarily used and thus is good. Mrs. Mitchell said her personal experience had been that watching shows all day had not bothered her eyes.

The speaker felt that a taste had been cultivated for the emotionally bad as movies make us see, hear, and feel, but rarely think, and children asked what they liked replied, "bloody, roaring killings," "big crooks," "ones that have the biggest kick." The movies speak the language of emotions and in this lies their great opportunity as most people are ruled by their emotions.

Educationally the motion picture has unlimited possibilities, according to her view. Already it is being used in many fields, medicine, army, by football coaches, in teaching immigrants, and in advertising. It can do much more. The speaker expressed her belief that the talkies were not an end but only a beginning, and added that even now there are revelations in filmdom being held back that they may be launched when the inevitable slump comes. She hinted that all-color films were one of these.

Parents can help by writing their congressmen in support of the Hudson and Brookhart bills, by forming study groups, selecting their children's movies, and demanding juvenile films. The speaker closed with a quotation, "Helping a little child and fotching him to his own is a durn sight better business than loafing 'round a throne."

Laws to aid parents in managing their children are of little use, in our opinion. A child is the victim of its parents' ineptitude or the beneficiary of their common sense. We have too many laws and any law favored by Senator Brookhart should not be approved by any responsible person without careful study—Editor.

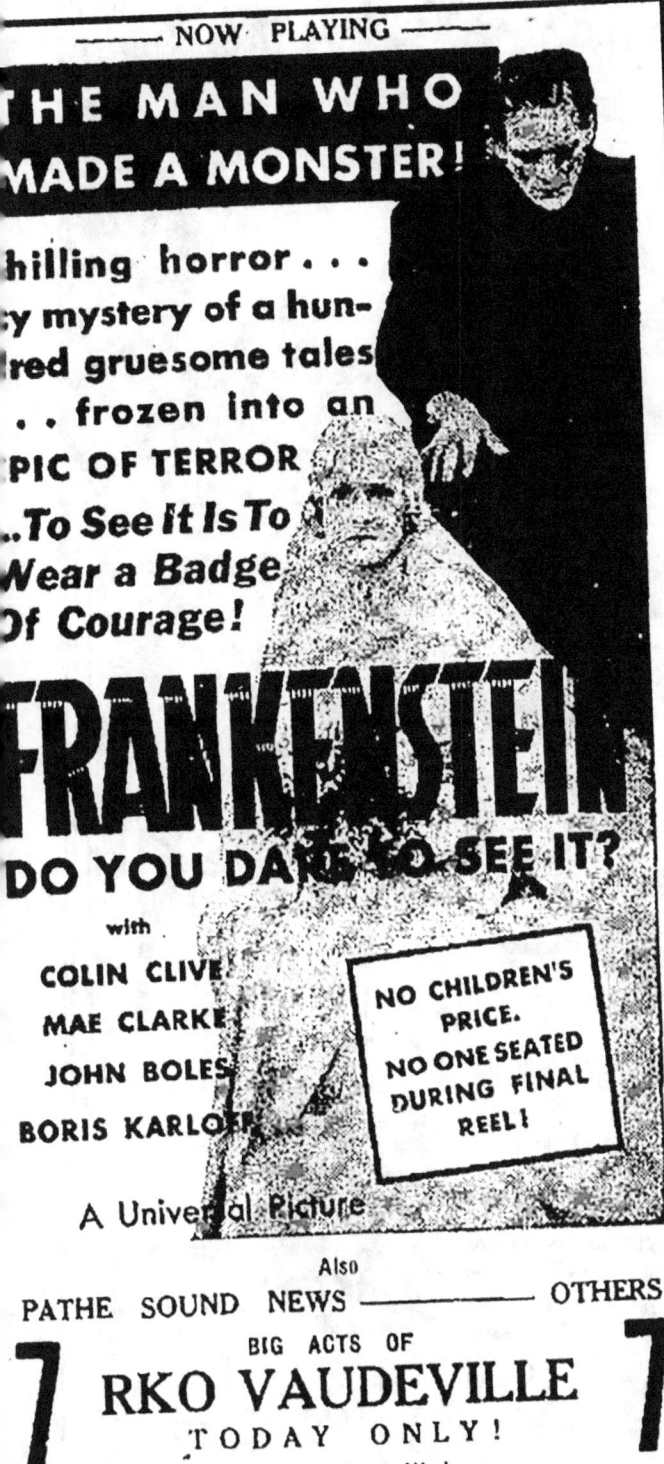

This Is How And This Is Why "Frankenstein" Was Made

Last year Carl Laemmle, Jr., flew in the face of Providence, as it were and made "Dracula." It had been offered to every other company and every other company had rejected it. Why? Because they didn't believe that a horror picture could possibly succeed. "Dracula" was, frankly and thoroughly a horror picture. No concessions were made to romance-loving frappers, to Cinderella formulas or the supposedly essential feminine. "Dracula" was a shocker, and "Dracula" shocked 'em. But it shattered box-office records and stood the industry on its astounded head. As an eye-opener it ranked second only to the astonishing success of "All Quiet on the Western Front" as a triumph for Carl Laemmle, Jr.

Such a success as "Dracula" proved could result in but one thing—a story that would go it one better. The Universal story department went into a huddle, and "Frankenstein," the remarkable story of a man who created a soulless monster bit by bit from graveyards, dissecting-rooms and giblets, was the result. "Frankenstein" was written by Mary Wollenstonecroft Shelley, the wife of the poet. It was best known work and was written under the inspiration of her immortal husband. As a story, it had much more romance, and much more suspense, than "Dracula" had, and these are elements which are highly desirable in any moving picture. For the direction of this one hundred per cent shocker, Carl Laemmle summoned James Whale, whose record for realism in "Journey's End" and "Waterloo Bridge" has raised him to the nth degree as a director.

Whale chose his cast with care and discernment. First he cabled to England for Colin Clive, who had been the mainstay as Captain Stanhope of "Journey's End." Clive is playing the title role, that of Dr. Frankenstein. Next, he chose Mae Clarke, whose work in "Waterloo Bridge" reminded scores of critics of the technique and success of the late Jeanne Eagles. Mae Clarke plays the role of Elizabeth, fiancee of Dr. Frankenstein. Then he chose two players from the cast of "Dracula." Dwight Frye, whose work as the maniac lawyer Renfield was so outstanding, plays the dwarf who assists Frankenstein in creating his monster. The other "Dracula" player is Edward Van Sloan, who plays Dr. Waldmann in "Frankenstein." John Boles has the role of the handsome unsuccessful suitor for the hand of Elizabeth, and Frederick Kerr, whose work in "Waterloo Bridge" was so delightful, plays Baron Frankenstein, father of Colin Clive.

Despite the entire witness and celebrity of this cast, a tremendous amount of the interest of "Frankenstein" centers in the role of the monster. This is the one role that Lon Chaney had longed to play, and what a role it would have been for his! The final choice for it fell upon Boris Karloff, whose most recent work is in "Five Star Final." The make-up devised for Karloff is an amazing and forbidding thing. So forbidding and so terrifying that James Whale was afraid to have the make-up exposed before the picture is actually shown. It consists of some, forty-five pounds of build-up and padding to add to Karloff's six feet of stature and his one hundred and ninety pounds of weight. Every precaution was taken to keep the make-up an absolute secret. A strictly guarded dressing-room was built just outside the stage and the stage and the dressing-room were guarded constantly from 7:30 in the morning, until 7:30 at night.

POWELL COMING IN NEW PICTURE

William Powell's second starring picture for Warner Brothers, and said to eclipse anything that this popular star has ever done is titled "High Pressure" and will be shown at the Lyric Theatre next Tuesday and Wednesday.

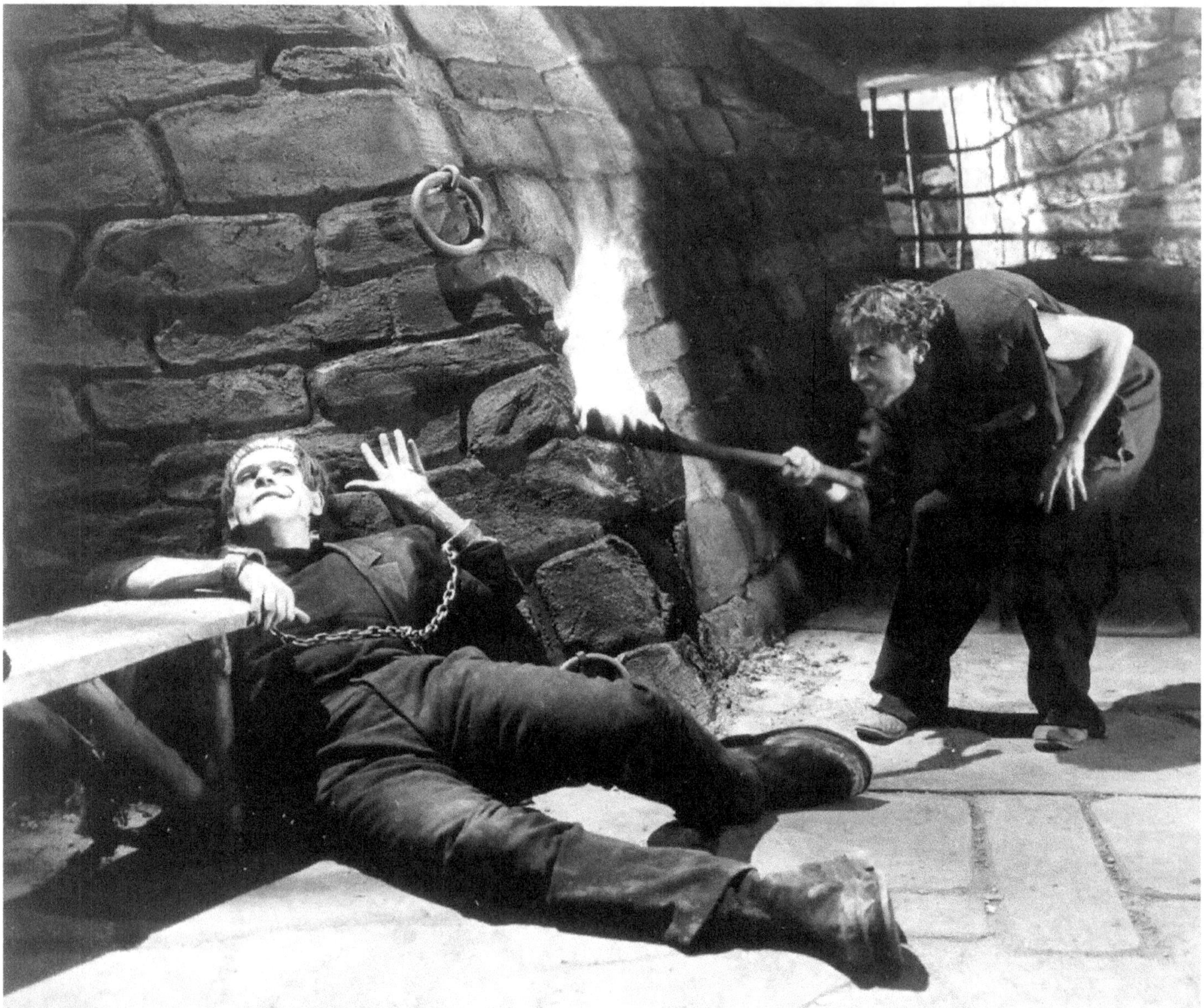

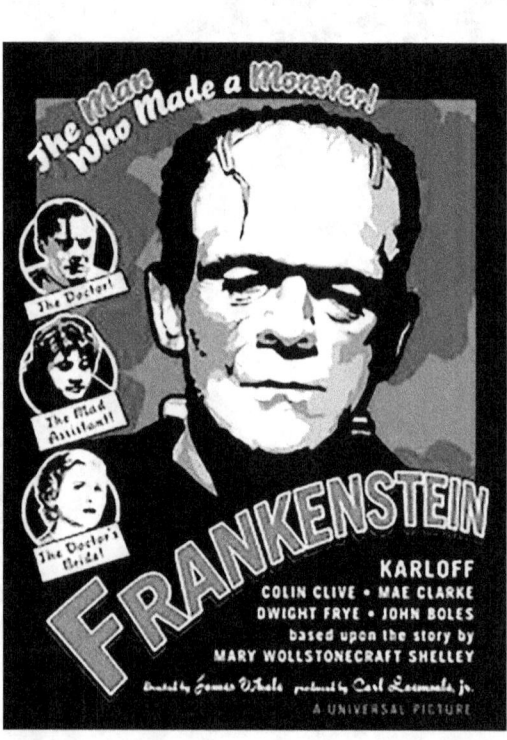

Dr. Jekyll and Mr. Hyde
Released U.S. Dec. 31, 1931

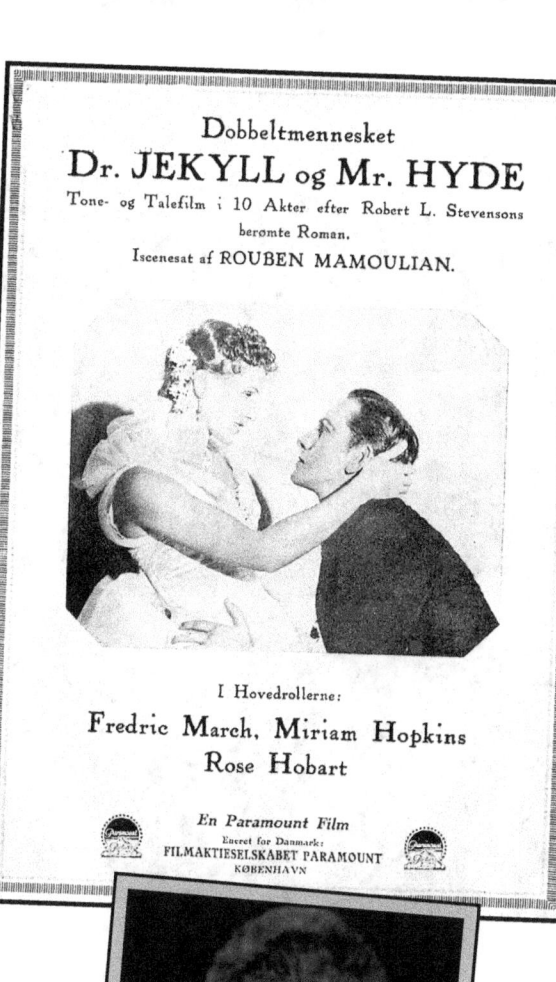

WEIRD

"DOCTOR JEKYLL and MR. HYDE," most famous of stories dealing with the conflict of a dual nature, comes to the screen with Fredric March in the title rôle. Easily the finest opportunity of this versatile actor, the story also provides attractive parts for two exceptional actresses, Miriam Hopkins and Rose Hobart.

BROOKLYN ON TRIAL

Laughed at 'Dr. Jekyll'—Puzzled Paramounters

The freakiest preview audience reaction in the history of pre-showings in eastern theatres has Paramount and other companies wondering. Whether a drama should be previewed on the same program with a comedy, vice versa, or whether it's just that—Brooklyn will be Brooklyn.

Across the bridge they laughed all through Par's horror feature, 'Hyde.' 'Sooky' was programmed as the feature and 'Dr. Jekyll and Mr. Hyde' the surprise.

If it happens again—this laughing at a drama after a comedy—the Paramounties say they will know that Brooklyn can't control over one emotion nightly.

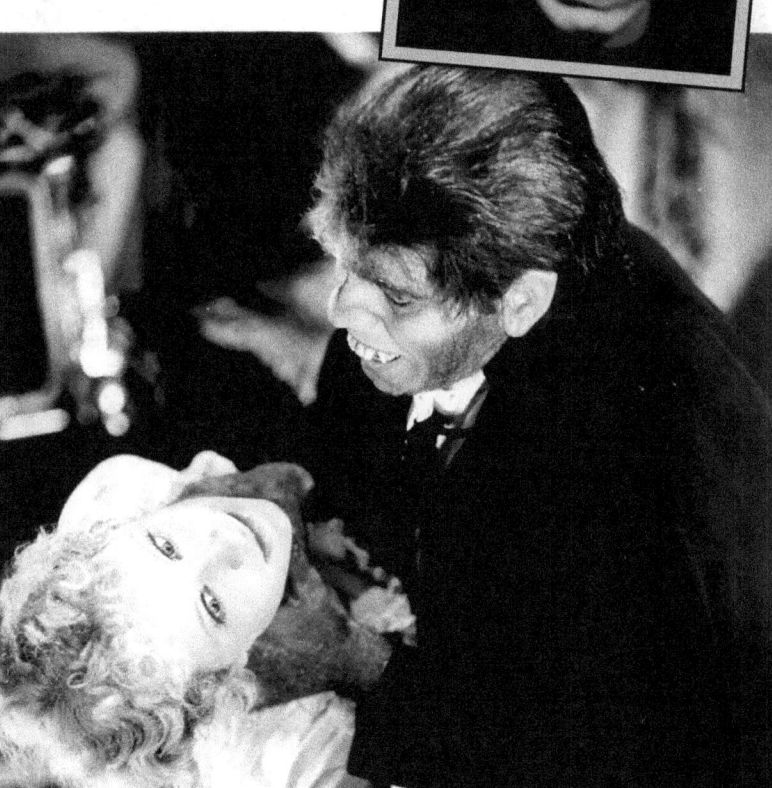

> Warner (WB) (2,000; 25-35-50)—
> 'Jekyll and Hyde' (Par). Great notices, but 'Frankenstein' so recent may have removed the edge; should do $13,000 and possibility of two weeks. Last week 'Manhattan Parade' (WB), seven days, under $10,000.

LOVER AND FIEND

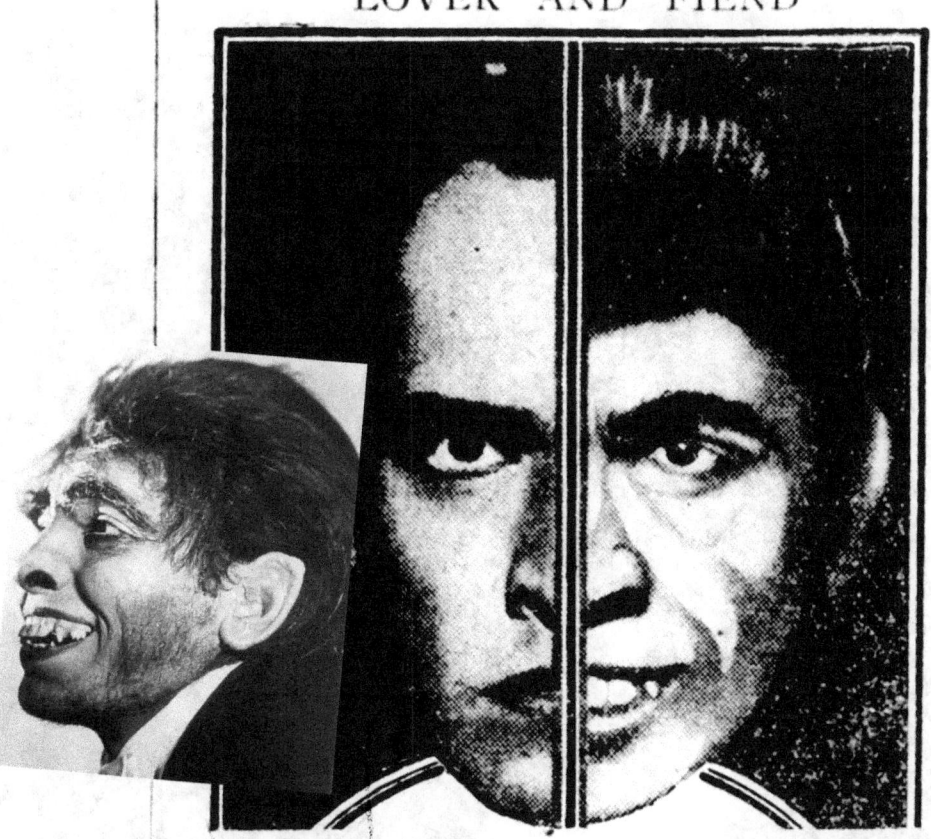

"Dr. Jekyll and Mr. Hyde" Paramount's sensation starring Fredric March, showing today and tomorrow at Brownsville's Capitol theatre.

MARCH STARS IN STRANGE, WEIRD TALE

"Dr. Jekyll and Mr. Hyde", Robert Louis Stevenson's immortal story of a man who dared to experiment with the good and evil sides of his nature, has been dramatized on the talking screen by Paramount. With Fredric March's peroformance (or Jekyll and Hyde, and Miriam Hopkins and Rose Hobart prominently featured in the supporting cast, this weird and strange production was shown for the first time at the Capitol Theatre at midnight Saturday.

"Dr. Jekyll and Mr. Hyde" tells of a young physician who defies the immutable laws of God and man and attempts to separate his being into two distinct entities, the good and the evil. This mad dream of the physician, Jekyll, is eventually realized, his evil self taking the form of a grotesque, deformed man known as Mr. Hyde. But once Jekyll discovers that, at will, he can be either Jekyll or Hyde, he is faced with a terrifying situation. For as Hyde he is cruel, brutal, wreaking horrible vengeance on innocent people who chance to cross his path. What happens when he realizes that Hyde is gaining complete dominance over his normal kindly self, makes "Dr. Jekyll and Mr. Hyde" distinctively different and fascinating entertainment.

Fredric March's performance(or performances) as Dr. Jekyll and Mr. Hyde ranks with the best he has ever attempted on the screen. As Mr. Jekyll you will see March as a handsome, kindly young man, tenderly in love with his fiancee. But as Mr. Hyde you will see this same actor grotesquely deformed and horrible, wreaking strange vengeance on an innocent girl.

'Jekyll & Hyde' Talker

London, March 31.
Paramount bought the talker rights to "Dr. Jekyll and Mr. Hyde." Robert Louis Stevenson's estate held them.

Par made "Jekyll and Hyde" as a silent in 1920.

Another Jekyll

Hollywood, April 7.
I. E. Chadwick, independent producer inactive three years, returns to production making "Dr. Jekyll and Mr. Hyde."

Paramount contemplates a production of the Stevenson chiller in New York, with Fredric March. Novel is in public domain.

65

Mamoulian's Party

Hollywood, Nov. 9.

More and more infrequent custom of a director throwing a party for the staff upon completion of the film was revived by Rouben Mamoulian when 'Dr. Jekyll and Mr. Hyde' was finished at Paramount.

Mamoulian had about 100 actors, technicians and others comprising the film's staff at the Russian-American club for dinner, which was topped by a number of skits and specialties all poking fun at the director and other staff members.

Cameramen gave their version of Mamoulian's moving shots with a camera that was passed from hand to hand like a basketball. Fredric March, star of the film, did a take-off on the director and Bob Lee, his assistant, discussing the next shot. Edgar Norton and Halliwell Hobbs did their version of 'Jekyll & Hyde' and the grips showed how the transformation scene was accomplished, with Oscar, the Paramount bootblack, as the Hyde character.

Karl Struss, head cameraman, modeled ladies' hats, while Travis Banton, Par designer, gave the vocal description, and Samuel Hoffenstein authored a skit, 'Dr. Balaban and Mr. Katz' in honor of the new Par finances.

ITALY'S FILM FESTIVAL AS A BIENNIAL EVENT

Venice, Aug. 27.

The first international festival of cinematography has just closed after registering a brilliant success. Venice, and the Lido especially, have had the most successful and fashionable season for several years, and the arrival of the Prince of Wales at the height of the season put the seal on it.

The Cinema festival is to be made a regular biennial affair. Count Volpi of Misurata, former Italian Finance Minister, Signor De Feo, chief of the Rome Institute for Educational Cinematography and the European representatives of the big American film producers were on the committee to arrange for the future festivals.

The most attractive feature of this year's festival was the sequence of first class films by producers of various nations. Several of these films were new, or were being shown contemporaneously in their country of origin for the first time.

Paramount's 'Dr. Jekyll and Mr. Hyde' was voted one of the successful pieces, as well as Universal's 'Frankenstein.' Some interesting Russian Soviet films were shown and a few novel shorts on art

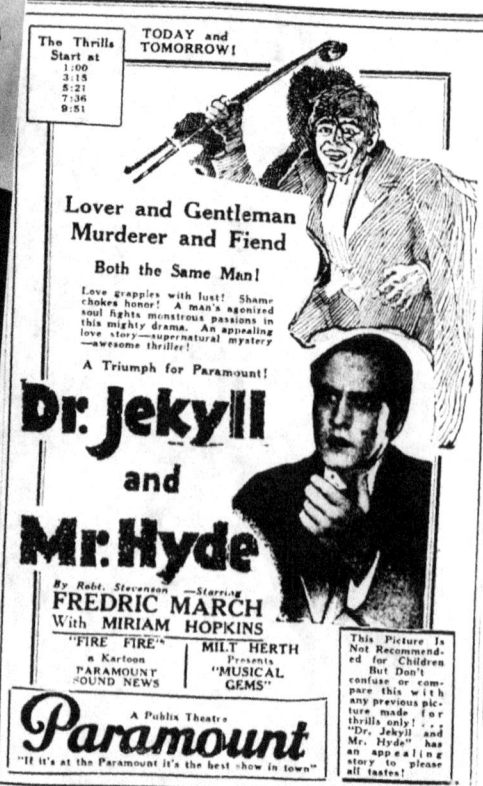

IN GRIM DRAMA!

FREDERIC MARCH and members of the cast reflect a moment between scenes of "DR. JEKYLL and MR. HYDE," at the Lyric theatre, next THURSDDAY - FRIDAY - SATURDAY.

"DR. JEKYLL AND MR. HYDE"

Long Awaited Dramatic Smash Coming To Lyric Next Thursday, Friday and Saturday

Few stories can truthfully be classed among the immortal works of fiction.

And of this number, only a small percentage are such as to lend themselves to motion picture greatness.

Yet not only is "Dr. Jekyll and Mr. Hyde" admittedly the mightiest drama of dual identity ever written, but it can be told far more powerfully on the screen than in book form or on the stage.

The years have proven the dramatic power of this compelling narrative.

In spite of the fact that it was written almost half a century ago, its fascination has not decreased. The basic situation is still regarded as the most startling ever conceived . . . and by its frightening suspense and tense action, it still remains the greatest writing achievement in the realm of imagination.

Following a book sale that ran into the millions, "Dr. Jekyll and Mr. Hyde" was dramatized with sensational success. It was thru his portrayal of the double characterization of Jekyll and Hyde that Robert Mansfield became the greatest actor of his day.

In 1920 Paramount brought "Dr. Jekyll and Mr. Hyde" to the silent screen, with John Barrymore enacting the dual role. That picture is a glorious chapter in motion picture history.

When Paramount decided to film this story as a talking picture, the greatest care was given to its preparation. The development of the scenario was accomplished only after detailed discussion by some of the finest writers and greatest picture minds in the industry. Wizards of motion picture making— no other phrase adequately describes them— achieved amazing means of reproducting on the screen the startling informations of Jekyll to Hyde— and Hyde to Jekyll. Eerie light effects—crawling shadows—weirdly swooping cameras—strange settings that contribute pictorial fascination to the amazing story—all these were perfected before production was started.

Rouben Mamoulian was chosen to direct "Dr. Jekyll and Mr. Hyde" because of his originality, and his keen sense of drama.

After weighing the qualifications of scores of actors who sought the opportunity to portray the dual role, Frederic March was selected. Weeks of study followed—test after test was made by Cameraman Karl Struss before the perfection of the make-up in which March will be seen as Hyde.

Never before have we known such care to be given to the production of a picture.

"Dr. Jekyll and Mr. Hyde" combines all the fascinating elements of the original story—the stage play—the silent picture—yet it is being given a treatment that is new and refreshing. It promises to be far greater than its predecessors.

FREDRIC MARCH   FRANK BORZAGE

In recognition of meritorious achievement in the motion picture world, the Academy of Motion Picture Arts and Sciences recently bestowed its traditional gold statuettes upon an illustrious few at its annual banquet in Hollywood. To Helen Hayes went the palm for the best performance of an actress during 1932 for her work in "The Sin of Madelon Claudet," hailed by the critics as one of the year's outstanding pictures. Miss Hayes is a product of the American stage, having appeared before the footlights for eighteen years before she attained stardom in the films. She began her career as an actress at the age of seven. The leader among the male actors, Frederic March, is also an American, a native of Racine, Wis. March, a graduate of the University of Wisconsin, is that rara avis, a banker who turned thespian. Though not nominally a star, March is considered by many critics as being head and shoulders above the rest of the crop of luminaries at Hollywood. He won recognition from the Academy for his portrayal of the dual role of Dr. Jekyll and Mr. Hyde, in the film of that name. Frank Borzage, named as the year's best director, is a native of Salt Lake City, the son of a wealthy rancher. He is the youngest of Hollywood's ace directors. Borzage has been on the stage and in the films since he was thirteen. His direction of the picture "Bad Girl" won him the academy award. This picture was listed among the six leading movies of the year.

Native Film Stars Head List For Meritorious Achievement

* * * * * *

Foreign Stars Eclipsed by Home-Grown Products as Annual Accolade of Academy of Arts and Sciences Goes to Helen Hayes and Frederic March.

MOTION PICTURE ACADEMY OF ARTS AWARDS FIVE FIRSTS TO PARAMOUNT

FREDRIC MARCH
awarded trophy for the best male performance of the year. His current picture is "THE SIGN OF THE CROSS."

HELEN HAYES
awarded trophy for the best female performance of the year. Starred in Paramount's "A FAREWELL TO ARMS."

FRANK BORZAGE
awarded trophy for the best directorial achievement of the year. Director of "A FAREWELL TO ARMS."

Trophy for photography third consecutive year for Garmes's "SHANGHAI EXPRESS."

Paramount awarded trophy second successive year for the best sound recording.

Warner (WB) (2,000; 25-35-50)—'Jekyll and Hyde' (Par). Great notices, but 'Frankenstein' so recent may have removed the edge; should do $13,000 and possibility of two weeks. Last week 'Manhattan Parade' (WB), seven days, under $10,000.

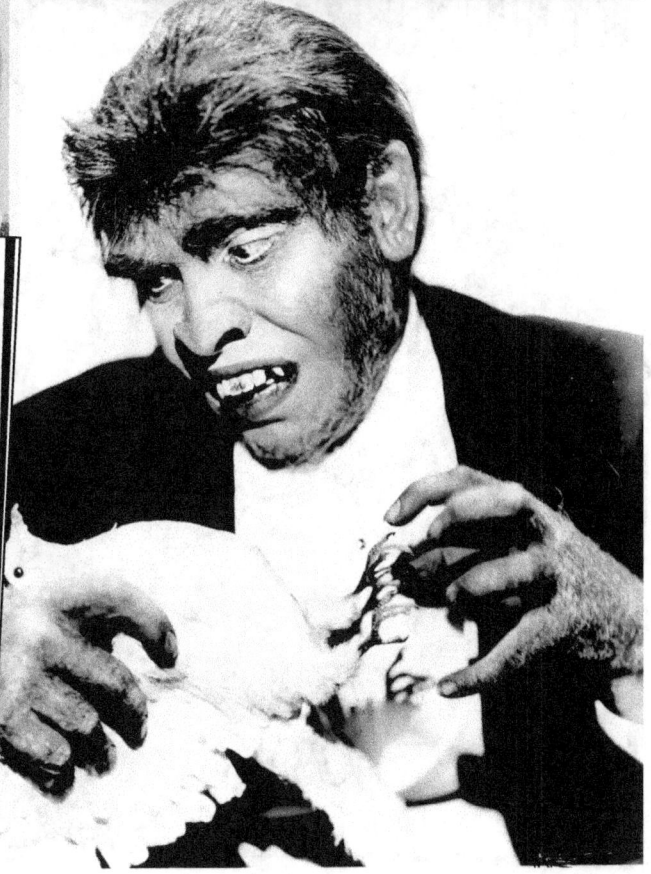

'Jekyll and Hyde' (Par). Elaborated, artistic version of the old standby. Promises abundant shocks and returns now that the fan public is horror conscious. Probably loses something in popular appeal by highbrow treatment, but will create talk. Runs 95 minutes in Broadway form, but easily adaptable to cutting.

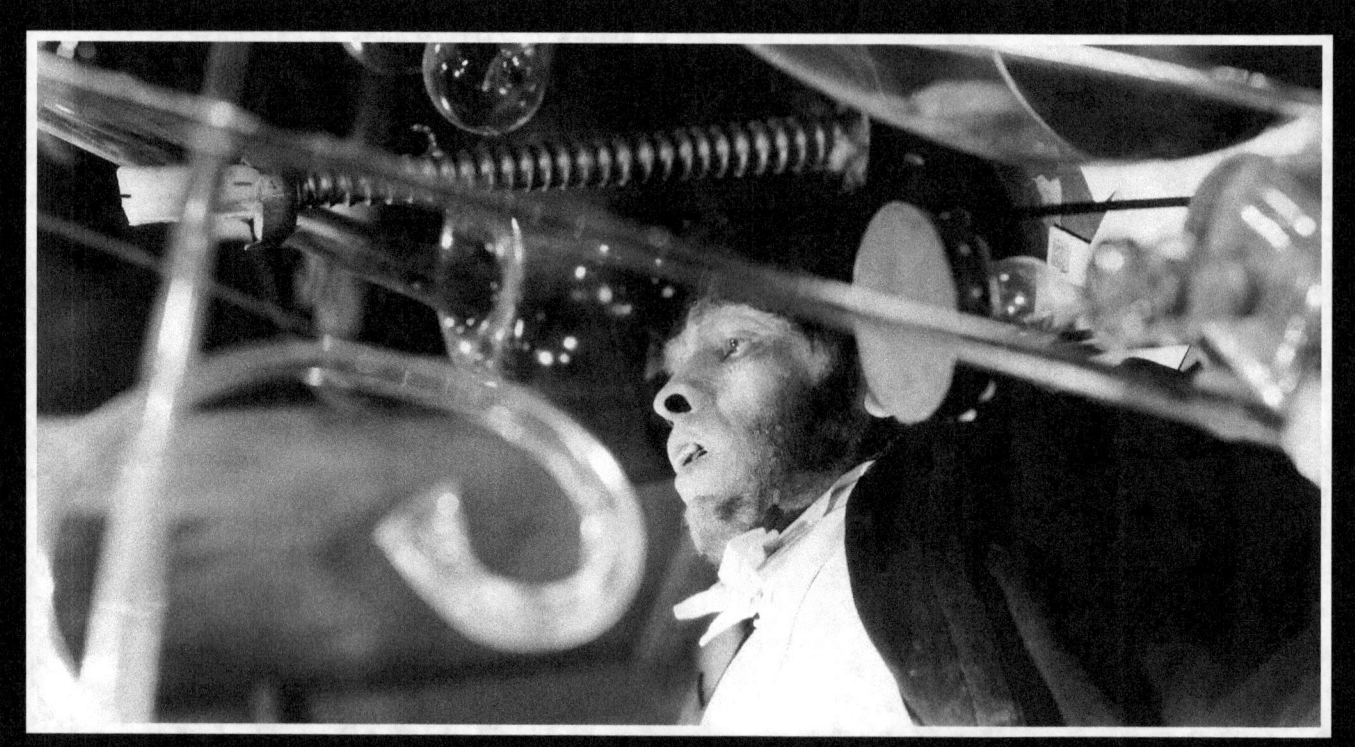

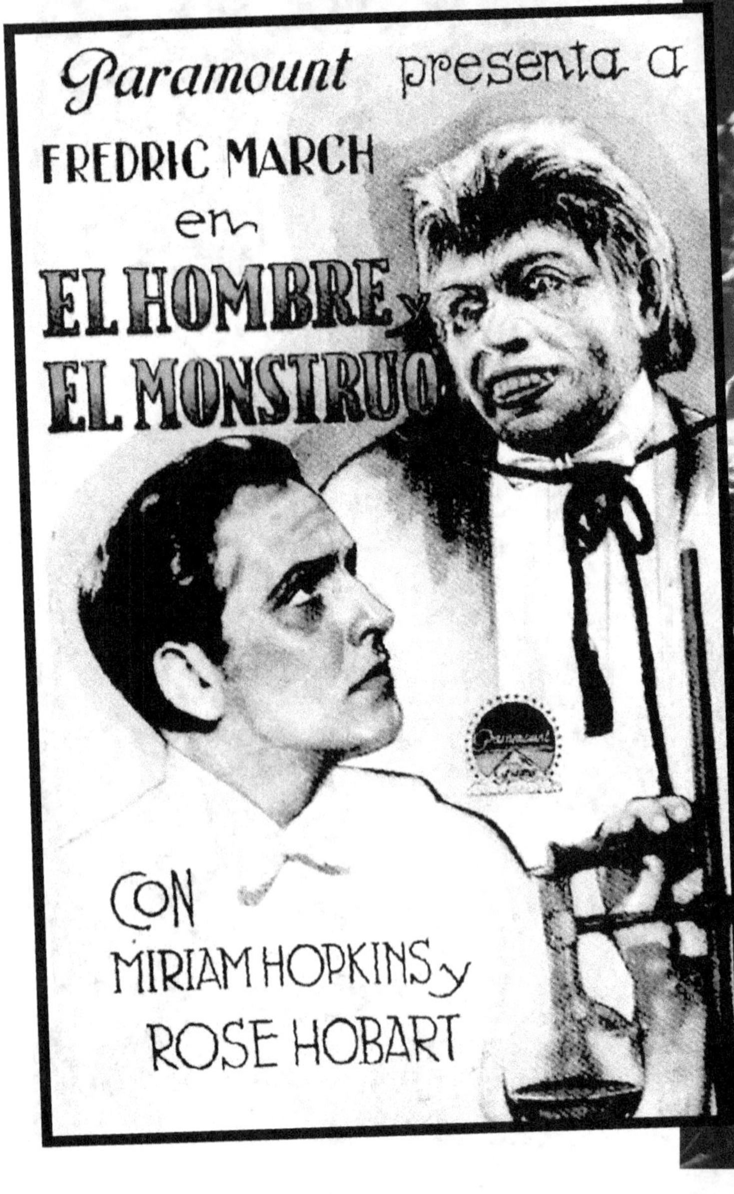
Paramount presenta a
FREDRIC MARCH
en
EL HOMBRE y
EL MONSTRUO
CON
MIRIAM HOPKINS y
ROSE HOBART

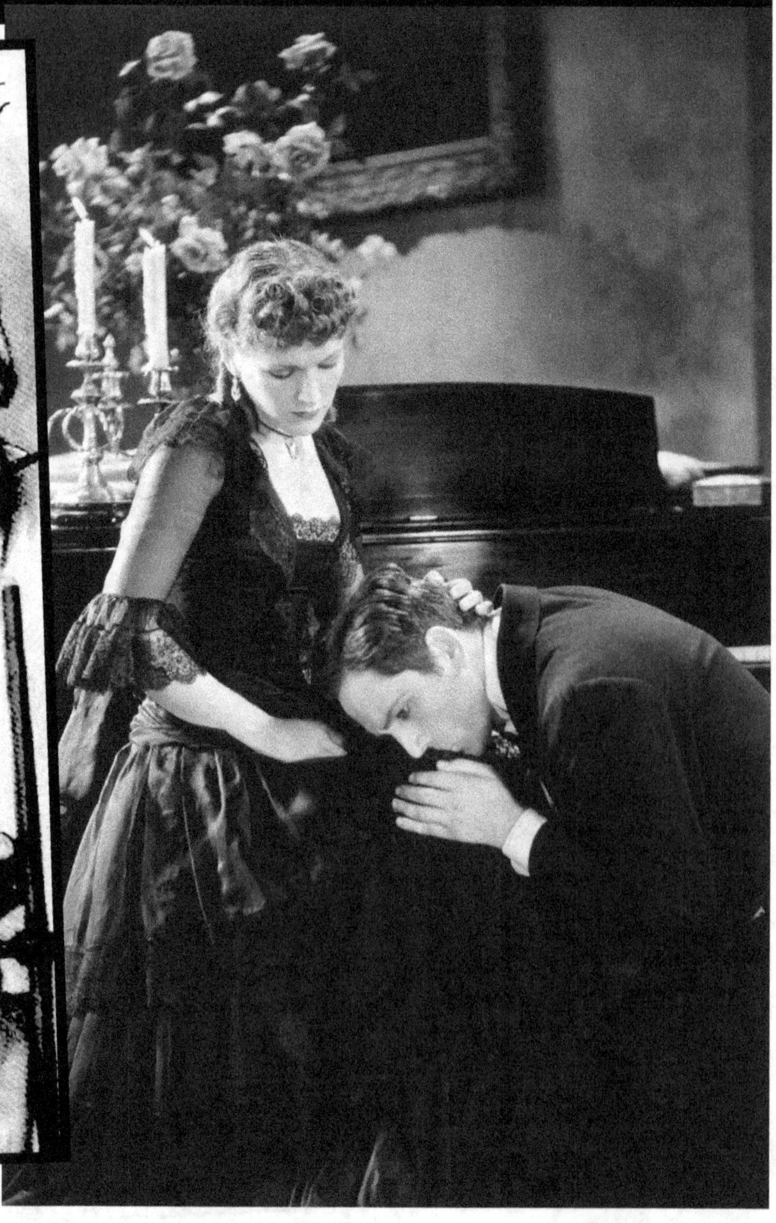

"Dr. Jekyll and Mr. Hyde."

The film of Robert Louis Stevenson's story, "Dr. Jekyll and Mr. Hyde," had the distinct advantage of camera wizardry coupled with a sterling performance by Fredric March. It was directed by Rouben Mamoulian, who succeeded in giving to his scenes an impressive conception of London in Victorian days. The gradual change in Dr. Jekyll when he became the hideous Hyde was wrought in a masterly fashion.

Genre films released in 1932

Murders in the Rue Morgue
Freaks (in Vol. 2)
Dr. X
White Zombie
The Most Dangerous Game (in Vol. 2)
The Old Dark House (in Vol. 2)
Mask of Fu Manchu
The Mummy
Island of Lost Souls

Murders in the Rue Morgue
Released U.S. Feb. 21, 1932

HIS name is Carl Laemmle Jr. and he is filled with the elation of a very young man in a fascinating job. As overlord of the production activities of Universal Pictures Corporation he made recently one of his annual pilgrimages to New York in search of stories for next season.

The fact that he hadn't found any, that prices for the rights to good plays were exorbitant, that money is scarce, worried him no more than the frigidity in the air. He gave crisp orders to secretaries, dictated enigmatic instructions to stenographers, spoke briefly into telephones and appeared to be having a high good time.

For the September season he has some interesting stories lined up and he was filled with enthusiasm about their prospects.

"Remember my prediction about 'Frankenstein'? We hit them with that one, didn't we? We've started a cycle of crime and horror stories and we're going to continue along that line. Robert Louis Stevenson's 'The Suicide Club' should make a peach of a film. 'The Invisible Man,' by H. G. Wells, is another good one.

Poe Story to Be Filmed.

Edgar Allen Poe's story, "Murders in the Rue Morgue," will be brought to the screen by Universal next season, Carl Laemmle announced yesterday. It will be the third of a series of horror films, the first of which was "Dracula." The second is "Frankenstein,"

THE air at Universal City is thick with rumors about the contemplated productions of "Frankenstein" and Poe's "Murders in the Rue Morgue." The real news, though, is limited to the announcement that Bela Lugosi, who played the title rôle in "Dracula," will have the lead in Mary Shelley's macabre story and probably also in the Poe mystery.

Sidney Fox, on for a vacation, went to see a picture with Charles Beahan, who wrestles script for Universal. It was a sad picture, so they cheered up by getting married Wed. (14) morning. Told in Conn. they would have to wait five days, they got spliced in Harrison, N. Y., where there are no residential requirements.

CHI CENSORS HALT U'S 'MORGUE'—DUE FEB. 3

Chicago, Feb. 1.
Possibility of 'Murders of Rue Morgue' not opening at the State Lake this Wednesday (3) as scheduled since the censor board has rejected the picture entirely on extra-comm horror grounds.
Universal exchange is trying to induce board to give the film another screening.

'Murders in the Rue Morgue' (U). In spite of macabre characterisations and backgrounds, fanettes are not unduly alarmed by highly colored, unrealistic melodrama. Neither are they entertained by a confused film more interested in being terrifying than projecting a credible story.

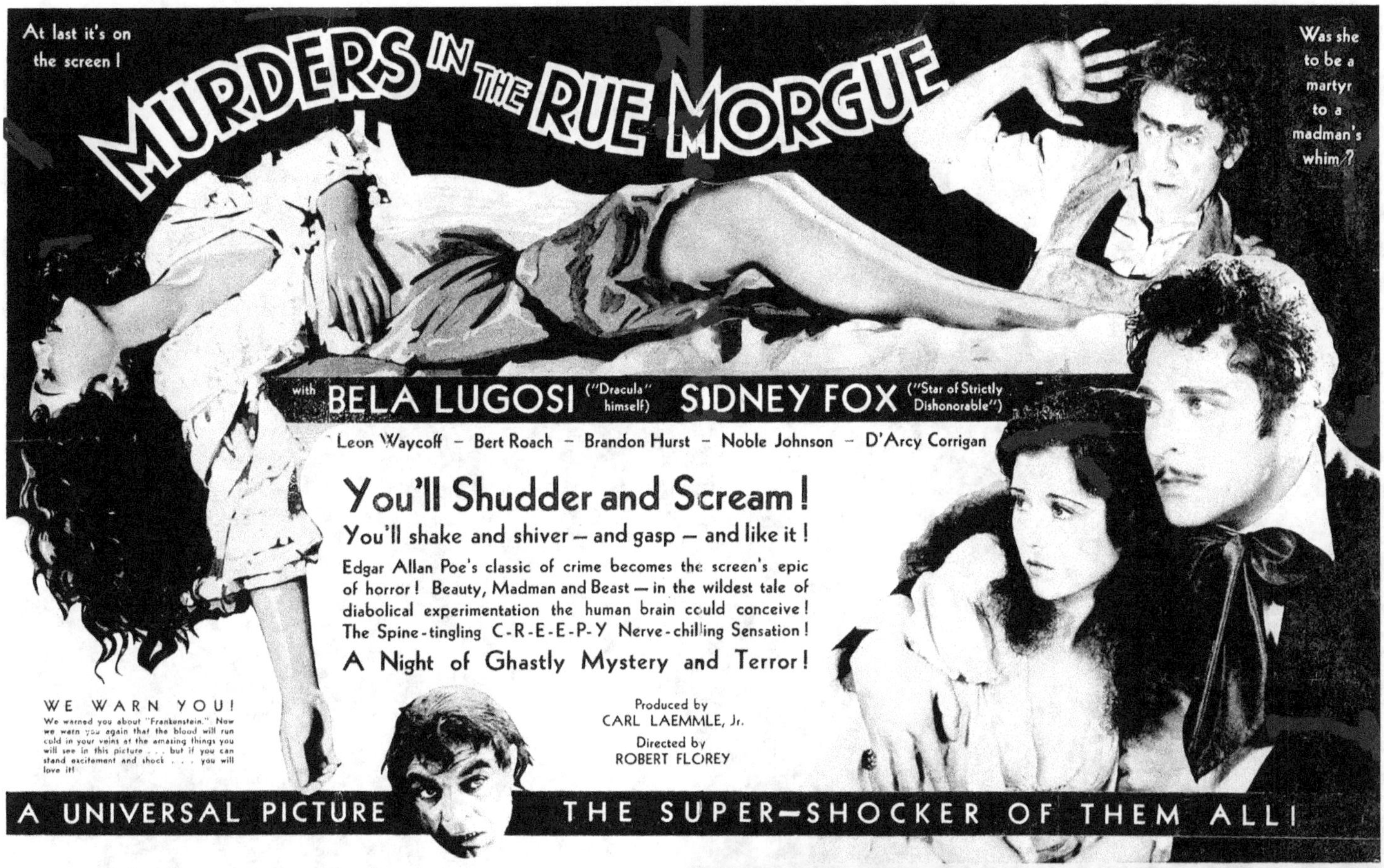

At last it's on the screen!
MURDERS IN THE RUE MORGUE
Was she to be a martyr to a madman's whim?
with BELA LUGOSI ("Dracula" himself) SIDNEY FOX ("Star of Strictly Dishonorable")
Leon Waycoff – Bert Roach – Brandon Hurst – Noble Johnson – D'Arcy Corrigan
You'll Shudder and Scream!
You'll shake and shiver – and gasp – and like it!
Edgar Allan Poe's classic of crime becomes the screen's epic of horror! Beauty, Madman and Beast – in the wildest tale of diabolical experimentation the human brain could conceive! The Spine-tingling C-R-E-E-P-Y Nerve-chilling Sensation!
A Night of Ghastly Mystery and Terror!
WE WARN YOU!
We warned you about "Frankenstein." Now we warn you again that the blood will run culd in your veins at the amazing things you will see in this picture . . . but if you can stand excitement and shock . . . you will love it!
Produced by CARL LAEMMLE, Jr.
Directed by ROBERT FLOREY
A UNIVERSAL PICTURE
THE SUPER-SHOCKER OF THEM ALL!

BRANDON HURST "Prefect of Police"
LEON WAYCOFF "Pierre Dupin"
SIDNEY FOX "Camille L'Espanaye"
BELA LUGOSI "Dr. Mirakle"
BETSY ROSS CLARKE "Mme. L'Espanaye"
BERT RO
The Super Shocker of Them All!
BELA LUGOSI ("Dracula" Himself)
IN
Edgar Allan Poe's
"MURDERS IN THE RUE MORGUE"
4 Days Starting Saturday, February 20th
Madison Ave. MAJESTIC Phone 4-0108
Direct From Roxy Theatre, N. Y. C.
He Who Laughs Best, Laughs At
WILL ROGERS
IN
"Business and Pleasure"
From Booth Tarkington's "The Plutocrat"
3 Days Starting Wednesday, February 24th
COMING
MARIE DRESSLER in "EMMA"
Presented by CARL LAEMMLE
MURDERS IN THE RUE MORGUE
A UNIVERSAL PICTURE
PRINTED IN U.S.

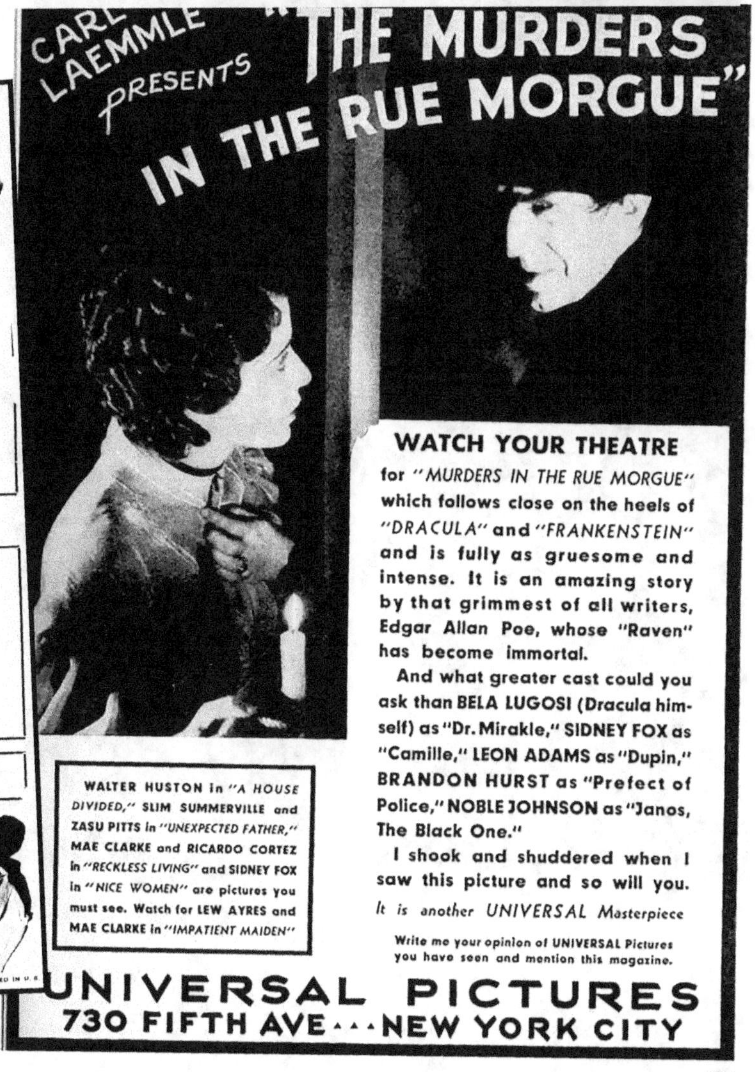

CARL LAEMMLE PRESENTS "THE MURDERS IN THE RUE MORGUE"
WATCH YOUR THEATRE
for "MURDERS IN THE RUE MORGUE" which follows close on the heels of "DRACULA" and "FRANKENSTEIN" and is fully as gruesome and intense. It is an amazing story by that grimmest of all writers, Edgar Allan Poe, whose "Raven" has become immortal.
And what greater cast could you ask than BELA LUGOSI (Dracula himself) as "Dr. Mirakle," SIDNEY FOX as "Camille," LEON ADAMS as "Dupin," BRANDON HURST as "Prefect of Police," NOBLE JOHNSON as "Janos, The Black One."
I shook and shuddered when I saw this picture and so will you.
It is another UNIVERSAL Masterpiece
Write me your opinion of UNIVERSAL Pictures you have seen and mention this magazine.
WALTER HUSTON in "A HOUSE DIVIDED," SLIM SUMMERVILLE and ZASU PITTS in "UNEXPECTED FATHER," MAE CLARKE and RICARDO CORTEZ in "RECKLESS LIVING" and SIDNEY FOX in "NICE WOMEN" are pictures you must see. Watch for LEW AYRES and MAE CLARKE in "IMPATIENT MAIDEN"
UNIVERSAL PICTURES
730 FIFTH AVE . . . NEW YORK CITY

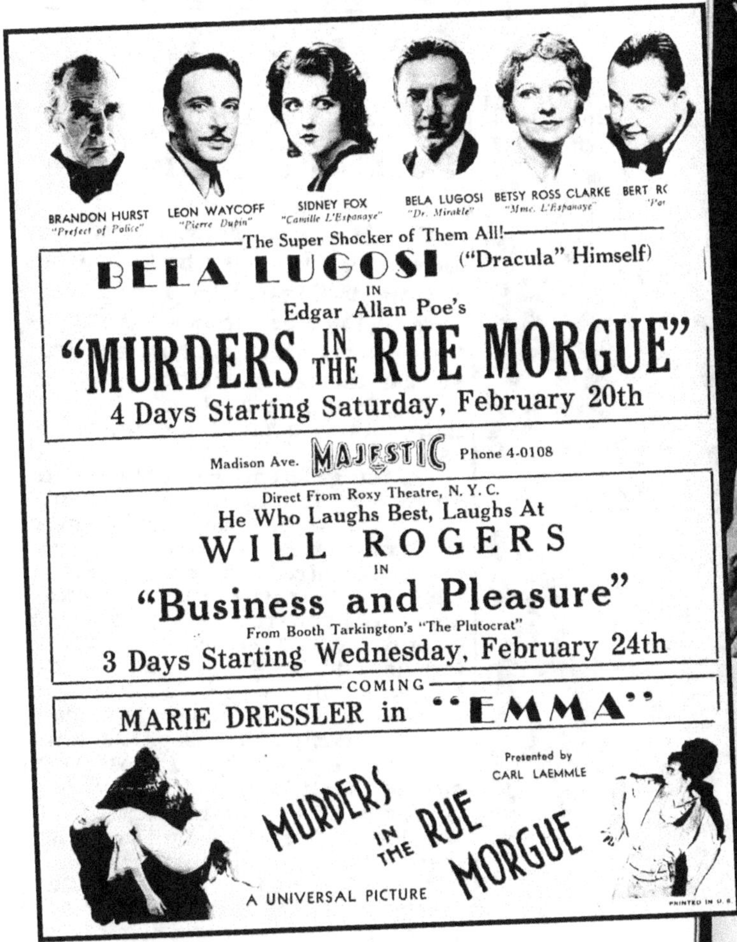

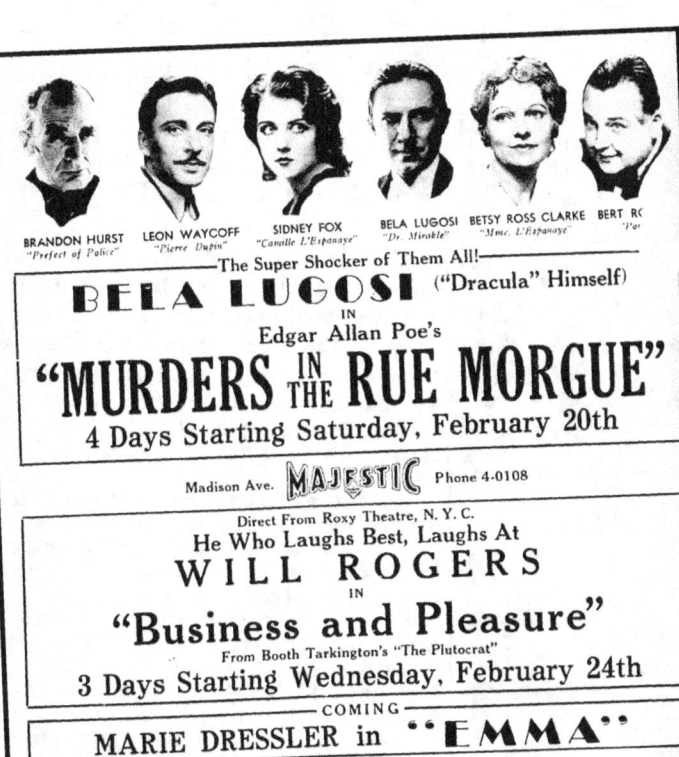

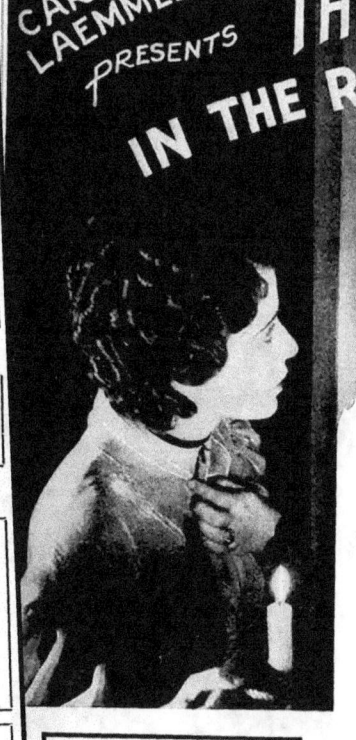

Bela Lugosi And Sidney Fox Appear At The Sheboygan

One of the strangest motion pictures ever shown at The Sheboygan theatre, is Edgar Allen Poe's "Murders in the Rue Morgue," the mystery drama, which is now showing at that theatre in addition to added units. Bela Lugosi, Sidney Fox and many others are in the outstanding cast.

All the gruesome weirdness of its story, and in the exciting events which follow one another in quick succession, this screen play constitutes a contribution to the screen which is nothing short of remarkable. Its power to work on the emotions of an audience is simply terrific, and it will be many a day before its like is seen again. It literally "out-Draculas Dracula," and this comparison is particularly appropriate since Bela Lugosi, who played the title role of "Dracula," is also seen as the menacing Dr. Mirakle of "Murders in the Rue Morgue."

"Safe in Hell," with Dorothy Mackaill has its grand opening run at the Sheboygan beginning Wednesday.

SEE MOVIES WITH POTATOES, EGGS

LENINGRAD, (AP)—Movie fans in Russia, who are short on currency, now obtain admission to some cinemas by tendering old clothing, potatoes, eggs, flowers and whatnot at the box office.

Particularly welcome in this land of heavy snows and long winters is the prospective patron who brings a pair of old galoshes.

The Krasnaya Gazeta says it is for the box office cashier to judge whether the articles presented are sufficient valuable to justify admission.

Radio Script

Universal is sending out a radio script on 'Murders in the Rue Morgue' for the benefit of those who may wish to locally air the picture. If there is no radio it might be possible, in spite of the lengty, to sell it to the audience as a sample radio script, making it a feature on the preceding bill. Three or four local amateurs and a cut in on the non-sync or any loudspeaker should put this over for a novelty, working back of a screen or showing how it is done as may seem best.

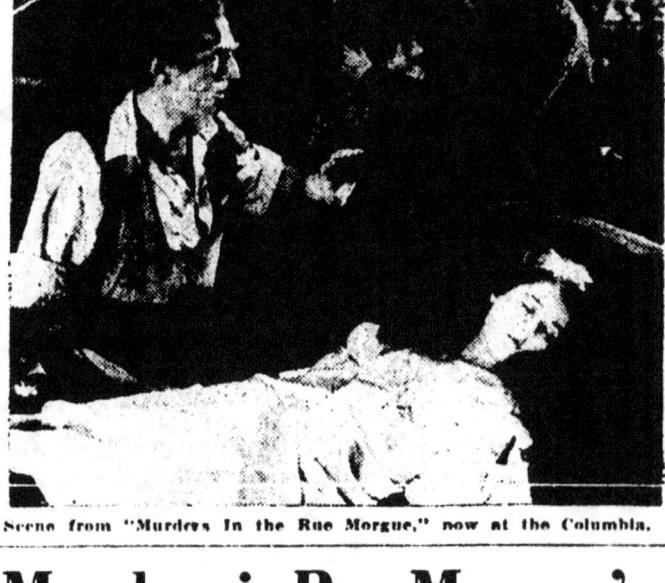

Scene from "Murders In the Rue Morgue," now at the Columbia.

'Murders in Rue Morgue' Opens at Columbia

The picturesque buildings of the Paris of a generation ago furnish the backgrounds for the story of Edgar Allan Poe's "Murders in the Rue Morgue," the weird Universal drama which comes to the Columbia Theater today, with Bela Lugosi and Sidney Fox in the leading roles.

Steeply pitching roofs surmount crazily leading structures; balconies line the upper floors; sharp church spires pierce the sky; strange shadows lurk in sheltered courtyards; the Seine River flows sullenly along behind its embankments. But even stranger are the interior settings of the picture, for many of them show the laboratory of the terrible Dr. Mirakle, scientist with a warped brain, whose constant companion is a gigantic gorilla.

This laboratory is a huge affair, located in the basement of one of the oldest buildings in Paris. Crazy ladders and winding stairs lead from the street level on both sides of the building to its rock paved floor. A scaffold is erected in the center. From this scaffold Dr. Mirakle can open a trap door, disclosing the dark waters of the Seine flowing beneath. Another scene depicts as accurately as careful investigation can ascertain, what an ancient Parisian city morgue was like.

There is also a set depicting three garret rooms of a typical Paris residential flat, and three very elaborate street scenes, one showing the house where Sidney Fox and her mother lived, one the Rue Morgue itself, and the other a street on the banks of the Seine. There is also an elaborate setting for a side-show somewhat on the order of the amusement park shown years ago in the Universal "The Man Who Laughs."

The association of ape and master is the basis of the story, since Mirakle is deep in a series of unbelievable experiments which have for their objects the introduction of the ape's blood into the veins of a living girl. Sidney Fox, in the character of Camille L'Espanaye, eventually becomes the object of Mirakle's pursuit, and subsequent events make of "Murders in the Rue Morgue" the most gruesomely exciting picture in the history of the talking screen.

In addition to Lugosi and Miss Fox, the cast of "Murders in the Rue Morgue" includes Leon Waycoff, Bert Roach, Brandon Hurst, Betty Ross Clarke, Noble Johnson, D'Arcy Corrigan and John T. Murray. The picture was directed by Robert Florey.

Doctor X
Released U.S. Aug. 3, 1932

"Doctor X," the mystery melodrama recently completed by First National, will be drifting into the Strand or Winter Garden some time next month. The cast includes Lionel Atwill, Lee Tracy, Fay Wray, Mae Busch and Preston Foster.

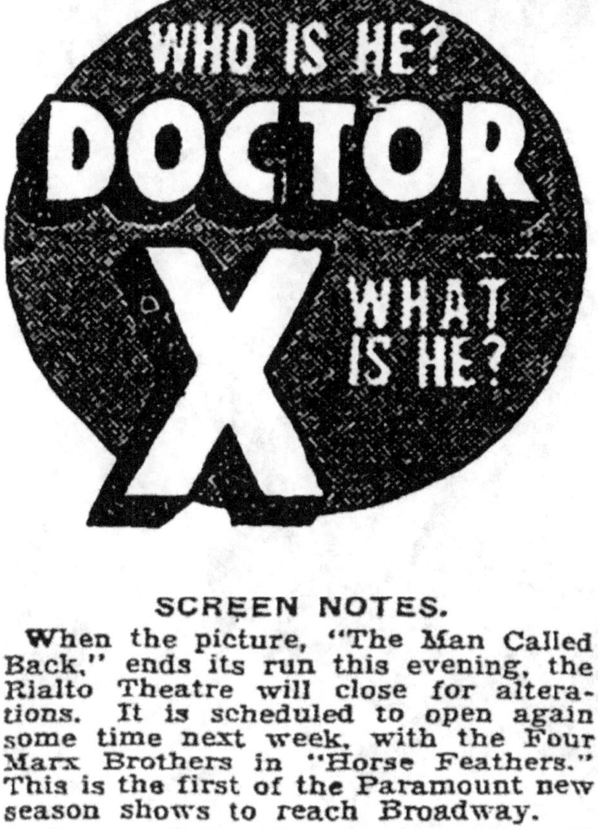

SCREEN NOTES.

When the picture, "The Man Called Back," ends its run this evening, the Rialto Theatre will close for alterations. It is scheduled to open again some time next week, with the Four Marx Brothers in "Horse Feathers." This is the first of the Paramount new season shows to reach Broadway.

"Doctor X," with Lionel Atwill, will open this evening at the Strand.

"Doctor X," a screen version of last season's Broadway mystery thriller, entered production last week at the West Coast studios of First National Pictures. Michael Curtiz is directing the film. In the cast are Lionel Atwill, Lee Tracy, Fay Wray, Preston Foster, John Wray, Arthur Edmund Carewe, Harry Beresford, George Rosener, Robert Warwick, Leila Bennett and Mae Busch.

Dittmann

— TODAY —

"Doctor X"

LIONEL ATWILL
FAY WRAY

RKO Pathe Comedy

Summer Price, 10c

STATE
WARNER'S
Now!
A First National Thriller filmed in gorgeous natural colors with LIONEL ATWILL, FAY WRAY, LEE TRACY
MOON DEMON TERRORIZES WHOLE CITY
DOCTOR X
It's the Fourth Dimension in Screen Thrills! New! Startling! Daring!
How Doctor X, SHOCK by SHOCK, Startled the World!
1—Six fiendish crimes cause panic.
2—Doctor X re-enacts gruesome killings.
3—Experimental murder turns out like real ones.
4—Daughter of Doctor X selected for new experiment.
5—Girl at mercy of Moon-demon.
6—Moon-demon's secret . . . Who is he? ? ?
NO ONE SEATED DURING FINAL REEL!
See it from the beginning. Feature at 1:59, 3:58, 5:57, 7:56, 9:55

REX
DOCTOR "X"
GREATEST THRILLER YET
GEORGEOUS TECHNICOLOR
REX
FROZEN CUSTA
ALL DAY
25¢
DOCTOR X
DOCTOR X
DOCTOR X
With
LEE TRACY
LIONEL ATWILL
FAY WRAY
ALL IN GEORGEOUS TECHNICOLOR

'Doctor X' Is Screen Feature At State Today

Well contrived mystery mixed with sturdy melodrama, brilliant comedy and Technicolor are features of "Doctor X," at the State Sunday through Tuesday. As a newspaper reporter, Lee Tracy, perennial newshound of both stage and screen, displays an excellent and novel quality of acting. Lionel Atwill, actor and director of stage plays, is cast as Doctor Xavier. Others in the cast are Fay Wray, Preston Foster, John Wray and Harry Beresford.

White Zombie

Released U.S. Aug. 4, 1932

'Zombie,' at U. A., Chi, $16,000;

'WHITE ZOMBIE' OPENS AT PALACE

Bela Lugosi Has Starring Role in This Masterpiece of Horror Films

An eerie, spooky motion picture which for sheer mystery outdoes all its predecessors is "White Zombie," which opened at the Palace yesterday for three days.

This picture may safely be said to be in a class by itself. For it deals with a subject which heretofore has been little short of superstition, and a not very well known one at that. Its story deals with occult practices in remote sections of Haiti, where Zombies, or dead bodies, are dug from their graves and, by a process of sorcery, re-animated and put to work in the fields and mills as slaves.

Whether or not you believe what you see in this picture, you will be enthralled by its presentation. Particularly when you learn that there is a wealth of evidence to bear out its authenticity.

She was not alive... nor dead... Just a WHITE ZOMBIE Performing his every desire

'White Zombie' Is Grotesque Story

"White Zombie." At the Queen. Screenplay by Garnet Weston. Photographed by Arthur Martinelli. Produced by Edward Halperin. Directed by Victor Halperin. Released by Regal Distributing Corporation. The cast follows:

Murder	Bela Lugosi
Madeleine	Madge Bellamy
Dr. Bruner	Joseph Cawthorn
Beaumont	Robert Frazer
Neil	John Harron
Driver	Clarence Muse
Silver	Brandon Hurst
Pierre	Dan Crimmins
Chauvin	John Peters
Von Gelder	George Burr McAnnan

Just to look at Bela Lugosi one would never think that he has the appeal of a Shirley Temple or an Ann Sheridan. And yet, without even baring his chief beauty, a fang, this satanic cadaver kept an amazingly large audience of would-be fans waiting for hours in the bitter cold yesterday until "White Zombie," the feature attraction, arrived at the theater.

After all that excitement the picture was almost incidental. This film is of a type that is now almost extinct. No studio produces this bold, melodramatic kind of horror which was so popular at the beginning of the present decade. The horror has nothing subtle about it and the actors really go about the business of terrorizing themselves as well as the audience in an efficient manner.

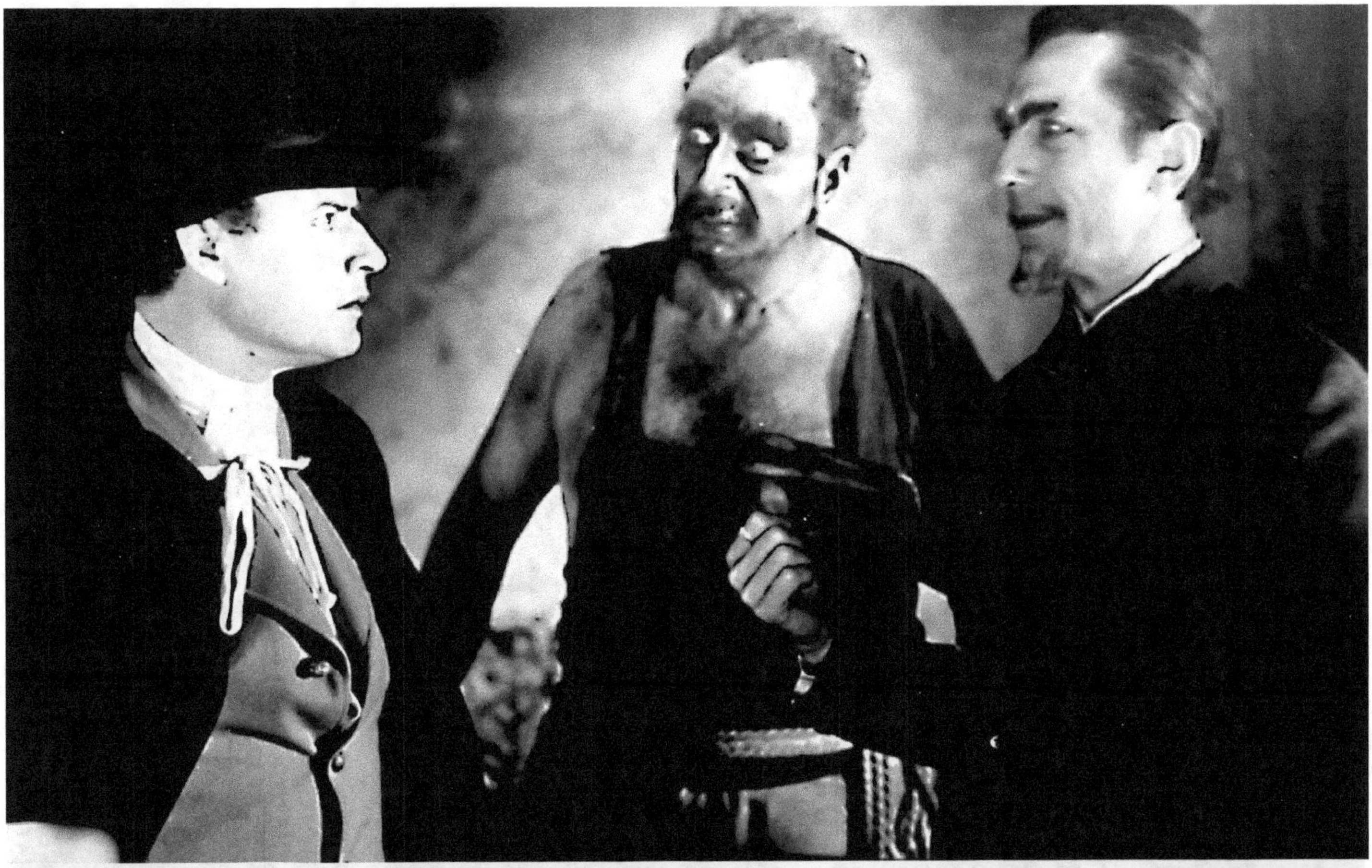

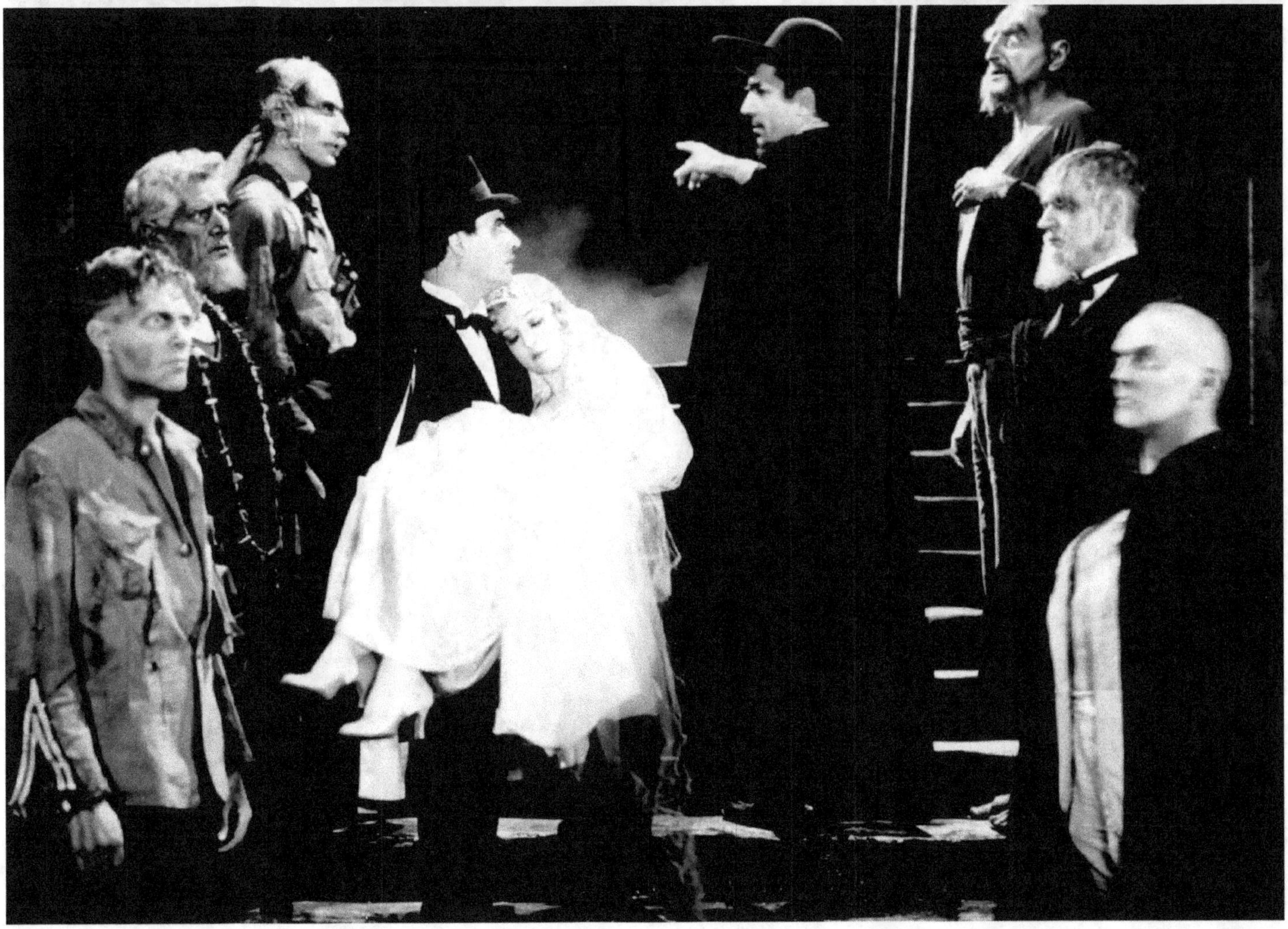

MIDNIGHT MATINEE

Weird Bela Lugosi will be presented at a midnight matinee Saturday night of "White Zombie" at the Mission.

Haitian superstition, dealing with persons only partly alive due to a spell of magic, is used as a basis for this picture.

Madge Bellamy is cast as leading woman, after an absence of more than two years from the screen. She is placed under the spell of Lugosi, as "Murder," a native magician. Held captive in a remote castle, without mental capacity, she is forced to attempt to murder her husband.

KLAN RECRUITING DRY VOTES ON RESUBMISSION

Long Beach, Cal., Aug. 8.

Ku Klux Klan has sprung up here again, opening a recruiting office and appealing to the bone drys.

That the Klan revival is apparently for the purpose of winning Republican votes in the south is gathered from literature issued here.

Pamphlets state the Klan is in favor of the party that advocates resubmission and against the one that has a repeal plank in its platform.

Local organizers declare that they are still affiliated with national headquarters in Atlanta, Ga., and that recruiting is going on all over the south.

"I'm Telling You"
By Jack Osterman

HERE'S MY COPY. YOU CAN GO TO PRESS NOW.

Observation

The little lady observes that there are enough half dead people walking up and down Broadway without going to see 'White Zombie.'

Appearing with this picture is an Olsen and Johnson short, so we took our little nephew. He laughed at 'Zombie' but Olsen and Johnson frightened him.

Bela Lugosi in 'Zombie' Film

Bela ("Dracula") Lugosi has another spine-chilling role in "White Zombie," the latest horror picture appearing on the Aztec theater screen for a seven-day engagement which opened Saturday. This road show engagement for one week marks a departure temporarily from the regular split week policy at the theater.

Based upon a fantastic superstition of the natives in Haiti, "White Zombie" deals with a form of superstition supported by many weird stories concerning the ability to bring to a half-life, bodies that have been freshly buried. This black magic at least is being practiced in the remote sections of this country, and natives live in dread fear of this superstitious belief. As the story opens Madge Bellamy is seen arriving on the island as the fiancee of John Harron, a young banker, who plans an early marriage. On the boat the girl has accepted an invitation from Bela Lugosi, a wealthy plantation owner, to be his guest at a bridal party. This he does as a trick to gain an opportunity to win the love of the girl. At the party he drugs her with a potion that dulls the senses and she drops to the floor apparently dead. At least physicians proclaim her so and her body is prepared for burial. Lugosi, known in the story as "Murder," is the one who administers the poison and after the trick has been worked removes the body of the girl to his castle where he has a small army of zombies, or living dead, in his power. The young bridegroom learns of the plot and in the company of an American missionary and a witch, goes to the castle to rescue his sweetheart from the spell of the fiend. From this point many chilling incidents follow.

Comedy short subjects of a diverting nature include a song cartoon, "Treasure Runt," a comedy, "East Meets West," and a comedy act, "In Your Hat." The Airplane edition of the Paramount Sound news shows several interesting news events on the screen.

Rivoli (2,200; 40-55-72-94-$1.10)— 'White Zombie' (UA). At $25,000 will be bringing to house best week it has had in over a month. Publix may spot 'Blonde Venus' (Par) in here next. Date unset. 'Igloo' (U), which preceded 'Zombie' and stayed only one week, failed to get anywhere at all, $8,000.

United Artists opened Thursday (28) with 'White Zombie' and used several stooges on the marquee in an animated goosepimple tableau to halt passers-by. This exploitation was most unusual for the house, and accumulated a sidewalk audience at the busy Randolph-Dearborn corner.

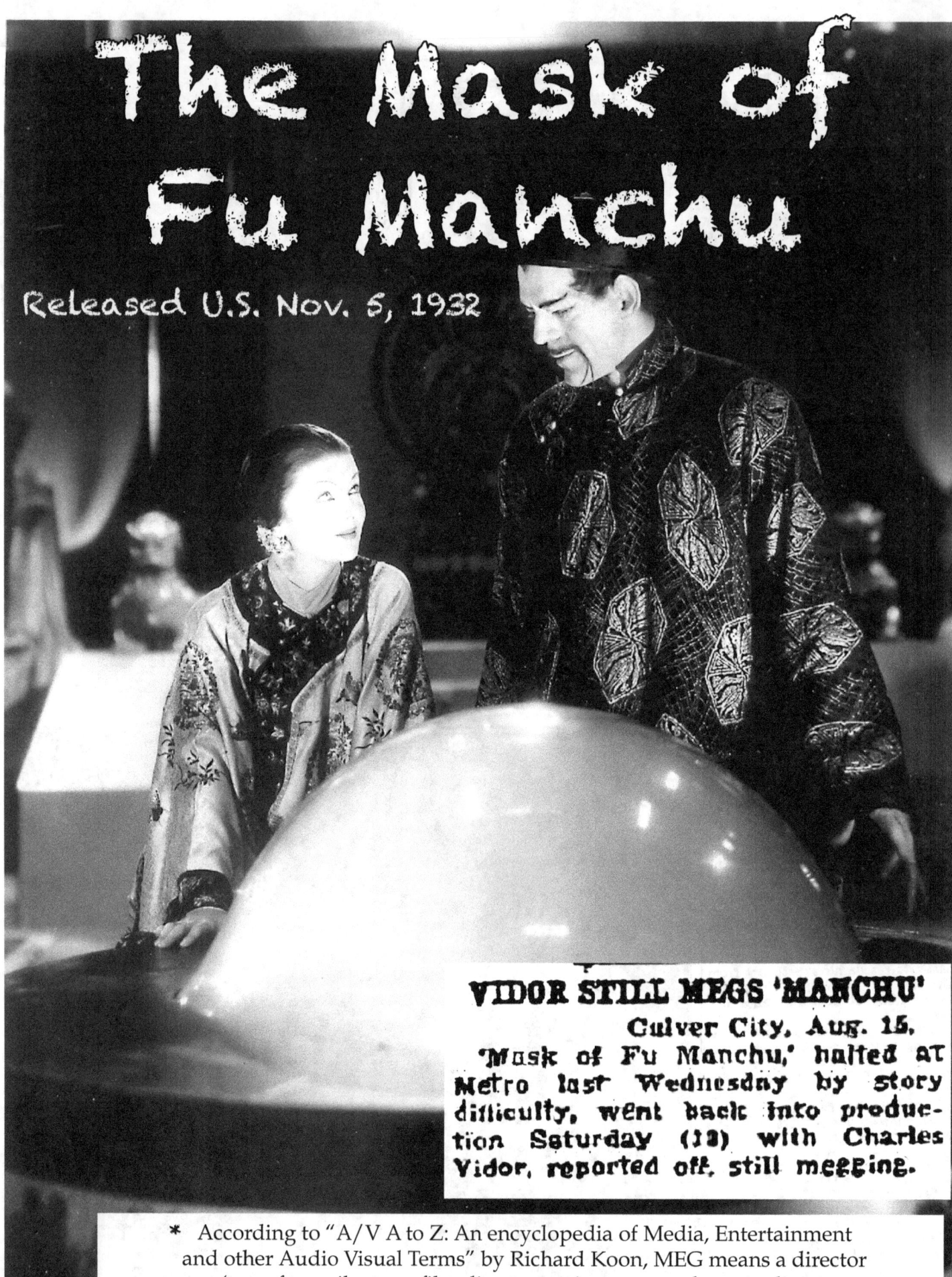

The Mask of Fu Manchu

Released U.S. Nov. 5, 1932

VIDOR STILL MEGS 'MANCHU'

Culver City, Aug. 15.
'Mask of Fu Manchu,' halted at Metro last Wednesday by story difficulty, went back into production Saturday (13) with Charles Vidor, reported off, still megging.

* According to "A/V A to Z: An encyclopedia of Media, Entertainment and other Audio Visual Terms" by Richard Koon, MEG means a director (term from silent-era film directors using a megaphone to direct.

THE FILM SHOP

By Harrison Carroll
Copyright 1932, King Features
Syndicate, Inc.

Hollywood, Cal., Aug. 9—And now for an even stranger tale of Dr. Fu Manchu.

After being an exclusive Paramount bogey man since way back yonder, the sinister old fellow has been sold down the river to Metro-Goldwyn-Mayer and suddenly finds himself in the lanky and unaccustomed frame of Boris Karloff.

Why Mr. Karloff instead of bland Warner Oland isn't explained; and I suppose doesn't matter.

The important thing is that the wily old oriental, master of a thousand tricks, is to be with us again, with new villainies. His latest adventure, "The Mask of Fu Manchu," will be directed by Charles Vidor, and his pretty victim will be Gertrude Michael, one of M. G. M.'s crop of Broadway starlets.

The picture goes into immediate production with Mr. Karloff, of course, loaned from Universal for the engagement.

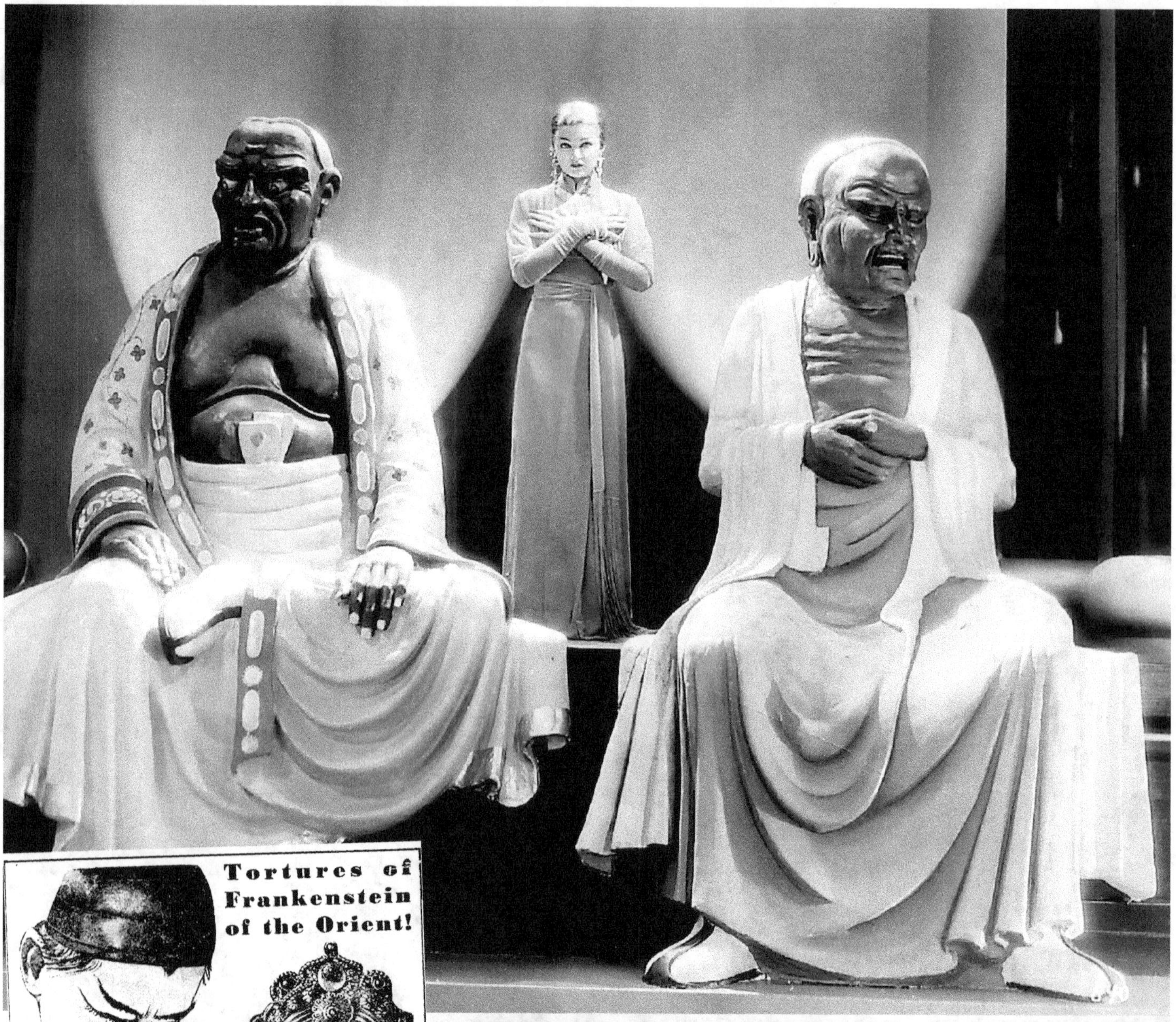

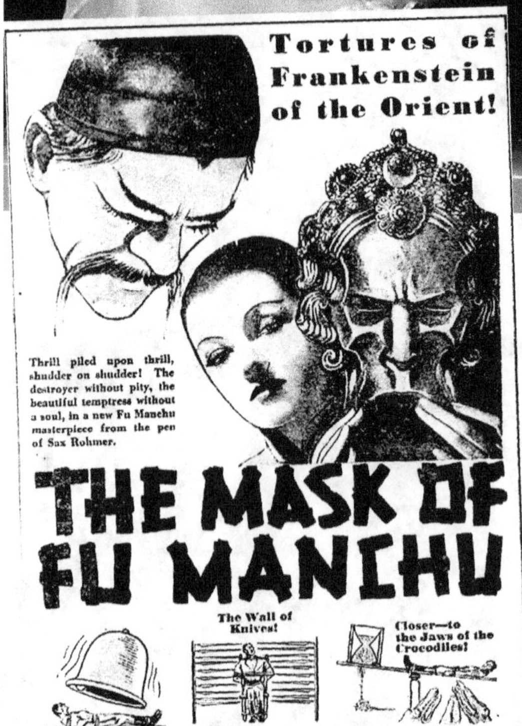

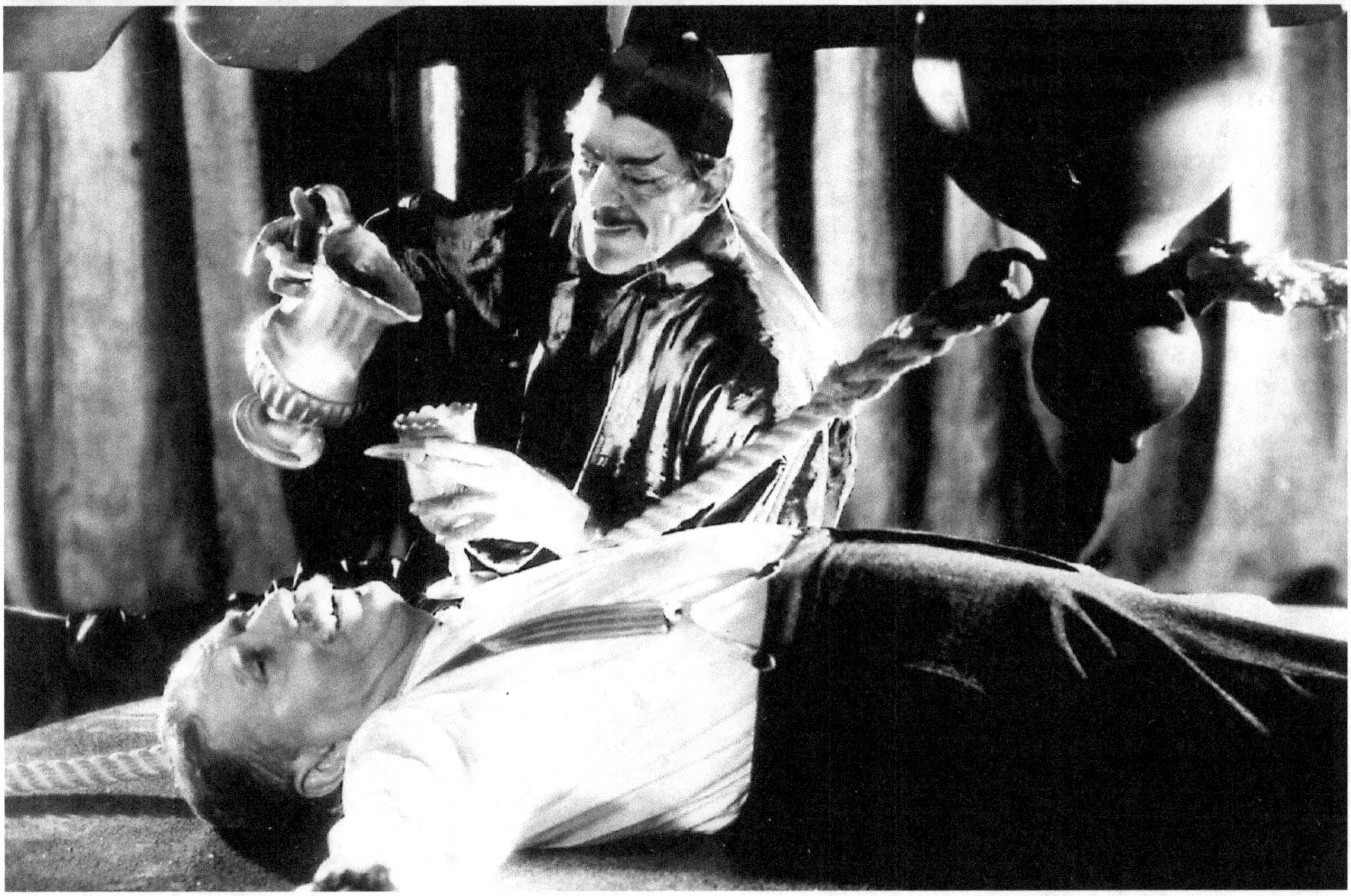

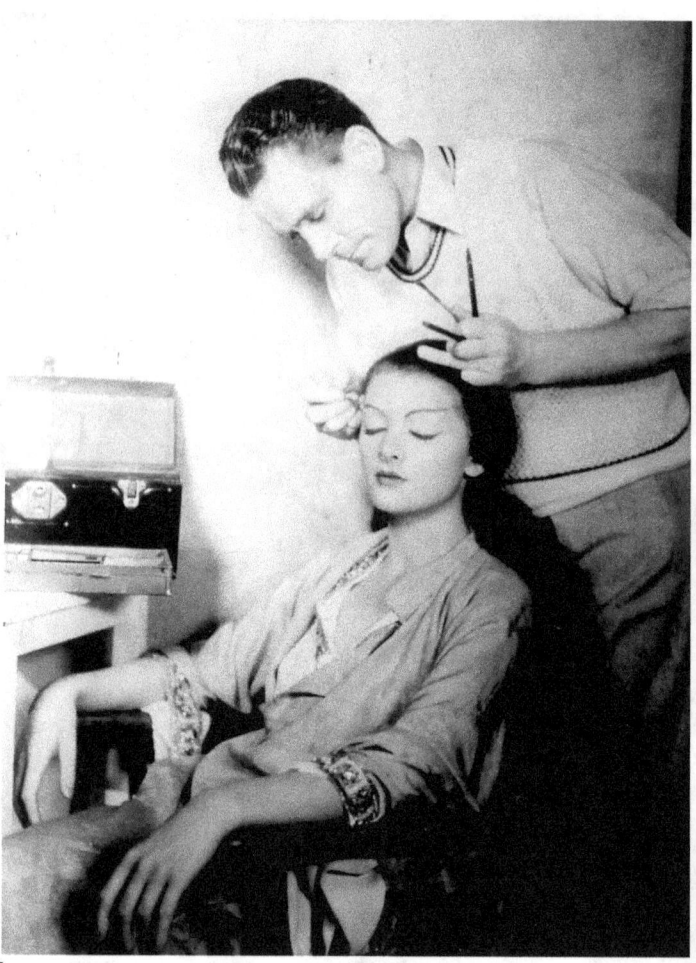

Dressing Shudder Roles

Myrna Loy's slanting eyes have gotten her into all sorts of pictures needing inscrutable Oriental women. None of them seem to mind her fresh young American voice, her red-white-and-blue pronunciation.

In "The Mask of Fu Manchu" she's been given some additional slant to her eyes. Fortunately for the help of her sinisterness, she has little to say. She's just got to stand by in glittering Chinese-through-Hollywood garb and look sadistically amorous, occasionally bursting into shrieks as she orders her slaves to beat her lover harder.

Karen Morley's throaty voice continually despairs of ever finding the loved ones that Fu Manchu snatches away so methodically. Miss Morley goes through a lot of trouble in riding clothes, only to find herself at the end garbed like a Greek maiden because she is going to be a sacrifice to some god somewhere in China. It doesn't check, but it's becoming.

NOW PLAYING Nancy Carroll in "HOT SATURDAY" Cary Grant

A *New* FU MANCHU THRILLER!

The sensational star of "Frankenstein" is here now in the finest story from the pen of Sax Rohmer.

A woman without a soul... A voice behind the Mask... A Mask that no man could look upon and live!

From the story by Sax Rohmer

with **BORIS KARLOFF** in his greatest role

Lewis Stone, Karen Morley, Charles Starrett, Myrna Loy, Jean Hersholt . . . . .

THE MASK OF FU MANCHU

INDIANA SUNDAY

GRAND
Pecos, Texas
Matinee 2 P. M., Night 7:15 P. M.

SATURDAY ONLY
"HE LEARNED ABOUT WOMEN"
STUART ERWIN

SUNDAY and MONDAY
"MEN MUST FIGHT"
PHILLIP HOLMES and RUTH SELWYN

TUESDAY and WEDNESDAY
"THE MASK OF FU MANCHU"
BORIS KARLOFF and KAREN MORLEY

THURSDAY and FRIDAY
"SIGN OF THE CROSS"
FREDRICK MARCH and C. COLBERT

FU MANCHU IS NOW AT IOWA

Chinese Mystery Play With All Star Cast Is a Thriller.

Admirers of Sax Rohmer's stories and there are many, will have an opportunity of seeing his greatest success "The Mask of Fu Manchu," on the screen at the Iowa theater. The picture is being shown now.

Mystery thrillers are supposed to give audiences a nightmare sometimes, but "The Mask of Fu Manchu" started by giving one to studio technicians at the Metro-Goldwyn-Mayer studios.

They had to collect cobras and king-snakes. They had to reproduce skeletons of dinosauri and peterodactyles. They had to counterfeit the mummies of ancient Egypt. They had to operate man-made lightning, latest wonder of science, and hurl millions of volts about.

All of which are incidental to some of the most amazing thrills ever seen, in the filmization of Sax Rohmer's weird story of Oriental mystery, with Boris Karloff, the famous "Frankenstein," in the leading role.

Mysteries of ancient Egypt and China blend with the ultra modern, in the strange laboratory of the Oriental fiend whose dream is world dominion. Technical research produced replicas of prehistoric beasts; of ancient sarcophagi, of the mysterious tortures of the Orient, such as the great bell which rings until the victim under it is driven mad—or the weird room of the spikes. Modern science supplied the Tesla coils, the artificial lightning, the strange "death ray" and such modern details.

Hundreds of Mongols and other Orientals appear in the scenes where the Asiatic horde plans world dominion. Great towering Buddhas in gorgeous Oriental palaces contrast with the weird catacombs of the dead and the grim torture chambers in which the thrilling action is set.

The picture was produced on a specially lavish scale. In one scene a huge gold-plated Buddha fifty feet high is seen in the great Feast of the of strang statues, flanking the of strange tsatues, flanking the weird devices that operate the strange robot that stalks through the cringing hordes.

What does a brachycesphalic skull look like?

How does artificial lightning work?

How is a paleontology laboratory equipped?

"The Mask of Fu Manchu" has been acquired by Metro-Goldwyn-Mayer for the screen and this Sax Rohmer story will be produced with Boris Karloff in the leading role. Charles Vidor will direct this picture which is expected to get under way in the near future, with supporting players now being assembled.

METRO, RADIO CO-OP. ON 'FU'

Chicago, Aug. 29.
Metro-Goldwyn-Mayer has asked and received assurances of 'protection' for its forthcoming 'Mask of Fu-Manchu' from N. Porter Caldwell, who controls the radio rights to all of Sax Rohmer's works. Radio adaptation starts over CBS from WBBM, Chicago, on Sept. 26, about two weeks before the Metro picture will be released. Entirely different story will be used on the radio program sponsored by the Italian Campagana Balm. Publicity tie-ups between radio and screen are likely.
Sax Rohmer, the English author, will appear on the first broadcast, being picked up in New York ahead of the Chicago dramatization. It's Rohmer's premiere radio talk.

Looney Toons cartoon (1938) features my favorite monsters!

I dropped in on the "Mask of D[r.] Fu Manchu" set to see Boris Karlof[f] as the Mandarin scientist and de[-]cided it's really great fun to be [a] character actor of this type. Karlof[f,] his eyes heavy with putty to giv[e] the correct lid and pulled at the side[s] with fishskin to get the correct slan[t,] had to behead a victim.

The papier mache figure was ar[-]ranged in kneeling position—dow[n] came the great two-edged sword—of[f] came the head with a dull sickenin[g] thud. Followed a sign from Directo[r] Charles Brabin who is working prett[y] hard these days and nights trying t[o] finish up and release some of h[is] actors to other pictures. The bloo[d] bag, concealed in the neck, didn'[t] burst. Another figure was brought[.] This time the great sword—made o[f] light weight gilded wood—broke of[f] just below the handle. Moans agai[n] from the director and loud laugh[s] from Jean Hersholt sitting near [a] cage of live pythons, rattlers and tw[o] jars of tarantulas used in the pictur[e.]

A third sword was brought. Kar[-]loff reached out for it. Doubled u[p] in dismay. The original bronze two[-]edged sword from which the other[s] were copied. Karloff went throug[h] his routine. This time his arm[s] failed him from the tremendou[s] weight of the sword, just before th[e] camera cut the scene.

I hated to leave. It was so in[-]triguing. Hersholt, Myrna Loy, Kare[n] Morely and Charles Starrett were[,] telling me how chummy they were[,] getting with the snakes. It seem[s] you don't mind them at all afte[r] you've worked with them for a while[.] After a hard day with all sorts o[f] mishaps Brabin was leaving order[s] for the technical staff. He fel[t] something pressing against his leg:

"Get out of my way . . . you!" h[e] growled, shoving a monster pytho[n] aside . . . "and stay out of the way!"

Butterfly

LAST TIMES TONIGHT

Boris Karloff

In His Greatest Role

"The Mask of Fu Manchu"

Never have you witnessed such gasp-producing spectacles — The terrible Pool of Crocodiles— The Wall of Knives—The Death Ray.

Comedy
"GOOD HOUSE WRECKING"
And Paramount News

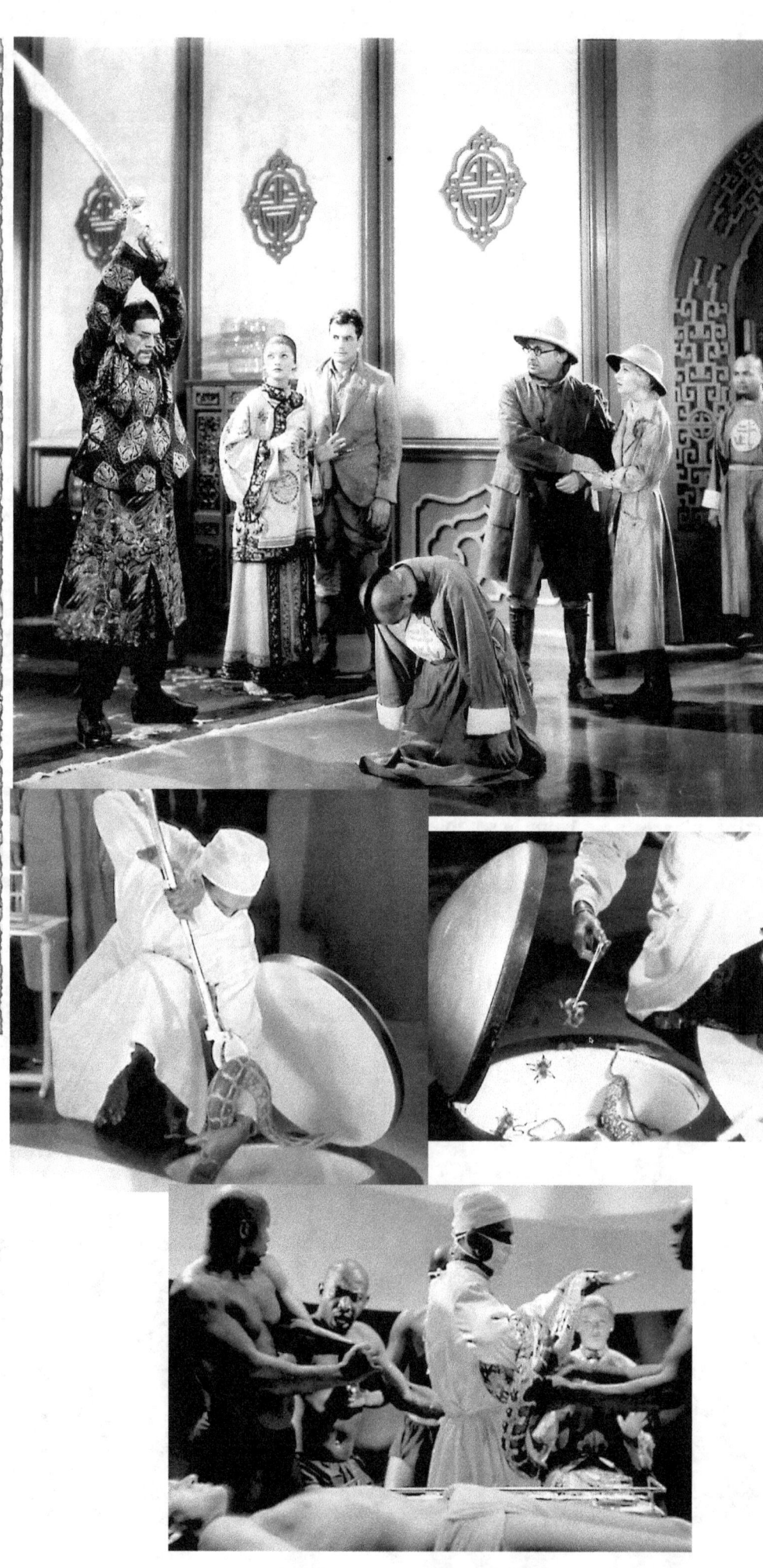

Collectibles!

Wow, this was sculpted by our friend Larry Elig!

BORIS KARLOFF FROM The MASK OF FU MANCHU

LAST TIMES TODAY
AMERICAN
The MASK OF FU MANCHU
With
BORIS KARLOFF
LEWIS STONE - KAREN MORLEY
MYRNA LOY - JEAN HERSHOLT
Also
MICKEY MOUSE
"LOST SPECIAL" AND NEWS

The Mummy
Released U.S. December 22, 1932

BORIS KARLOFF'S latest and possibly most startling face will be turned to New York audiences soon when "The Mummy" reaches Broadway. The man of many visages plays the part of an Egyptian mummy risen from the tomb after something like 3,700 years of death. Mr. Karloff sat for six hours in the make-up chair while layer after layer of cotton, spirit gum, clay and colored paints were applied to him. The process was arduous but interesting. First the actor's face was dampened and then covered with thin strips of cotton, over which collodion was applied, with spirit gum to hold it in place. Nothing was neglected, not even the eyelids. The ears were pinned back. At intervals work ceased and the electric machine was applied to dry and set the wrinkles. The hair was smoothed back and plastered down with make-up clay, pressed close to the scalp and then carefully dried. On the base of cotton and collodion a total of twenty-two different varieties of make-up paint were applied. His body was then swathed from head to foot in acid-eaten bandages which had been passed through a warm oven. The illusion of age was completed by a thin application of Fuller's earth over the body.

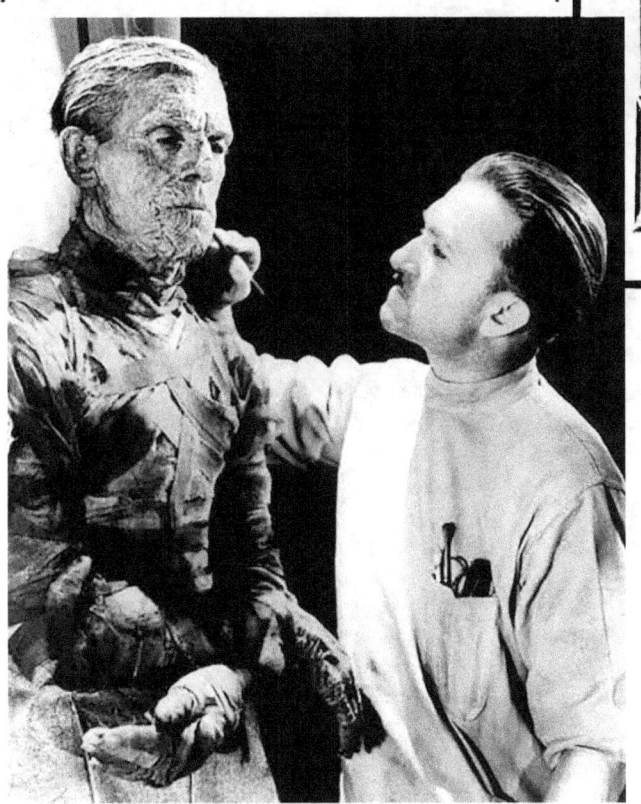

"The Mummy," Tale Of Mysterious Egypt, Showing At Grand

All the mystery, intriguing beauty, splendor and spectacle of the days of the Egyptian Pharaohs will come to the Grand Theatre when Universal's amazing drama of reincarnation, "The Mummy," opens a feature engagement tonight and Thursday.

"The Mummy," conceived by Nina Wilcox Putnam and Richard Schayer and adapted to the screen by the eminent British writer of the occult, John L. Balderston, deals with an ancient sacrilege committed by a High Priest of Osiris and a Priestess of Isis. A British archeological expedition unearths the mummy of the Priest who had been embalmed alive as a penalty for his crime. When a sacred scroll is unearthed, the mummy comes to life, bringing to the modern world his ancient occult secrets. He discovers the reincarnated soul of his unholy love in a beautiful Anglo-Egyptian girl, and his efforts to carry her back through the ages so that their love may be consummated provides one of the most singular and strangely fascinating themes of any recent screen drama.

The film is replete with spectacular sets of Ancient Egyptian splendor executed by the noted stage designer and artist, Willy Pogany. Costumes and relics of the past enhance the unusual beauty and effectiveness of "The Mummy," which presents the great make-up artist, Karloff, in the starring role of the reincarnated mummy. His uncanny make-up is his greatest achievement, surpassing the unforgettable monster of "Frankenstein." Zita Johann, alluring Hungarian actress, and David Manners provide the love interest of today, which struggles against the power of the past, exemplified by Karloff. Arthur Byron, Edward Van Sloan and Bramwell Fletcher enact the other important parts in the film under the direction of Karl Freund, whose artistic camera eye is evident throughout "The Mummy."

Wednesday and Thursday
"The Mummy"
Boris Karloff and David Manners

Watch this paper for our programs each week

STARTING TODAY
KARLOFF as 'THE MUMMY'
A UNIVERSAL PICTURE

also

Morton Downey and Vincent Lopez and his Orchestra
in Special Featurettes

25c Till One

R. K. O. HILLSTREET THEATRE

KARLOFF IS BACK AT SPENSLEY IN ROLE OF MUMMY

Picture Is Described as Being Both Weird and Fantastic

Whether or not you believe in reincarnation, you will certainly be intrigued and thrilled to your very marrow by Universal's fantastic "The Mummy" which opened an engagement at the Spensley Theatre Saturday. It is the most weirdly fascinating film with the most unusual and bizarre theme ever produced.

"The Mummy" reaches back into the mists of antiquity and uncovers a love which existed 3700 years ago in the days of the Egyptian Pharaohs, but its main story is modern in background and theme.

Karloff makes his starring debut in this picture. His mummy is so real, so death-like, that it is almost unbelievable. The great makeup artist proves conclusively that he is supreme in his field of characterization. Zita Johann is a new exotic actress who will be well remembered by those who saw her on Broadway. David Manners, Arthur Byron, Edward Van Sloan and Bramwell Fletcher also carry off dramatic roles with finesse.

"The Mummy" possesses some of the most arrestingly beautiful sets seen in a long time, designed by Willy Pogany. The work of Karl Freund, who moved up to a director's chair for "The Mummy" is splendid. See it—you'll enjoy every minute of "The Mummy."

'The Mummy' Tells Tale of Mysterious Egypt; At Dittmann

All the mystery, intriguing beauty, splendor and spectacle of the days of the Egyptian Pharoahs will come to the Dittmann Theatre when Universal's amazing drama of reincarnation, "The Mummy," opens a feature engagement on Sunday.

"The Mummy," deals with an ancient sacrilege committed by a High Priest of Osiris and a Priestess of Isis. A British archeological expedition unearths the mummy of the Priest who had been embalmed alive on the mainland of North America.

Dittmann

Today — Tomorrow

KARLOFF, The Uncanny, in

"The Mummy"

Universal Comedy

Admission 10c

 What Terrible Message did the heiroglyphics tell? What ghastly thing did the young archeologist see -- to drive him mad? What power pulled a beautiful girl to the arms of a revivified mummy! What secret beyond the knowledge of the greatest scientists of today, did the ancients know?

See "The Mummy" it comes to life--to woo the girl it loves--while her sweetheart tries in vain to save her!

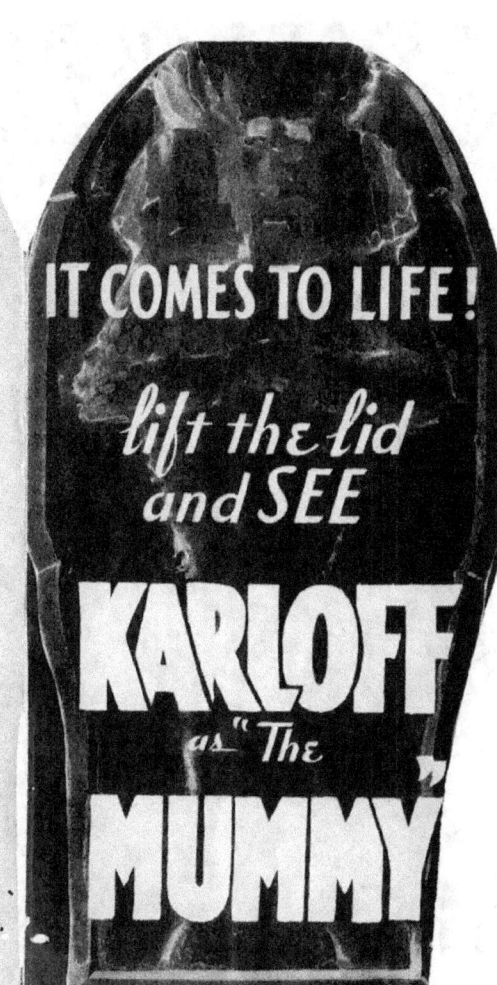

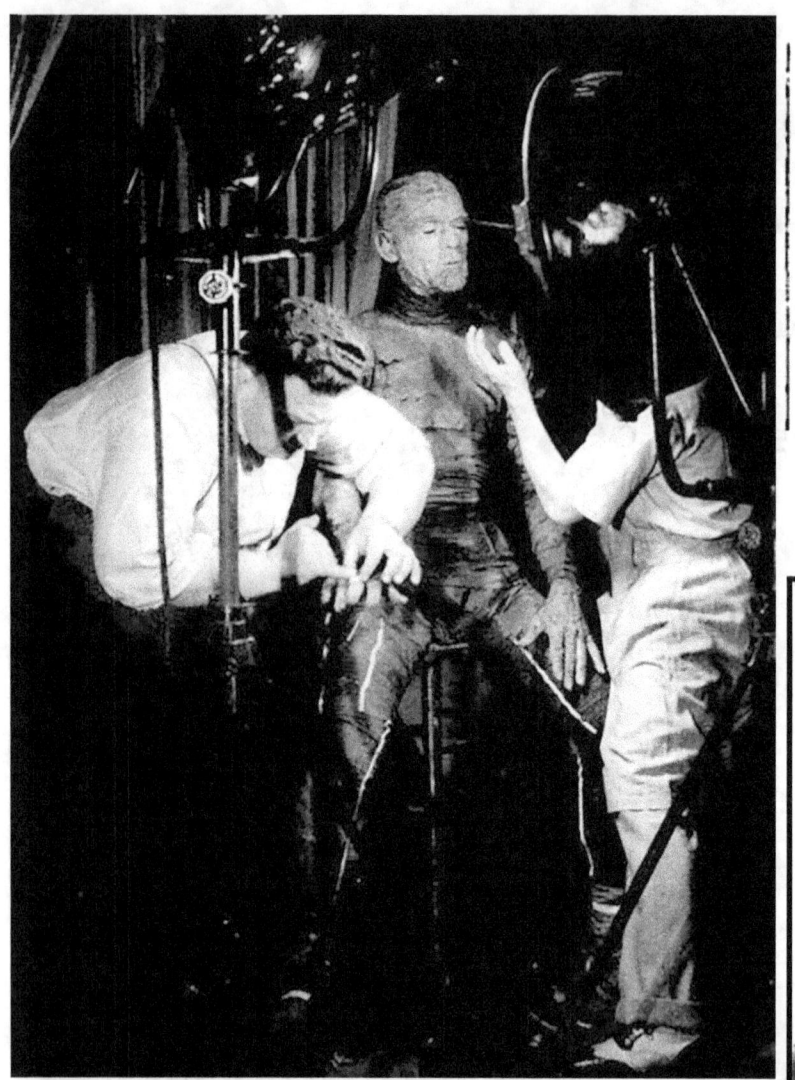

At Universal City the make-up department points out that twenty-two kinds of paint, several hundred yards of rotted bandages, collodion, cotton, gum and tiny pieces of rubber tissue all played an important part in the process which transformed Boris Karloff into a mummy for the picture of that name.

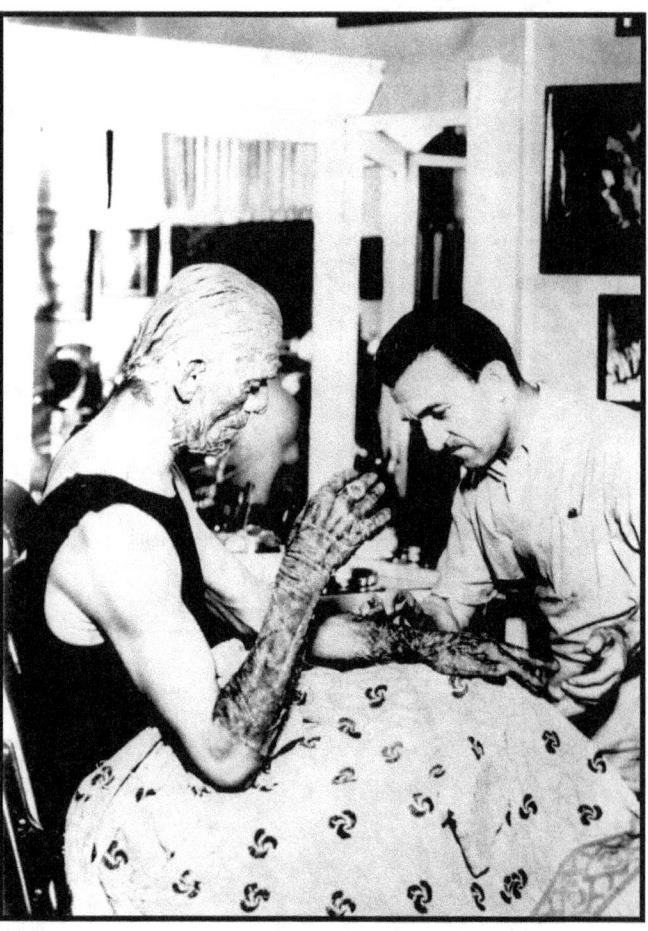

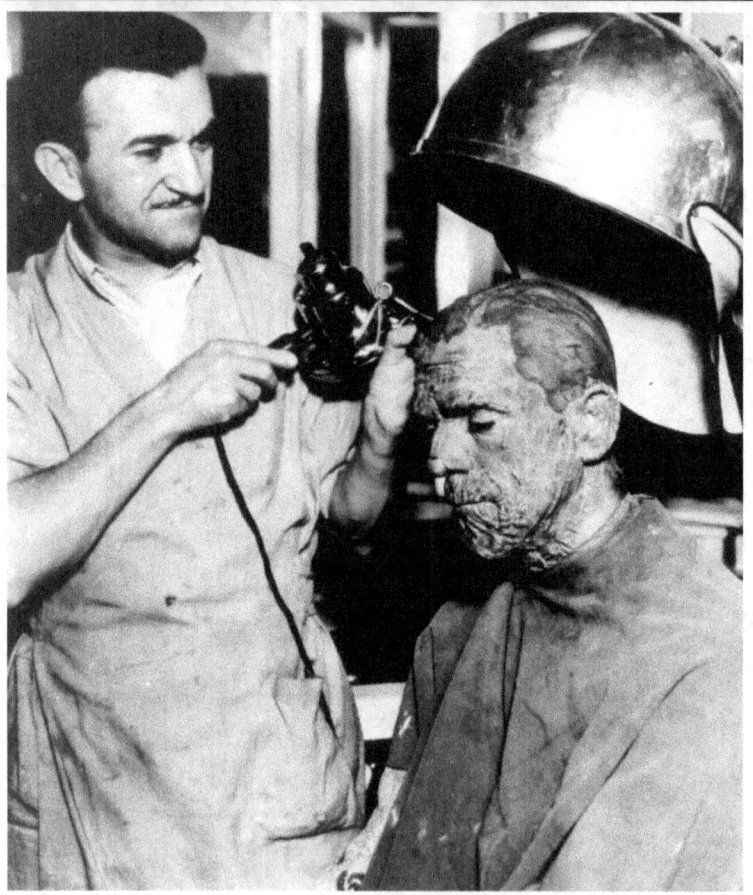

**WARNER BROS.'
HIGHLAND
THEATRE
79th & ASHLAND AVE.**

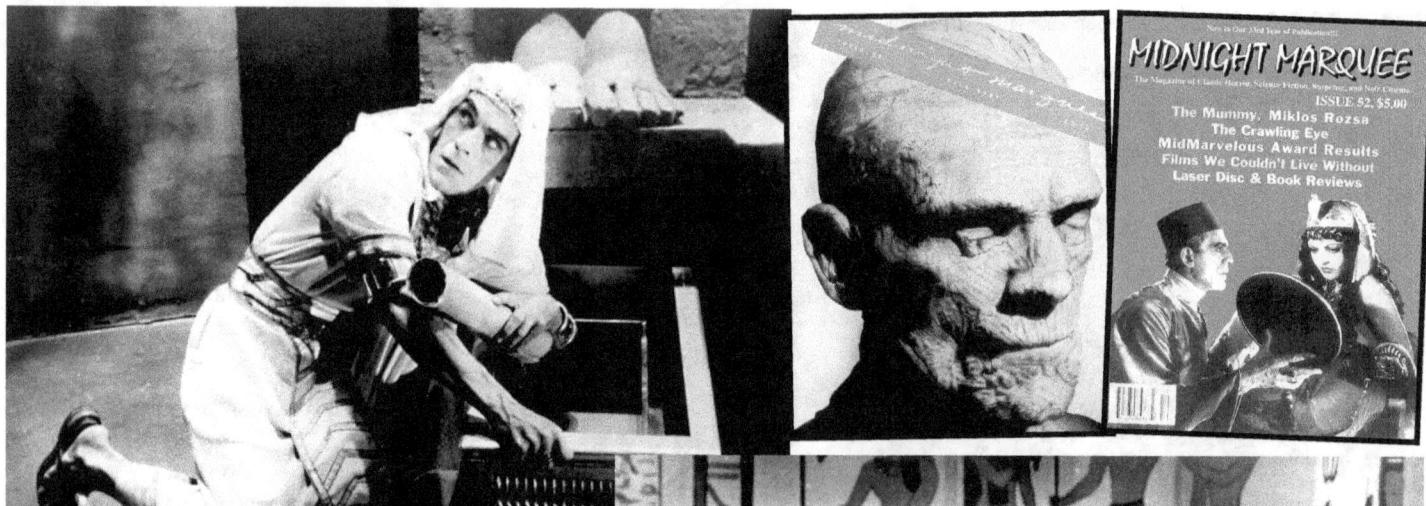

EN ROUTE TO BROADWAY

BORIS KARLOFF'S latest and possibly most startling face will be turned to New York audiences soon when "The Mummy" reaches Broadway. The man of many visages plays the part of an Egyptian mummy risen from the tomb after something like 3,700 years of death. Mr. Karloff sat for six hours in the make-up chair while layer after layer of cotton, spirit gum, clay and colored paints were applied to him. The process was arduous but interesting. First the actor's face was dampened and then covered with thin strips of cotton, over which collodion was applied, with spirit gum to hold it in place. Nothing was neglected, not even the eyelids. The ears were pinned back. At intervals work ceased and the electric machine was applied to dry and set the wrinkles. The hair was smoothed back and plastered down with make-up clay, pressed close to the scalp and then carefully dried. On the base of cotton and collodion a total of twenty-two different varieties of make-up paint were applied. His body was then swathed from head to foot in acid-eaten bandages which had been passed through a warm oven. The illusion of age was completed by a thin application of Fuller's earth over the body.

In Ägypten, im Sandmeer der uralten Totenstadt, arbeitet eine Expedition des British Museums. Eine 3000 Jahre alte Mumie wird ausgegraben. Neben ihr findet man eine versiegelte Goldtruhe, auf deren Siegel ein furchtbarer Fluch in Hieroglyphen zu lesen ist. Wehe dem, der die Truhe öffnet! Sir Joseph Whemple und sein Freund, der Arzt Müller, untersuchen die Funde. Der Arzt ist ein hervorragender Ägyptologe und ist auch in den okkulten Wissenschaften bewandert. Er stellt fest, daß die Mumie aller Wahrscheinlichkeit nach lebend einbalsamiert wurde. Das galt als schreckliche Strafe, die nur in

The Universal company, which evolved the "Frankenstein" make-up for Boris Karloff, now announces an even more grotesque rôle for the easy-going English character actor. The rôle is that of an Egyptian mummy, 3,000 years old, who, or which, is reincarnated, according to the yarn of which Nina Wilcox Putnam is co-author. The studio title for the picture is "Im-Ho-Tep." The cast so far gathered about Mr. Karloff includes Zita Johann, David Manners and Edward Van Sloan. The film, incidentally, will be the first directorial work of Karl Freund, the German photographer, whose camera tricks and artistic effects have made him one of Hollywood's most celebrated camera men. He has filmed more than 500 pictures, one of the outstanding among them being the German film, "Variety." Mr. Freund has introduced many of the camera devices that Hollywood now uses as a matter of course.

Island of Lost Souls

Released U.S. Dec. 31, 1932

Paramount keeps giving Norman Taurog some of the more important assignments on the lot. The director, winner of the Academy award for "Skippy" and currently directing George M. Cohan in "The Phantom President," is to get H. G. Wells's "The Island of Lost Souls," which will be one of Paramount's larger pictures during the coming year.

ARLEN APPEARS IN WELLS STORY

Charles Laughton Offers Unusual Portrayal in Iowa's "Island of Lost Souls"

Using the unbeatable formula of creepy thrills, adventure and fast romance plus splendid acting, "The Island of Lost Souls" is one of these pictures that should not be missed.

It's a film that will be talked about —starring Richard Arlen, Charles Laughton, Bela Lugosi and Leila Hyams. "The Island of Lost Souls" was written by H. G. Wells.

Laughton, the English actor who has become one of filmdom's leading box office attractions during this year in America, has the role of Dr. Moreau who uses an island for his experiment where he turns beasts into men and women.

Lota, the Panther Woman, is the ultimate in Moreau's experiments, having been changed into a human from a panther. She and Arlen fall in love, but he does not know at first that she is the result of one of the half-mad scientist's experiments.

Eventually Arlen is saved by a searching party of which his fiancee is a member. The climax of the film is reached when the scientist's beastmen turn on him in rebellion.

Laughton presents a wonderful portrayal and never lets the audience feel that here is an arch criminal or fiend, but rather a scientist who has allowed his genius and a single idea carry him almost to madness. "The Island of Lost Souls" is at the Iowa now.

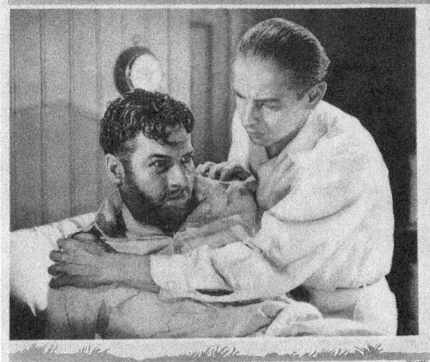

Stenog Now Is Panther Girl Out in Hollywood

As magically as she was transformed from office girl to featured film player, Kathreen Burke (inset) dons her makeup to become the glamorous Panther Girl in the larger photo.

By DAN THOMAS,
NEA Service Writer.

Hollywood, Nov. 28.—It's a long way from Chicago to Hollywood and an even greater distance to the interior of Hollywood's gigantic film factories.

Yet Kathleen Burke made it in a single step. Until a few weeks ago Kathleen was an office worker in Chicago. Now she is a featured film actress, playing one of the leading roles in "Island of Lost Souls." Furthermore, she outclassed some 60,000 other girls to get the job. They also competed in the nation-wide Panther Girl contest which Miss Burke won.

However, the winning of her film contract isn't half as interesting to me as her reactions to everything since she arrived here. A few days ago I discovered that she has been keeping a diary. By dint of much persuasion I finally managed to get hold of it and am printing here her entries for a few days.

* * *

Monday—

The picture starts tomorrow.

I can't sleep. I have been calm and collected through five chaotic weeks following my arrival here for the final tests but now I'm jittery and jumpy. Even when I went dancing at the Coconut Grove with Jack Oakie I didn't get nervous.

When Fred Datig sent for me to come to the casting office this morning, I was afraid the news would be disappointing. While he was telling me that I had been selected for the part, I wondered why I didn't scream for joy. Instead I sat there and cried and twisted my handkerchief.

This afternoon I moved to the Ambassador Hotel. The room is part of the laurels for winning the contest. And the studio has placed a car and driver at my disposal. It's all too luxurious for words.

I wish I could go to sleep. I feel lonesome.

* * *

Tuesday—

My first day's work and what a day.

Wally Westmore helped me put on my makeup. Then I got into my costume, a string of beads and a piece of bright painted silk.

Eric Kenton, the director, Dick Arlen, Charles Laughton and Leila Hyams all came up to congratulate me and wish me luck when I walked on the set.

What a thrill it was when Mr Kenton called "Camera" and I knew that every movement and sound I made was being recorded. I am too quick in my movements. Mr. Kenton has to keep reminding me to take it slowly.

* * *

Wednesday—

Ran into my first trouble today, but Dick Arlen tells me that all players have trouble in some scenes. I just couldn't get my scene. Mr. Kenton was very patient. We worked all morning until I was so tired I hardly could walk. Mr. Kenton called lunch and said we would try it again in the afternoon. I had lunch with Sylvia Sidney and Cary Grant. What a thrill that was. And Fredric March and Claudette Colbert sat at the table right next t ous. Now to go on location. Thats' going to be fun.

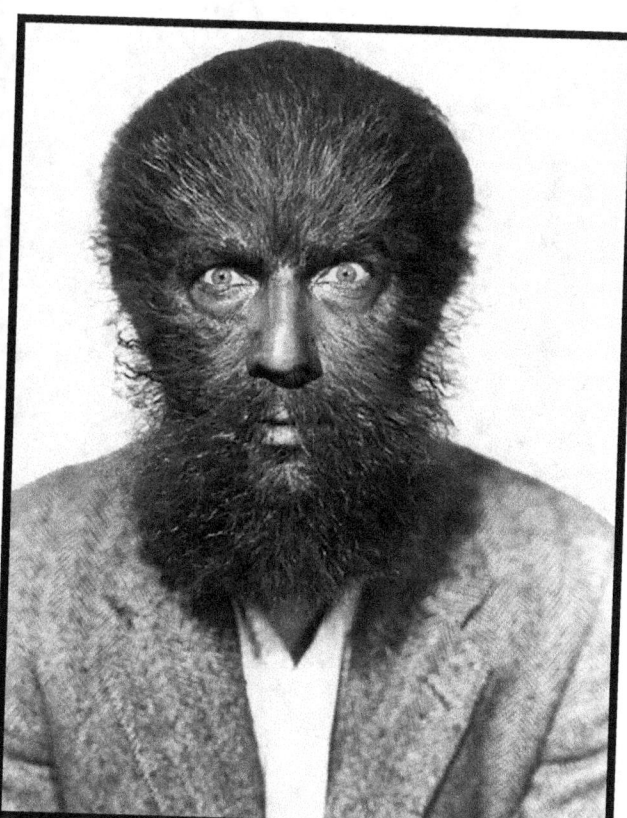

National Panther Winner
Kathleen Burke of Chicago was named national winner of Paramount's panther woman contest and gets the part offered as prize in 'Island of Lost Souls.' Maxine Land, Verna Hillie and Lona Andre, other contestants brought here, were tested for stock possibilities.

H.G. WELLS'
"ISLAND of LOST SOULS"
WITH
CHARLES LAUGHTON
BELA LUGOSI
RICHARD ARLEN
LEILA HYAMS
and
The PANTHER WOMAN
a Paramount Picture

Just in Case....

The young lady who will witness alone a special showing of "Island of Lost Souls" should faint, our Modern Ambulance Service will be instantly available.

Such a service will probably not be needed, however our two modern ambulances and trained attendants are at your call to render an efficient and considerate service when any emergency arises.

RICH & THOMPSON AMBULANCE SERVICE

PHONE 1077

He took them from his mad menagerie...nights were horrible with the screams of tortured beasts...from his House of Pain they came re-made...Pig-men...Wolf-women...thoughtful Human Apes and his masterpiece—the Panther Woman throbbing to the hot flush of love.

ISLAND OF LOST SOULS

From H. G. Wells' surging rhapsody of adventure, romance and terror, "The Island of Dr. Moreau" with CHARLES LAUGHTON BELA LUGOSI RICHARD ARLEN LEILA HYAMS, AND THE PANTHER WOMAN

A Paramount Picture

H. G. WELLS'
ISLAND OF LOST SOULS
With CHARLES LAUGHTON, BELA LUGOSI
RICHARD ARLEN, LEILA HYAMS
and The PANTHER WOMAN

"ISLAND OF LOST SOULS"

"Island of Lost Souls," movie version of H. G. Wells' eerie adventure story, comes to the Strand Theatre Saturday, with a cast headed by Charles Laughton, Bela Lugosi, Richard Arlen, Leila Hyams, and Kathleen Burke, who was chosen as the "Panther Woman" from among 60,000 competitors in a nation-wide contest.

The story centers around a skilled scientist, who has become half-mad because of his fanatical desire to create men out of beasts. Outlawed from civilized countries, he has set up headquarters on a remote South Seas Island, where he has succeeded in transforming apes, dogs, lions and other animals into new creatures, resembling men, able even to talk like men.

A shipwrecked American is rescued and given shelter on the doctor's island. There he is horrified at the beast-men; shocked beyond endurance when he discovers Lota, a beauteous young girl, is really another of the mad-man's creations.

Aid reaches him on the island when his sweetheart charters a vessel and rushes to the scene. But their escape is blocked, and their lives endangered when the beast men taste blood for the first time, and turn on their creator. The revolt and the attempt at escape bring the picture to a dramatic climax.

Charles Laughton plays the role of the mad doctor. Richard Arlen, the American; Leila Hyams, his sweetheart; Lugosi, leader of the beast men, and Miss Burke, the "Panther Woman."

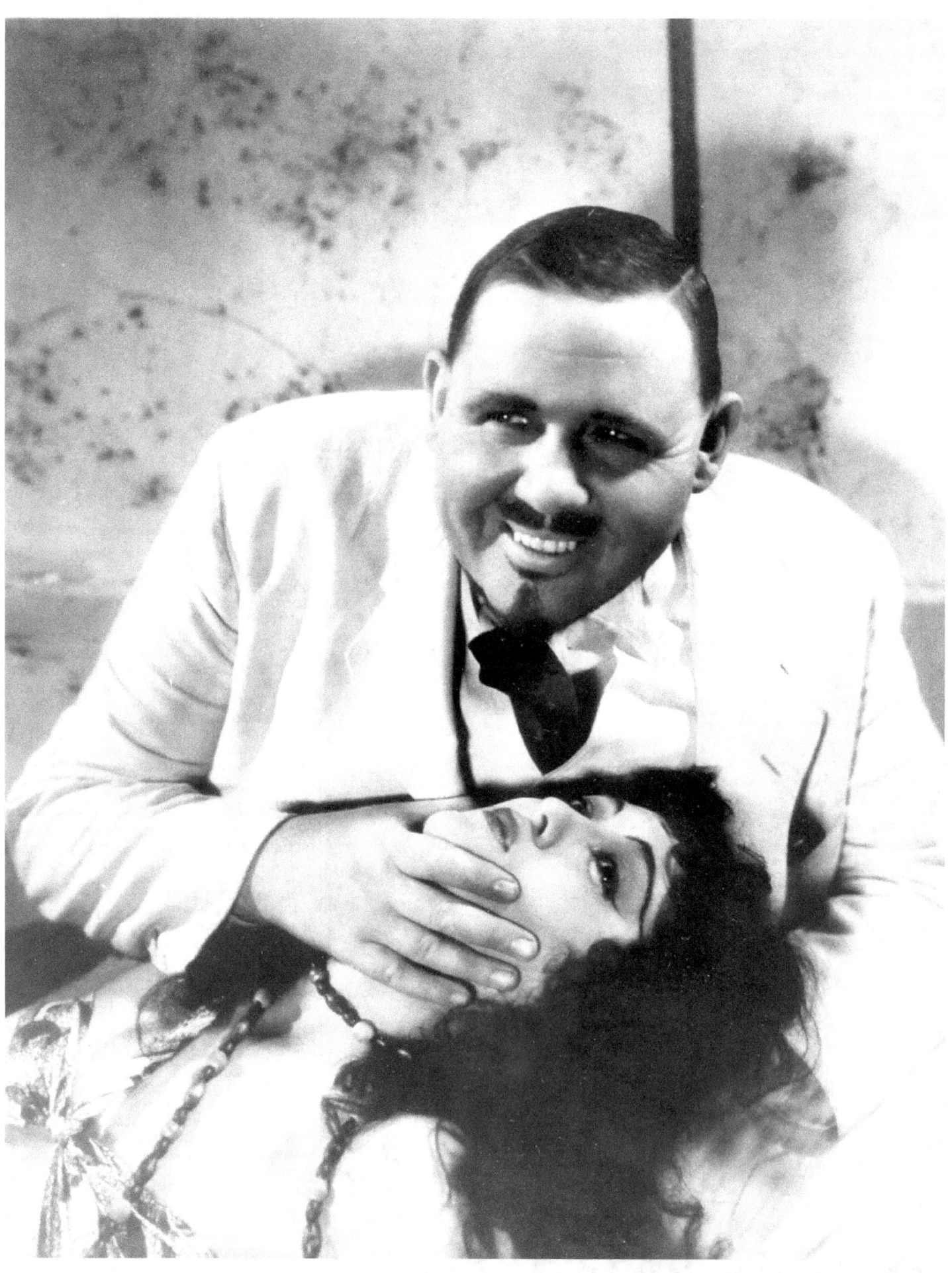

1933

The Vampire Bat
The Mystery of the Wax Museum
King Kong
The Invisible Man
The Ghoul (in Vol. 2)

The Vampire Bat

Released U.S. Jan. 31, 1933

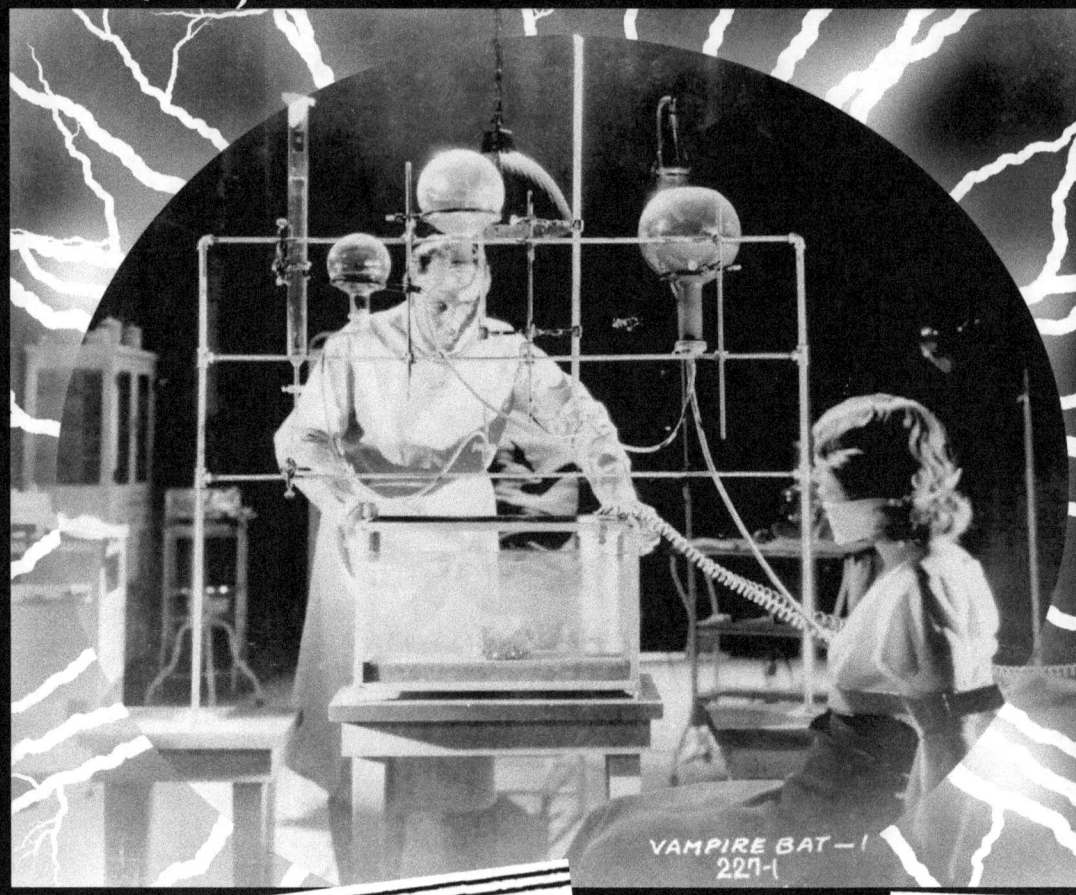

BABY VAMPIRE BAT IS BORN IN THE ZOO

"The Vampire Bat."
In conjunction with this big attraction Lionell Atwill and Fay Wray, who have co-starred in several pictures as "Dr. X" and "Wax Museum," will appear in their latest mystery picture, "The Vampire Bat." In this production Lionell Atwill will be seen in the role of a physician and scientist, with Miss Wray as his assistant. The story concerns a small town which has had many deaths, due to what they were able to find out as the "Vampire Bat!" How one lone believer finds out the real fiend is a part of the story.

EXPLOITATION

"THE VAMPIRE BAT" is made to order for the live showman. It has more red-hot exploitation possibilities than a dozen ordinary pictures. A complete campaign is discussed in detail on the inside back cover of this press sheet. Look it over. There are a flock of ideas that will definitely bring money to your box office.

STATE
11 A. M. TO 11.15 P. M.
TODAY
LAST TIMES TOMORROW
3 HITS ON ONE PROGRAM
COMEDY FEATURE
LAUREL and HARDY
—In—
"THEIR FIRST MISTAKE"
STAGE ATTRACTION
KING BRAWN
Escape Artist. Emperor of the Impossible.
Appearing at 3.10, 7.15 and 9.30 P. M.
FLIP THE FROG AND METRO NEWS
Jack Oakie
In His Best Picture. Written For Him By VINA DELMAR Author of "Bad Girl"
UPTOWN NEW YORK
A Human Story of a Boy and Girl Who Were Just Human.
SHIRLEY GREY and LEON WAYCOFF
Directed by VICTOR SCHERTZINGER
At 11.25 A. M., 1.15, 3.30, 5.25, 7.40 and 10 P. M.
REGULAR STATE PRICES — THREE SHOWS FOR THE PRICE OF ONE
FRIDAY, SAT. AND MON.
The Greatest, Modern Railroad Picture Ever Produced
"THE PHANTOM EXPRESS"
with
J. Farrell MacDonald
William Collier, Jr.
Sally Blane
STARTS FRIDAY
SPLIT WEEK ATTRACTIONS
Two Complete Program Changes
NEXT. TUES., WED., THURS.
A Picture of Shudders, Fears, Thrills and Chills
"THE VAMPIRE BAT"
starring
Lionel Atwill
Fay Wray
Melvin Douglas
SATURDAY MATINEE AT 10.00 A. M. FOR CHILDREN

MAJESTIC PICTURES PRESENTS
"The VAMPIRE BAT"

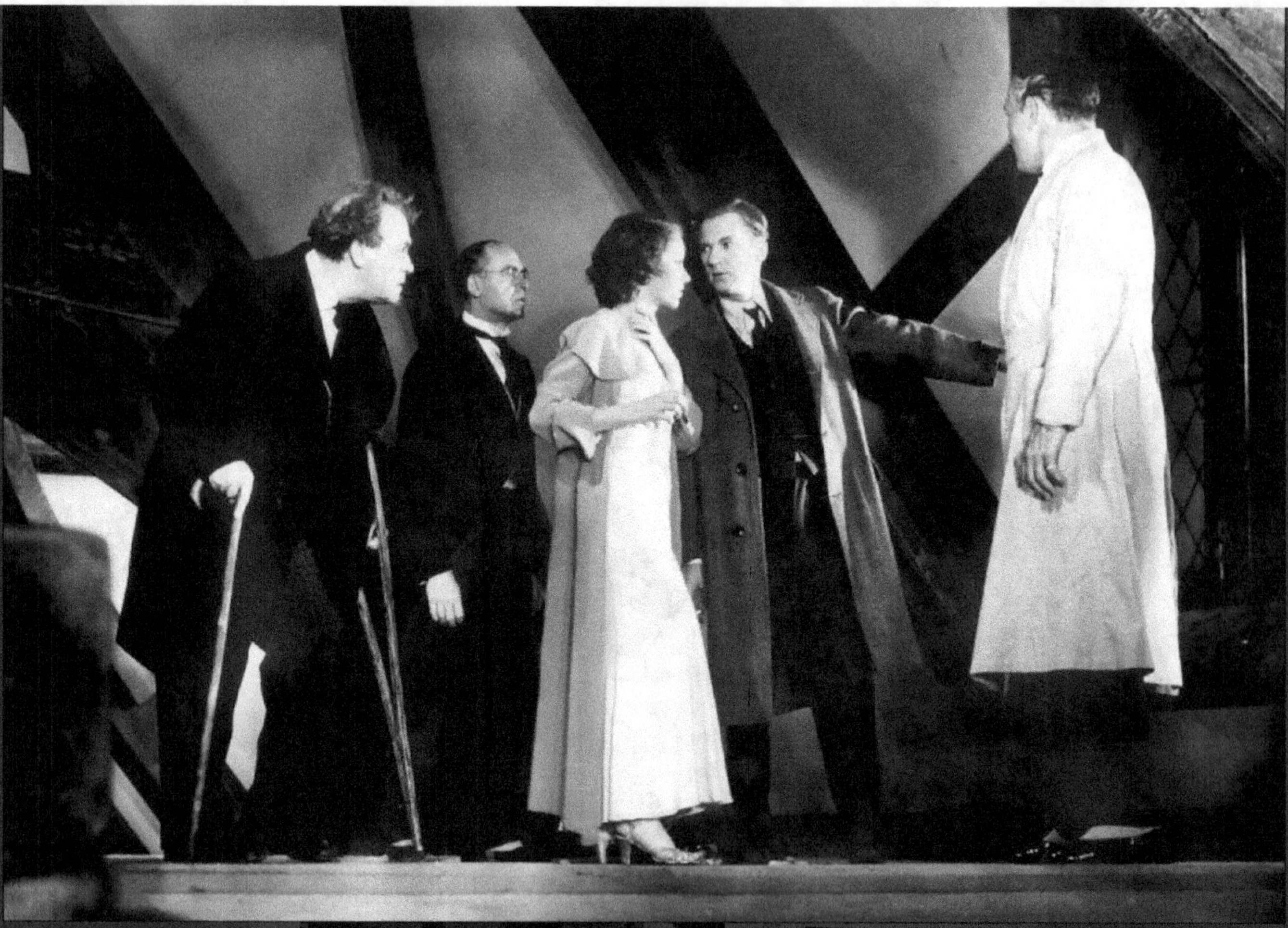

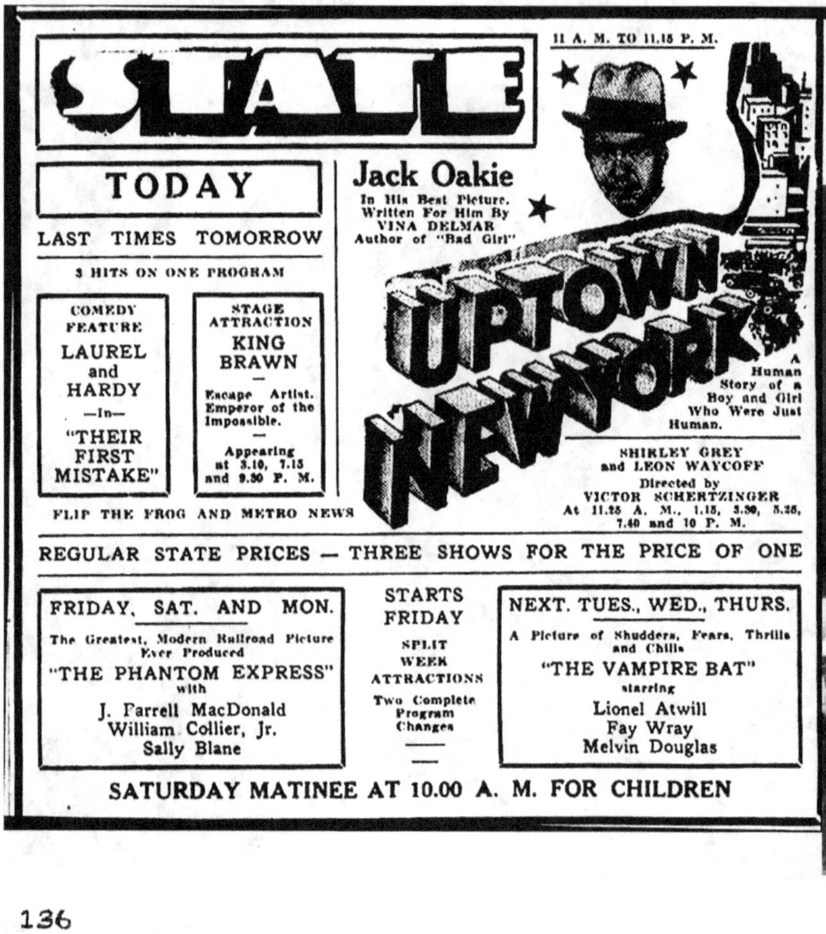

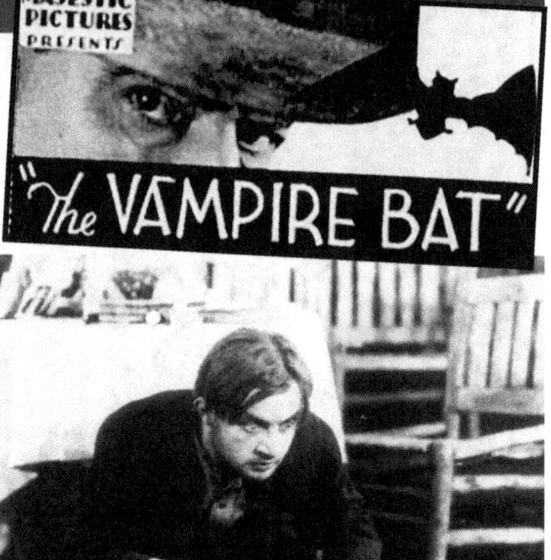

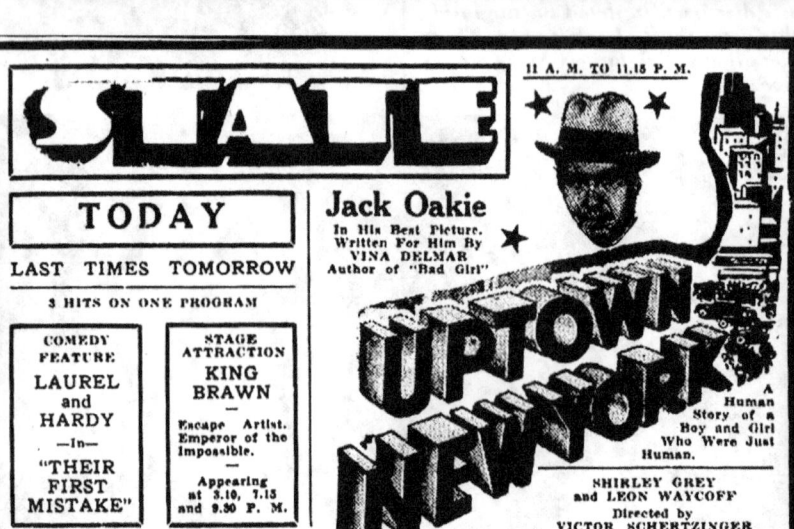

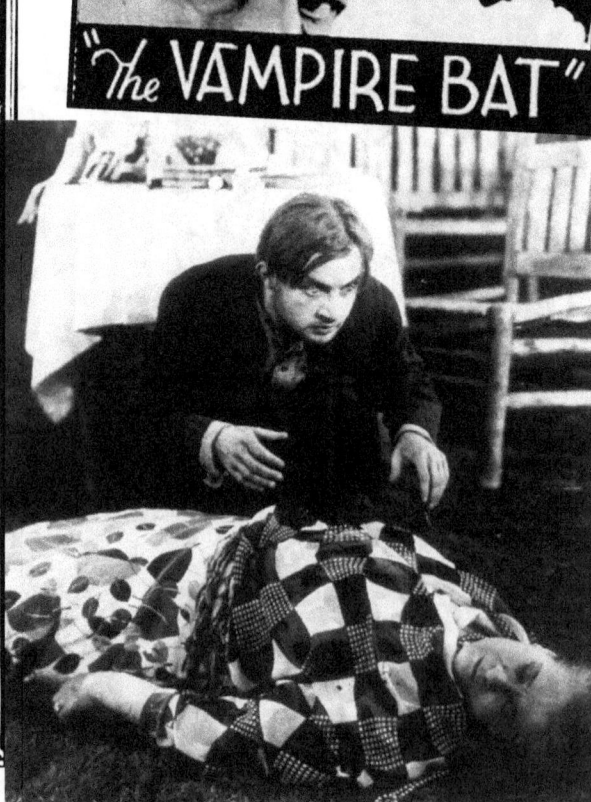

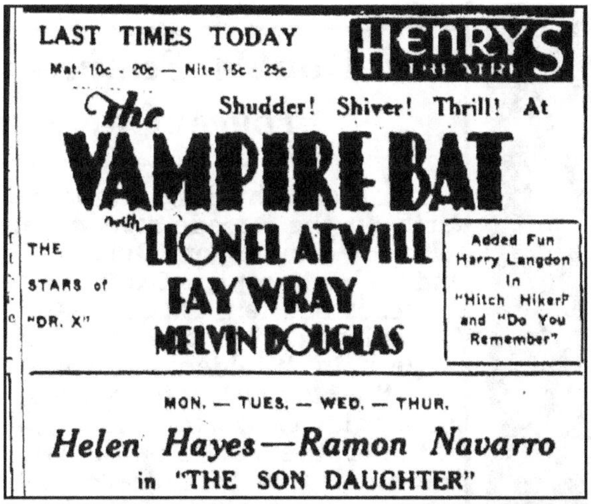

LAST TIMES TODAY — **HENRYS THEATRE**
Mat. 10c - 20c — Nite 15c - 25c

Shudder! Shiver! Thrill! At

The VAMPIRE BAT
with **LIONEL ATWILL**, **FAY WRAY**, **MELVIN DOUGLAS**

THE STARS of "DR. X"

Added Fun Harry Langdon in "Hitch Hiker?" and "Do You Remember"

MON. — TUES. — WED. — THUR.
Helen Hayes — Ramon Navarro in "THE SON DAUGHTER"

MYSTERY THRILLER COMING TO SCREEN

"The Vampire Bat," the new thriller, will be shown for the first time locally at the Park theater next Tuesday. Lionel Atwill, who has been specializing in screen thrills lately, will be seen in the role of the physician, who believes he has discovered the secret of eternal life.

"The Vampire Bat" is shown on a double bill, with "Before Dawn," starring Stuart Erwin.

These are the Eyes of THE VAMPIRE BAT

MAJESTIC PICTURES PRESENTS
THE VAMPIRE BAT
with **LIONEL ATWILL**, **FAY WRAY**, **MELVIN DOUGLAS**
Produced by PHIL GOLDSTONE

New Double Feature Program at Arcade

Tense and thrilling drama will hold forth on the Arcade screen Saturday, with the showing of "Golden Harvest" and "The Vampire Bat."

Richard Arlen, Chester Morris and Genevieve Tobin are the featured players in "Golden Harvest," which tells the story of two brothers, raised on a midwest farm, and a girl. One of the brothers stays on the land while the other goes to Chicago to become a power in the grain market. There are farm strikes, powerful drama and a thrilling romance.

"The Vampire Bat" is a mystery tale of a blood-thirsty doctor, who cared little for lives. Lionel Atwill, Fay Wray and George E. Stone head the cast.

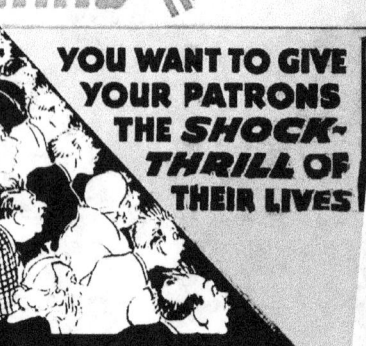

Lionel Atwil   Fay Wray
Melvyn Douglas
'THE VAMPIRE BAT'
And George Vanderbilt's
Sensational South Sea
Adventure
'THE DEVILS PLAYGROUND'
FOX PANTAGES Hollywood

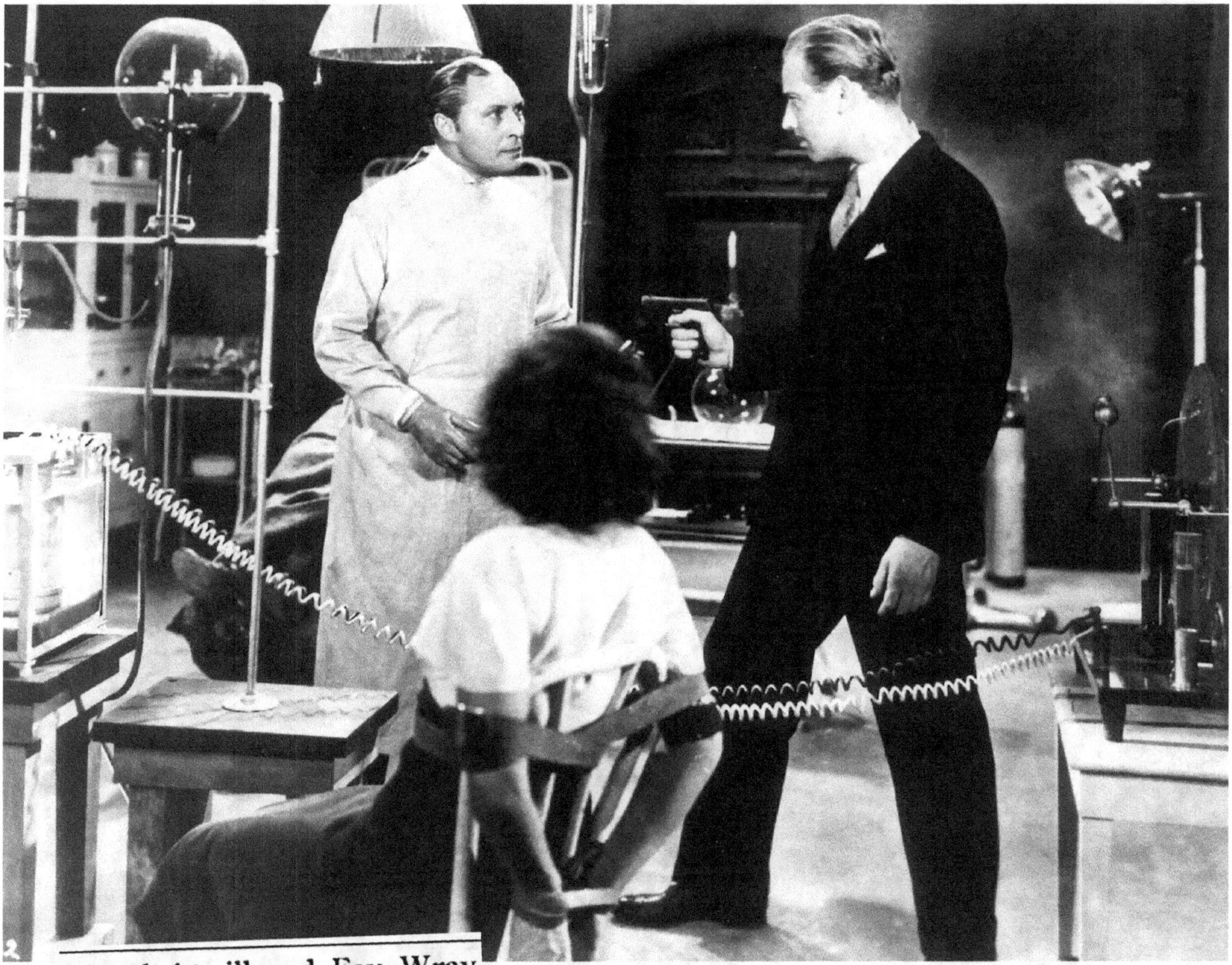

Lionel Atwill and Fay Wray

2 Col. Star Cut or Mat No. 2

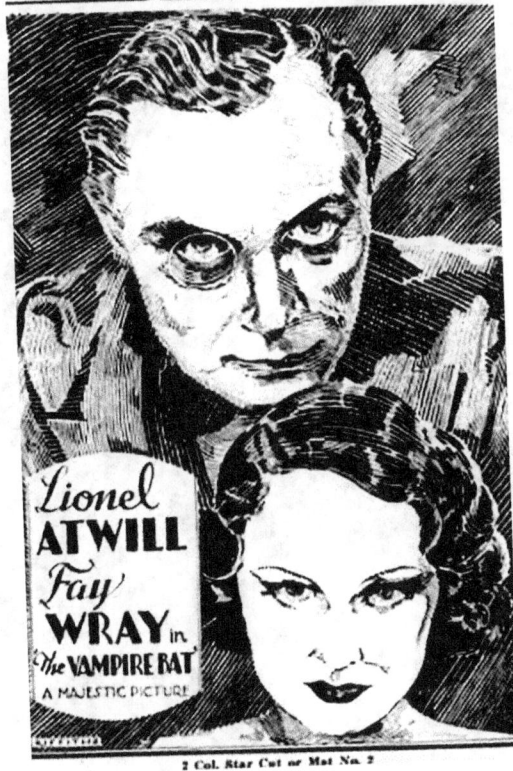

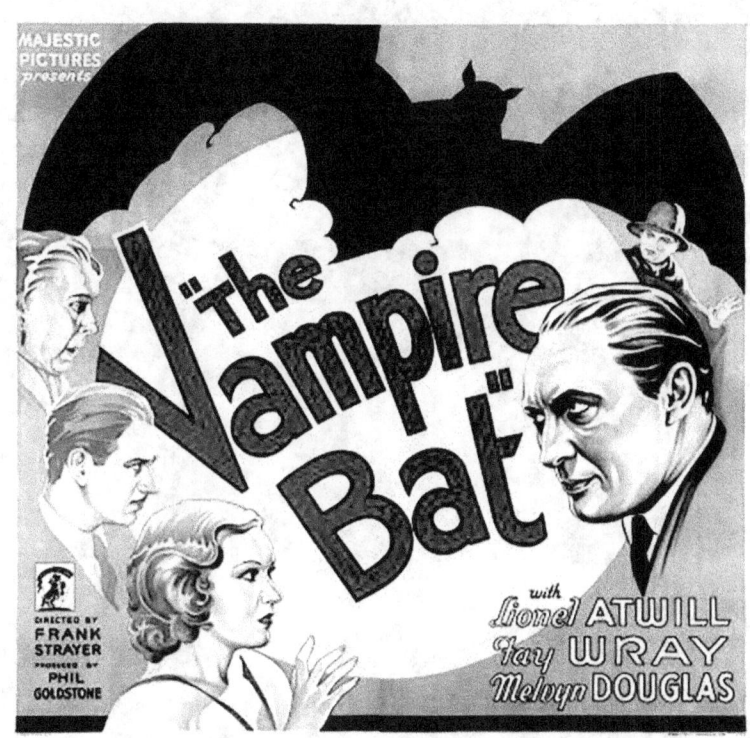

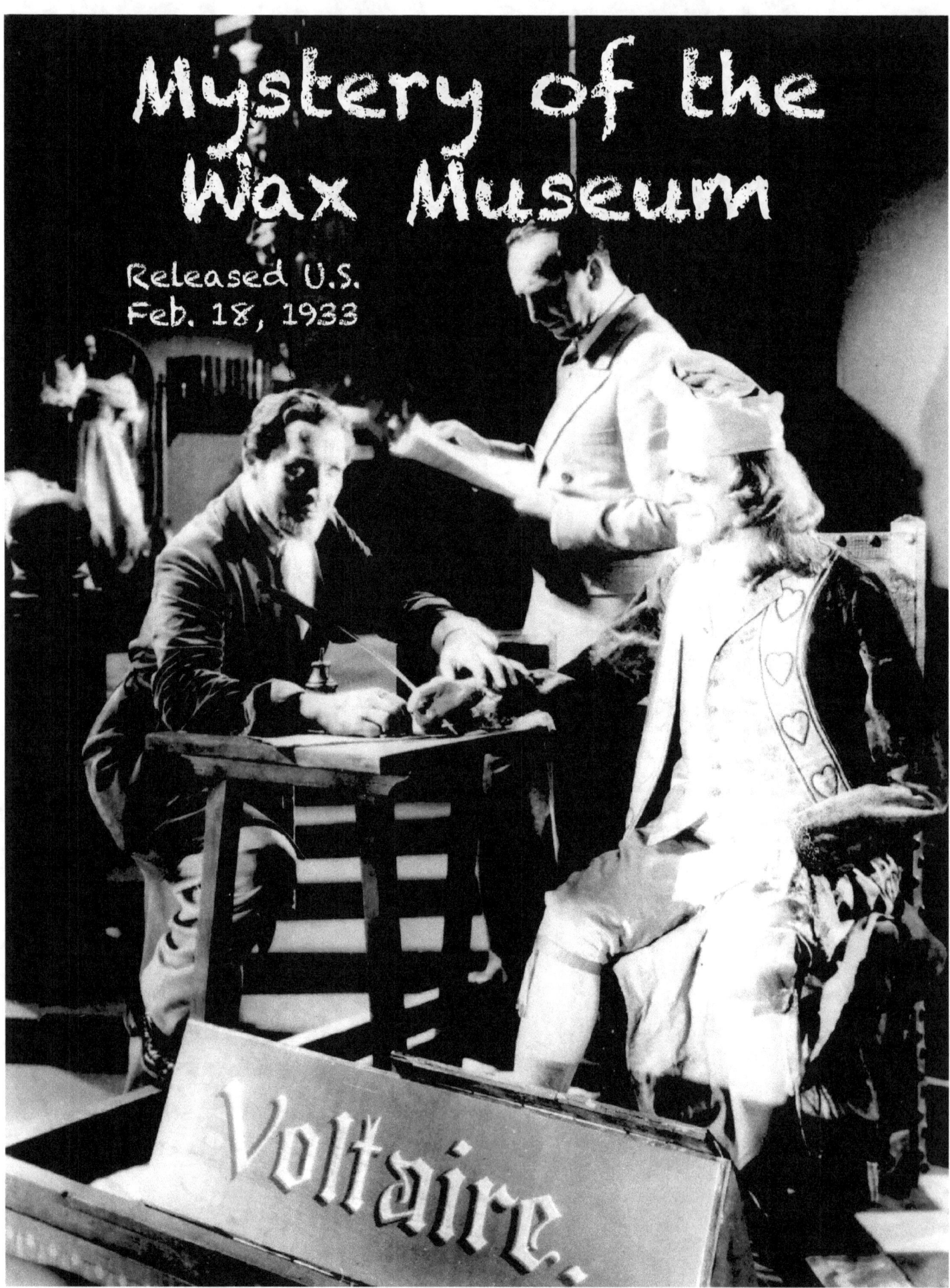

THE SCREEN

Lionel Atwill and Fay Wray in a Gruesome Narrative About a Mad Modeler of Wax Figures.

THE MYSTERY OF THE WAX MUSEUM, based on a play by Charles S. Belden; directed by Michael Curtiz; a Warner Brothers production. At the Strand.

Ivan Igor	Lionel Atwill
Charlotte Duncan	Fay Wray
Florence Dempsey	Glenda Farrell
Jim	Frank McHugh
Ralph Burton	Allen Vincent
Harold Winton	Gavin Gordon
Joe Worth	Edwin Maxwell
Dr. Rasmussen	Holmes Herbert
Sparrow	Arthur Edmund Carewe
Detective	Thomas E. Jackson
Captain of Police	De Witt Jennings
Hugo	Matthew Betz
Joan Gale	Monica Bannister
The Janitor	Bull Anderson

By MORDAUNT HALL.

Its ghastly details accentuated by being filmed in Technicolor, there is at the Warners' Strand a new shocker bearing the title of "The Mystery of the Wax Museum." In it the producers appear to have sought to outdo all the horror perpetrated by those old masters—Frankenstein, Dr. Moreau and the redoubtable Dr. X—and the result is too ghastly for comfort.

It is all very well in its way to have a mad scientist performing operations in well-told stories, but when a melodrama depends upon the glimpses of covered bodies in a morgue and the stealing of some of them by an insane modeler in wax, it is going too far. Michael Curtiz depicts the burning of a wax-works museum, which was suggested by the destruction of Madame Tussaud's in 1925. This section of the film is harmless, but when Ivan Igor, played by Lionel Atwill, undertakes to model new wax figures for a museum in New York, the film starts on its far from pleasant course.

Don't know what this was, but would have loved to see it!!!

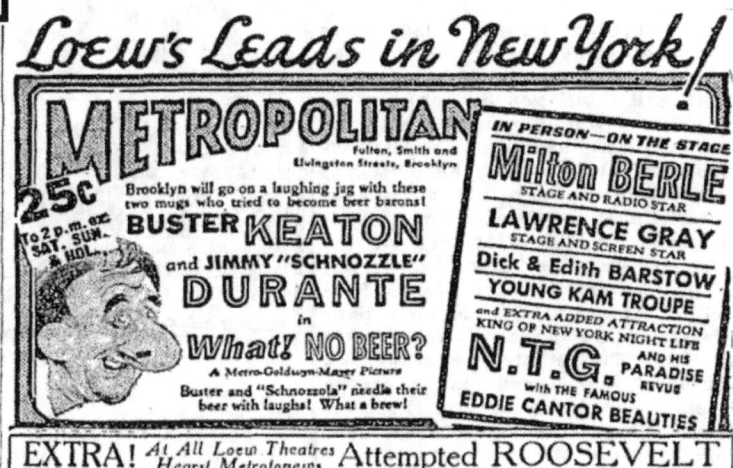

The Woman's Angle

'Nagana' (U). The jungle, tom-toms, wild animals amuck, disease and a siren all getting in the way of each other's phoniness. The girls won't believe a bit of it.

'The Great Jasper' (Radio). Matrons will enjoy following the life story of Richard Dix as an engaging rogue, dominating a cast of likeable, convincing characters—including the new Bruce Cabot, destined for flapperish attention.

'The Mystery of the Wax Museum' (WB). Well-produced thriller with properly hideous idea, much of whose power to terrify the girls leaks away in the scattered treatment of its denouement.

'Face in the Sky' (Fox). Spencer Tracy the lone mitigating feature for the femmes in this disorganized, inane fairy tale padded with inept whimsy.

'The Ghost Train' (Gainsborough). American femmes are accustomed to sturdier, more clearly defined mysteries than this overplayed British picture. Its male lead is not the boy to set their hearts aflutter.

'Lucky Devils' (Radio). Glorifies picture stunt men, fearless lads who may be heroes to small boys, but the girls won't find the motive for their daring romantic enough.

"WAX MUSEUM" AT THE CALUMET

The thrill of a lifetime is in store for you! "The Mystery of the Wax Museum" is a mystery indeed—one that will thrill you and chill you— one that will hold your interest from its brilliant beginning to its exciting finish. One of the most unusual stories ever told unreels at the Calumet theater tonight and tomorrow, as "The Mystery of the Wax Museum" is unraveled.

Other characters are Glenda Farrell, Frank McHugh, Monica Bannister, Allen Vincent and Gavin Gordin. "The Mystery of the Wax Museum" is filmed in gorgeous Technicolor, bringing you the most beautiful settings you have ever laid eyes on. It is a "mystery" to us—how anyone can afford to miss "The Mystery of the Wax Museum."

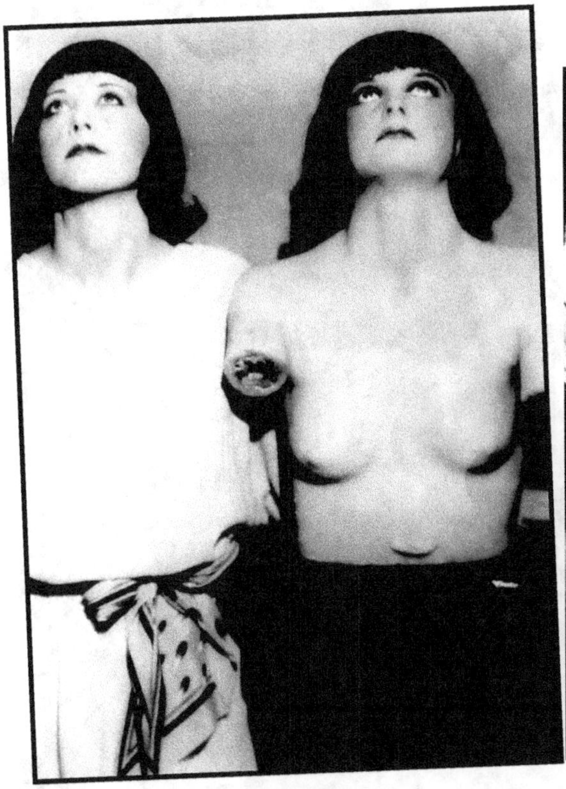

"The Mystery of the Wax Museum" at Paramount Friday

Many of the scenes in "The Mystery of the Wax Museum," the Warner Bros. picture, coming to the Paramount theatre next Friday which is said to be hte most exciting thriller of the year, were of necessity made behind locked doors, as the girls who appear as models for a wax sculptor, were required to appear in what is known to the art world as "the altogether." In order to reproduce exact likenesses of these girls' figures, plaster casts were made of their bodies first. Then the casts were used for the wax reproductions.

Lionel Atwill, who plays the leading role as the sculptor is said to give a performance of haunting power and uncanny reality. After a fire which melts and totally destroys his London collection of wax effigies of famous beauties and infamous characters of history, he comes to a large American city, where his increasing display of amazing lifelike "statues" in the nude arouses the suspicions of the police.

Glenda Farrell plays the feminine lead as an up-to-the-minutes girl reporter who ferrets out the mystery, saves the life of a girl "model" who is about to be the victim of a mania, sees that a number of twisted love affairs including her own go straight.

Playing the feminine lead in "The Mystery of the Wax Museum" at the Strand is Fay Wray, who was born on a Canadian farm. She migrated southward to Salt Lake City, where she saw her first motion picture and celebrated her thirteenth birthday. When her older brother landed a job in Hollywood, he brought his father and mother and young Fay out to the cinema capital to join him. Fay entered the Hollywood High School, became a leader in school theatricals, and during one Summer vacation won an extra's job at one of the studios—with her mother's permission. Three days after her début she was given the lead in a slapstick comedy called "Gasoline Love." Miss Wray had pies thrown at her by some of the best comedians at Roach's, Universal and other lots. The Universal people started her in Westerns, from which she drifted to the type of tear-jerkers that never see the light of Broadway. Discouraged, she decided to drop the whole thing. Then one day she learned that Erich von Stroheim was seeking a leading lady for "The Wedding March." She was admitted to his office and was picked on the spot. Paramount engaged her after that. She appeared in "The Street of Sin" with Emil Jannings and with Gary Cooper in "The Legion of the Condemned." Some of her other films were "The Kiss," "Four Feathers," "Pointed Heels," "Thunderbolt," "Dirigible," "The Finger Points," "The Unholy Garden," and not so long ago "The Most Dangerous Game" and "The Vampire Bat." Miss Wray is the wife of John Monk Saunders, writer.

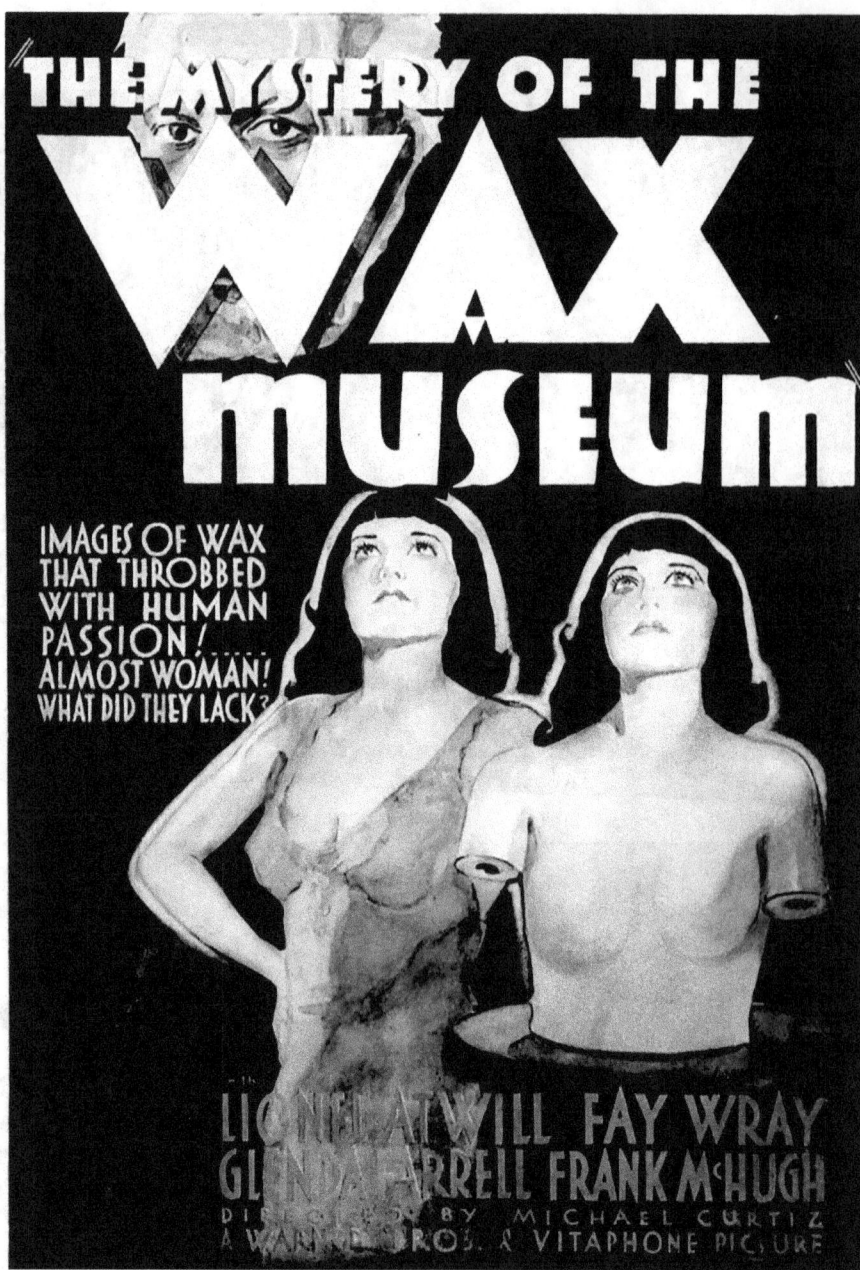

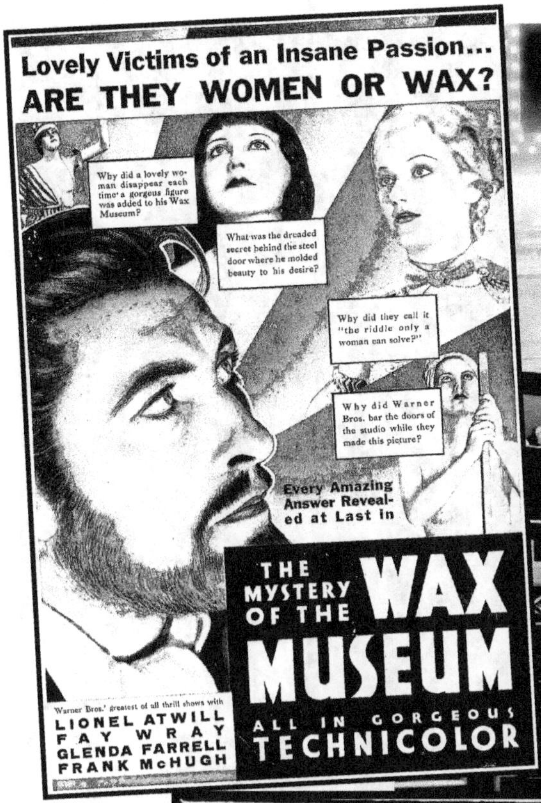

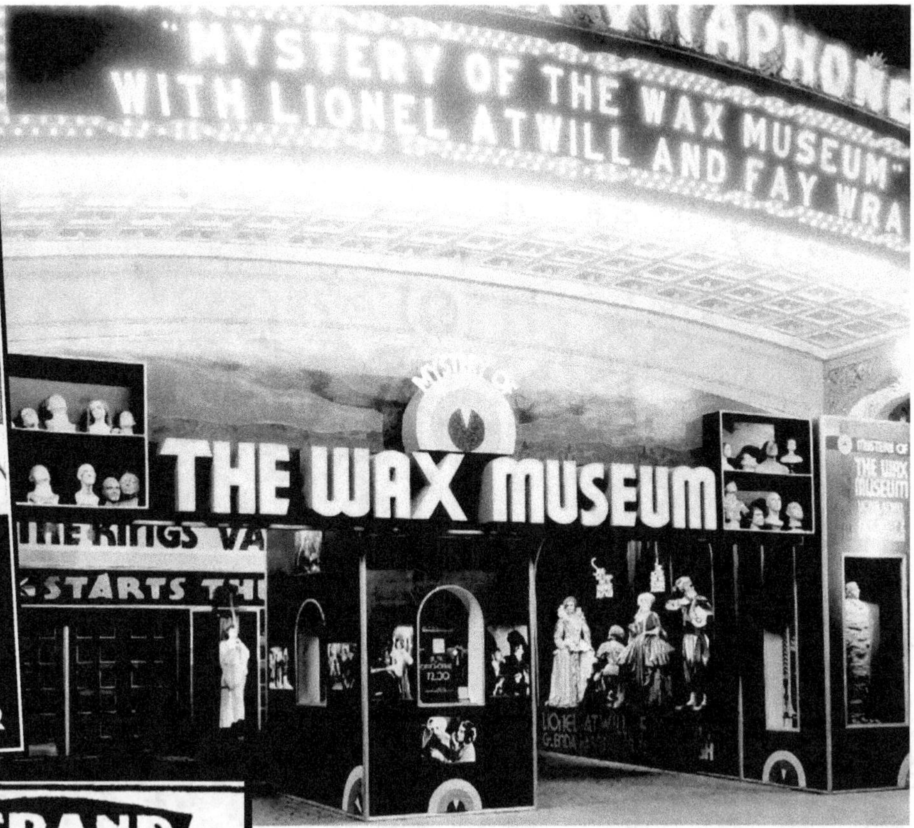

Loew's State (3,218; 60)—'Mystery of Wax Museum' (WB), and F & M unit. Very light and will only gross $8,000. Last week 'Employees Entrance' (WB) got profitable $11,000.

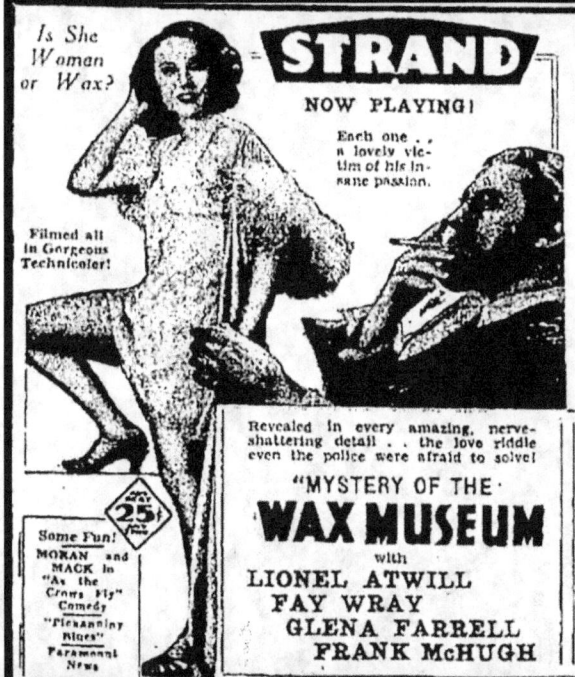

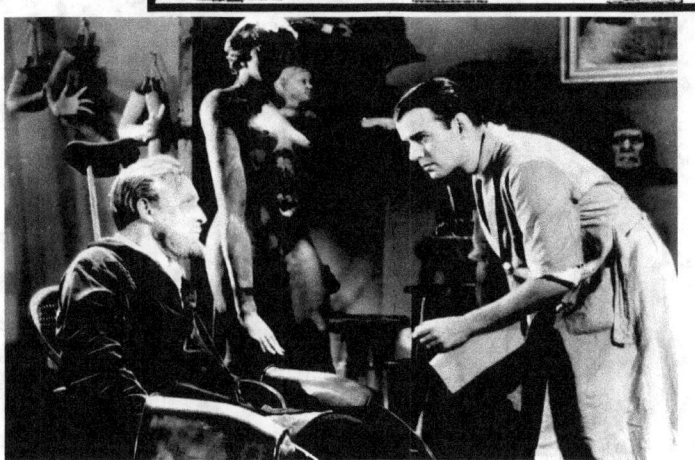

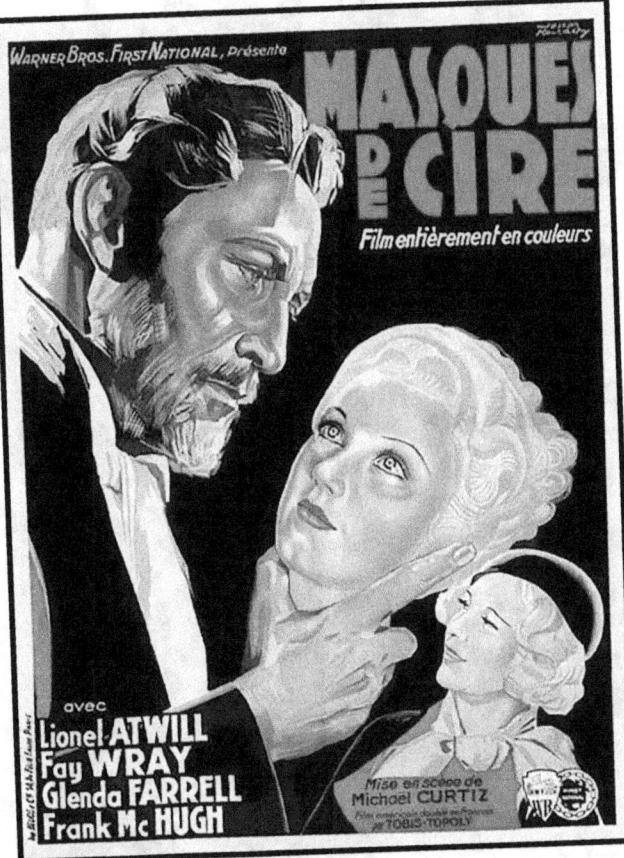

'KING KONG' AT MENLO THEATRE

Playing all this week at the Menlo Theatre, is the great RKO picture "King Kong," said to be the strangest story ever conceived by man. It is the tale of a prehistoric ape, which is taken captive and brought to New York, where it escapes, throws the metropolis into pandemonium, creates terrible devastation, and is the ultimate in goose flesh producing terror.

"King Kong's adventures are like something never seen before by movie fans. Besides the great beast there is a beautiful story of the two adventurers, the parts taken by Fay Wray and Robert Armstrong, who are seeking to get a motion picture of a legendary ape and to make a drama out of his reactions to the beauty of a woman. The modern thrill adventure is from an idea conceived by Edgar Wallace and Merian C. Cooper. It is the ultimate in motion pictures.

NOVELTIES THAT HELP IN A BIG CAMPAIGN
KING KONG

A 50-FOOT APE

MERIAN C. COOPER, who went out into the wilds to film "Chang" and "Grass," remained at home in the studio to manufacture the bizarre adventures in "King Kong," which is at the Music Hall and RKO Roxy this week. Producing this story, which shows prehistoric monsters battling in the jungle and a gigantic ape running amuck in modern New York, was by far the most arduous task of Mr. Cooper's unique career.

Three months were spent investigating scientific records before a single scene was photographed on the RKO-Radio sets where "King Kong" has been in the making since 1931. Geographical data concerning the vegetation, location and population of an imaginary island pictured in Edgar Wallace's story were checked with experts and university research departments. Paleontologists were consulted by Willis O'Brien, whose job it was to animate the dinosauria and other prehistoric monsters that figure in the jungle scenes. Murray Spivak, the studio expert on sound effects, had the task of giving voice to the ape-hero and other weird creatures. He went for suggestions to Dr. O. A. Paterson, curator of mammalian paleontology at the Carnegie Museum, and Dr. J. W. Lytle, vertebrate paleontologist of the Los Angeles Museum.

It was discovered, for example, that the most likely place for an island such as the late Mr. Wallace imagined, where prehistoric monsters might exist, was off the Malay Peninsula. The backgrounds were prepared with this locale in mind. More than 600 hand drawings, with quantities of detail, were made by the scientific artists, Mario Larrinaga and Byron Crabbe, to visualize the backgrounds needed for some of the sequences. Many of these master drawings were then reproduced in segments with dozens of detailed action sketches before "shooting" began on the constructed settings.

SCREEN NOTES.

"King Kong," produced by Merian C. Cooper and Ernest B. Schoedsack for RKO, will be presented at both the Radio City Music Hall and the RKO Roxy this morning. Fay Wray, Bruce Cabot and Robert Armstrong are the principals.

'King Kong' for R. C.

Hollywood, Jan. 16.

Radio has been ordered by its home office to rush the editing of 'King Kong,' with an intention to world premiere the trick animal picture in Radio City Music Hall.

Publicity department working overtime on similar orders on material to fit into a heavy New York campaign.

'King Kong' was in production over a year, bulk of which time was devoted to trick stuff of the 'Lost World' order.

THE CAPITOL
BOMBAY'S LEADING TALKIE HOUSE
DIRECTION: GLOBE THEATRES LTD.   MANAGEMENT: KOOKA, SIDHWA & CO.

Vol. 6   NOVEMBER 30th, 1933   No. 45

WHILE A CITY SHRIEKS IN TERROR

...an apelike monster from the prehistoric world...strangely stirred by woman's beauty...rushes over streets and rooftops...wrecking autos...breaking walls!

KING KONG

Out-leaping the maddest imaginings!
Out-thrilling the wildest thrills!
From an idea conceived by
EDGAR WALLACE
and **MERIAN C. COOPER**
With
FAY WRAY, ROBT. ARMSTRONG
BRUCE CABOT — David O. Selznick, exec. producer

RKO-RADIO Picture

Merian C. Cooper — Ernest B. Schoedsack Production

Commencing Thursday, November 30th
Daily at 4, 6-30 & 10 p.m.
BOOKING OFFICE OPEN FROM 9-30 A.M. TO 8 P.M.
Telephone: 20422.

Seats booked by Telephone must be claimed 15 minutes before the commencement of each show.

Motorists are requested to assist the W.I.A.A. car park attendants in the parking of their cars

Fay Wray and Bruce Cabot by Ernest A. Bachrach for *King Kong* directed by Merian C. Cooper, 1933

WATCH FOR THIS GREAT ARRAY OF RKO RADIO PICTURES!

ANN HARDING—LESLIE HOWARD
in THE ANIMAL KINGDOM
with Myrna Loy and William Gargan

Philip Barry's brilliant stage success that ran for two solid years on Broadway... The picture selected as the opening attraction at the New RKO Roxy Theatre in Radio City, New York, the new amusement center of the world...Now being shown throughout the country.

JOHN BARRYMORE
In the noted stage play that was a triumph in London, Paris and New York..."Topaze"...The story of an honest man who found it wiser to be a thief.

LIONEL BARRYMORE
In "Sweepings," with Allan Dinehart, William Gargan, Gregory Ratoff...From the best-selling novel of Lester Cohen... Barrymore in his most thrilling character part—a role really big enough for his great talents.

CONSTANCE BENNETT
More alluring than ever before—wearing her most gorgeous gowns—in "Our Betters"... From the celebrated stage play by W. Somerset Maugham.

KING KONG
The Eighth Wonder of the World!
With Robert Armstrong, Fay Wray, Bruce Cabot... From the prehistoric past, a monster ape—towering like a skyscraper—invades our civilization!

RICHARD DIX
In "The Great Jasper"...From the novel by Fulton Oursler... Dix in the fascinating role of a modern Don Juan who worked at love and loved his work!

RKO RADIO PICTURES — RKO BUILDING — RADIO CITY — NEW YORK

King Kong.

It is King Kong, not the Legislative Council, that people in Kingston are now talking about; it is King Kong of whom they will be talking all over the island presently; King Kong is the modern version of Santa Claus for grown-ups as well as children, King Kong is the giver of Christmas thrills in this island in this year of grace. A Dean of the American Episcopal Church first told this writer about him some months ago, though one would have thought that a fabulous gorilla-like monster, some forty or fifty feet high, would not have interested so grave and reverend a gentleman as the Dean of any Church, Episcopal or otherwise. But all America was talking about King Kong; and then all England began to talk about him; now it is Jamaica's turn, and opinion is furiously divided in regard to him.

Stupid Creatures.

This picture, "King Kong", then, is highly interesting because of its recreation of the animal life of a previous age, a life of which scientists tell us, of which a record has been preserved in fossils embedded in rocks and ancient mud, but of which the average reader can form no conception. Such a word as Tyrannosaurus conveys nothing to him; but when he sees the big beast fighting and screaming on the screen—and, of course, the picture was made under the direction of competent zoologists and paleontologists—he gains some slight idea of former conditions of existence on this earth of ours. Men did not exist then. And these huge animals perished, giving place to smaller and more intelligent ones; for with all their size the prehistoric brutes were extremely stupid, though they are certainly depicted in "King Kong" as possessed of an intelligence equal to that of the lower animals of our day. But they were extremely stupid, and they were unadaptable. Conditions changed: climate for, instance: food supplies may have diminished, and perhaps also the beasts went down before smaller and more intelligent creatures. They could not survive their age and particular terrestrial environment.

"We stay slim...or we lose our contracts"
...say Bruce Cabot and Fay Wray

How to keep weight down and energy *up* .. that's the problem movie stars face.

IF THERE'S one place in the world where excess weight isn't wanted —*it's in the movies!*

A few extra pounds can cost a star a contract. Keeping slender in Hollywood isn't a hobby—it's a requirement for success.

That's why every movie star is an amateur dietician. Knows exactly what foods will yield the nourishment and energy every star *must* have —yet not add a jot to the waistline.

Heavy lunches—taboo!

At lunch time, for example, you'll find few stars eating heavy, fattening lunches. They need energy—plenty of it—to carry them through the grind of the afternoon. But they get it in a nourishing, non-fattening lunch. A lunch that's become famous on the lots as the "Hollywood lunch."

If you had dropped in at the R-K-O Radio Studios around noontime, when Fay Wray and Bruce Cabot were making "King Kong" — the chances are you would have seen them enjoying it—*a sandwich and a glass of malted milk!*

Get the "Hollywood lunch" habit

If you want to stay slim, take a tip from the movies and pass up the heavy lunches. Instead, order a sandwich and the grandest, creamiest malted milk you ever drank— Borden's Malted Milk.

Why Borden's is better

Borden's is a richer malted milk. Richer in energy-building nourishment. Richer in Vitamins A, B and G. And every attendant at a Borden fountain is an expert—knows how to mix the *best* malted milk, and is so instructed by Borden's.

Start your "Hollywood lunch" habit tomorrow! And remember— you can also buy Borden's Malted Milk in handy bottles for home use.

Borden's Richer Malted Milk

GO TO THE FOUNTAIN THAT 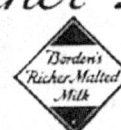 DISPLAYS THE BORDEN DIAMOND

Says "King Kong" is Impressive

"King Kong" is certain to be one of the sensational pictures of the year. There has been nothing comparable with it since "The Lost World" and this far exceeds that classic in clever process photography and dramatic story interest. No more thrilling climax ever was filmed than that giant 50-foot ape atop the Empire State Building, with Fay Wray in his massive paw, as a squadron of Army airplanes shoot him down with machine guns.

The picture made a tremendous impression at the preview, with experts like Sid Grauman predicting it will be an outstanding box office attraction.

From a production standpoint it stands as one of the most unusual novelties in the history of pictures, combining as it does amazing camera tricks and animations with powerful dramatic story, which keeps the audience on the edges of their seats.

Exploitation possibilities seem unlimited.—Meehan Hollywood.

King Kong Jig Saw Puzzle Contest To Be Staged In City

Arrangements are to be made this week for the big King Kong jig saw puzzle contest that is to be held next Saturday.

Prizes in the amount of $20 are to be given. The first person to complete the puzzle by properly fitting all pieces in place will receive $10; the second $5; the third, $3, and the fourth, $2.

The Laredo Times now has several hundred of these King Kong puzzles on hand for sale for 15 cents each.

Entrants are required to turn in their names this week for the contest. These entries must be made to the King Kong Puzzle Contest Editor of The Laredo Times.

It is suggested persons expecting to enter the King Kong Puzzle Contest come to The Laredo Times office this week and obtain one of the puzzles, and take it home and practice on it.

For the reason more practice may be had on the puzzle to better enable the entrants to work fast next Saturday, it is further suggested that the people expecting to enter get their puzzles Monday. That will leave five days for practice and it is said contestants will need much practice because the puzzle is hard.

When you come to The Laredo Times to get your King Kong puzzle, stop outside and in the window you will see one of the puzzles already worked.

One of the rules of the contest will be that no employe of The Laredo Times or R. and R. Theatres in Laredo, or any member of their families, will be allowed to win a prize. They may indulge in the contest for the pleasure, if they so desire.

The time and place for the contest will be announced later. Each person entering will be given an entirely new King Kong jig saw puzzle at the time of the contest.

For further details, communicate with the King Kong Jig Saw Puzzle Contest Editor of The Laredo Times.

GEM Theatre
Etowah, Tennessee

Thursday and Friday,
April 27 and 28

Presents

"KING KONG"

Out thrilling the wildest thrills

Also Vitaphone comedy.
"Wrongorilla"

'King Kong' Made By Secret Way

"King Kong," RKO-Radio Pictures' startling film featuring Fay Wray, Robert Armstrong and Bruce Cabot and showing at the Lyric Sunday, Monday and Tuesday, was made behind locked and guarded doors.

Merian C. Cooper, who produced and directed it with Ernest B. Schoedsack, says that the secrets used in making the picture will never be revealed.

He does reveal, however, that three new technical processes were invented to make possible the scenes where "King Kong," the fifty-foot ape, clambers up a 1000-foot skyscraper and then, with Fay Wray in its grasp, fights a squadron of planes, finally picking one out of the air and hurling it into the streets below.

One of the most difficult scenes in the picture, Cooper admits, is where the ape picks the clothes off Miss Wray. It was photographed 14 times before given an okey.

THE STRANGEST STORY EVER CONCEIVED BY MAN!—Out-leaping the maddest imaginings! Out-thrilling the wildest thrills!

You won't believe your eyes!

ADVENTURE that will make you wonder if it's true. THRILLS that will make the blood race in your veins. STRANGE PASSION that will make your blood stand still!

What if such a thing could happen!

The primitive drama titanic!

Live the screaming hours when it does!

WHILE A CITY SHRIEKS IN TERROR—an apelike monster from the pre-historic world...strangely stirred by woman's beauty...rushes over streets and roof-tops...wrecking autos...breaking walls!

SEE THE LIVING DINOSAUR...the flying lizard...the hairy mastodon...the giant reptiles...and KONG...monsters of Creation's dawn...rediscovered in the world today!

"KING KONG"
GREATEST THRILLS EVER CONCEIVED BY THE MIND OF MAN

Pre-Historic Drama Bro't Into the Living Present By Camera's Most Advanced Art

THRILLING SCENES FROM "KING KONG"

Paramount Acquires Two Broadway Hits

The Invisible Man
Released U.S. Nov. 13 1933

"THE MOST AMAZING PICTURE EVER SEEN"
THE INVISIBLE MAN
RIALTO

The Year's Best Thriller — Fiction's Most Fascinating Novel by H. G. Wells

BEGINS OWL SHOW SATURDAY NIGHT, SUNDAY AND MONDAY

IT'S UTTERLY IMPOSSIBLE TO DESCRIBE THIS PICTURE IN PRINTED WORDS: YOU MUST SEE IT FOR YOURSELF

DON'T MISS IT!

PRICES 10c - 25c - 35c

ALTHOUGH two English studios have offered Universal to keep Boris Karloff busy in Blighty until the late Summer, Carl Laemmle Jr. has cabled Mr. Karloff to return to Hollywood as soon as he finishes "The Ghoul," now being filmed in London by British-Gaumont. Mr. Karloff left England for America in 1909 and this is his first return since he became a stage and screen actor. Upon his arrival in Universal City he will be featured in "The Invisible Man," which R. C. Sherriff is now adapting from the novel by H. G. Wells.

UPTOWN

NRA Code member of the motion picture industry registration No. 42-7.

TODAY
Our New Admission
5c - 15c Day and Night
John Mack Brown
Judith Allen
in
"Marrying Widows"
Also
Vitaphone Comedy

TONIGHT IS Bank Night

Tonight at 11 p. m.
One Show Only
5c and 15c Admission
Claude Rains
in
"The Invisible Man"
Remember, we warn you if your heart is weak—please stay at home for this picture tops "Frankenstein."
Come dressed in a costume and be admitted free.

Thursday - Friday
5c and 15c Day or Night
Every woman and man, married or single, will thrill to this picture.

"Housewives"
with
Geo. Brent
Bette Davis
Ann Dvorak

Also Vincent Lopez and his Orchestra in a Musical Short

OVER in the Tyrolean Alps, where Luis Trenker produced the mountain scenes for "The Doomed Battalion," another picture is being planned, also under Mr. Trenker's supervision. "The Rebel" it will be called, and in addition to Mr. Trenker the cast will include Victor Varconi and Vilma Banky. Miss Banky left Hollywood soon after the talking pictures arrived and she has spent the last two years polishing up her English. "The Rebel" will be made in English, German and French.

An actor built along herculean lines and possessed of a desire to share close-ups with a lion can find a job at Paramount these days for the masculine lead in "King of the Jungle," an African adventure film soon to enter production. Metro-Goldwyn-Mayer went outside of Hollywood and made Johnny Weissmuller the star of "Tarzan," and Paramount would like to do something like that. Athletes from many fields, some of them Olympic contestants, have had screen tests, and the search goes on. "King of the Jungle" is one of the big outdoor thrillers that Paramount is concentrating on this Fall. Two others now being prepared are "The Lives of a Bengal Lancer" and "Island of Lost Souls."

For "Wax Museum," which will begin its macabre march past the Warner cameras within the next month, the company has begun to assemble a cast. Lionel Atwill, Fay Wray, Frank McHugh and Glenda Farrell are among those already selected. The film is based on an unproduced play by Charles S. Belden.

The Universal company, which evolved the "Frankenstein" make-up for Boris Karloff, now announces an even more grotesque rôle for the easy-going English character actor. The rôle is that of an Egyptian mummy, 3,000 years old, who, or which, is reincarnated, according to the yarn of which Nina Wilcox Putnam is co-author. The studio title for the picture is "Im-Ho-Tep." The cast so far gathered about Mr. Karloff includes Zita Johann, David Manners and Edward Van Sloan. The film, incidentally, will be the first directorial work of Karl Freund, the German photographer, whose camera tricks and artistic effects have made him one of Hollywood's most celebrated camera men. He has filmed more than 500 pictures, one of the outstanding among them being the German film, "Variety." Mr. Freund has introduced many of the camera devices that Hollywood now uses as a matter of course.

E. A. Dupont Leaves for Hollywood

E. A. Dupont, German director of "Variety" and other films, left New York for Hollywood yesterday to make pictures for Universal. The first will be "The Invisible Man," adapted from the novel by H. G. Wells, with Boris Karloff in the leading rôle.

THE BEST TEN.

Cavalcade, with Diana Wynyard, Clive Brook and others; based on Noel Coward's Drury Lane drama and directed by Frank Lloyd under the supervision of Winfield Sheehan.

Reunion in Vienna, with Diana Wynyard, John Barrymore and Frank Morgan, an adaptation of Robert E. Sherwood's play, directed by Sidney Franklin.

Morgenrot, a German production, with Rudolf Forster, directed by Gustav Ucicky; a story of submarines in the World War.

State Fair, with Will Rogers and Janet Gaynor, adapted from Phil Stong's novel of the same title, directed by Henry King.

Dinner at Eight, with several stellar performers, including Marie Dressler, John and Lionel Barrymore; based on the stage work by George S. Kaufman and Edna Ferber, directed by George Cukor.

Berkeley Square, with Leslie Howard and Heather Angel; a version of John L. Balderston's play, directed by Frank Lloyd.

The Private Life of Henry VIII, a British production, with Charles Laughton and Binnie Barnes, directed by Alexander Korda.

Little Women, with Katharine Hepburn, Joan Bennett and Paul Lukas, adapted from Louisa May Alcott's immensely popular novel, directed by George Cukor.

The Invisible Man, with Claude Rains, based on an H. G. Wells story, directed by James Whale, from a script written by R. C. Sherriff.

His Double Life, a pictorial version of Arnold Bennett's novel, "Buried Alive," directed by Arthur Hopkins, with Roland Young and Lillian Gish in the principal rôles.

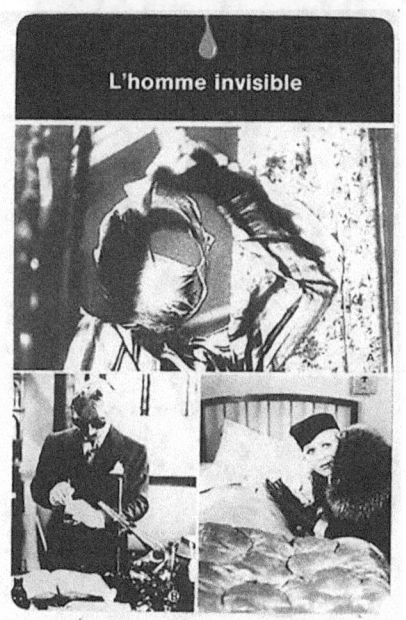

REGULAR ADMISSION PRICES TONIGHT AT HALLOWE'EN SHOW

If you think this fellow "Frankenstein" was a fiend, wait until you see the "Invisible Man" tonight at the Uptown Theatre's big Hallowe'en show which starts at 11 p. m.

Those of you who have a weak heart or can't stand shocks and excitement are advised to stay at home, for this picture is full of excitement from start to finish.

People who come in costume will be admitted free. The regular admission will be 5c and 15c, the Uptown's regular prices, which started yesterday.

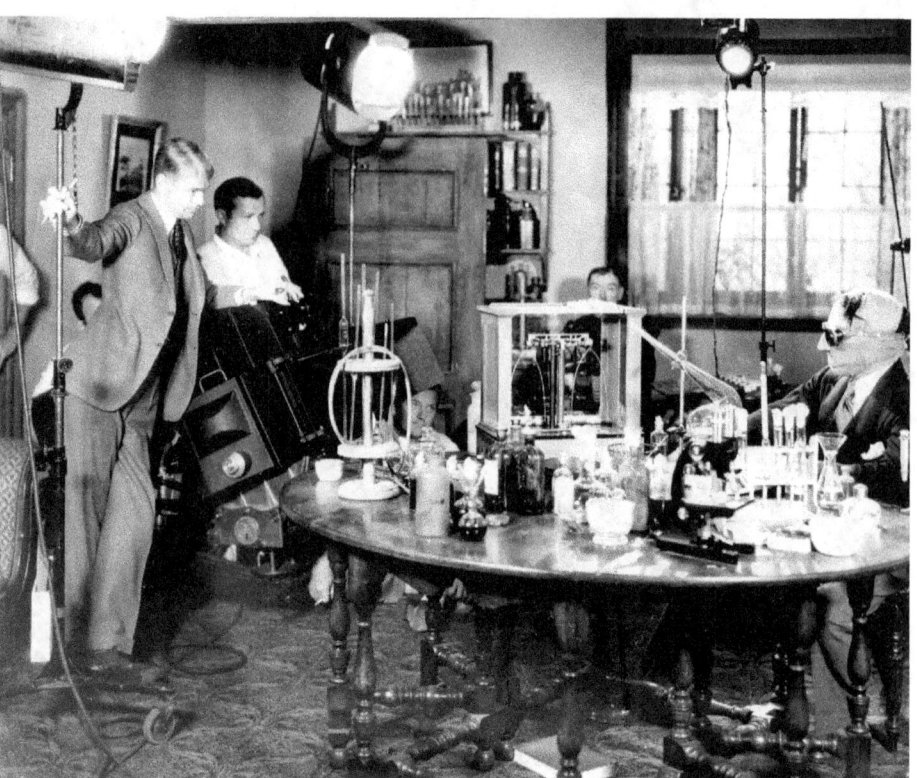

SCREEN NOTES.

James Whale, director of "The Invisible Man," will arrive on the Europa tonight after a two months' holiday in London. He is bringing with him the completed script of "A Trip to Mars," by R. C. Sherriff, in which Boris Karloff will probably be starred by Universal Pictures.

"The Invisible Man" Is Coming Here Soon!

"Dracula" chilled a nation; "Frankenstein" thrilled the world.

Now "The Invisible Man" is coming!

Monday and Tuesday the most starting, utterly amazing picture in years—the picture is causing a sensation wherever it is being shown—the master imaginative creation of H. G. Wells' great mind, which Universal has filmed to make a picture unparelleled in uncanny thrills — "The Invisible Man" at the Orpheum theatre.

The weird screen story of a scientist who meddled in things men must leave alone, the tremendous screen capture of an idea which has intrigued the minds of the world for centuries actually achieves realization in "The Invisible Man." It is nothing short of marvelous in its bizarre, supernatural suspense and excitement. The astounding story of a man whose strength was his weakness, who had lost the power to be normal and who gloried in it and a girl who loved a man she couldn't see.

Plan now to see this unusual, most absorbing of all screen dramas. As long as you live, you'll never forget "The Invisible Man."

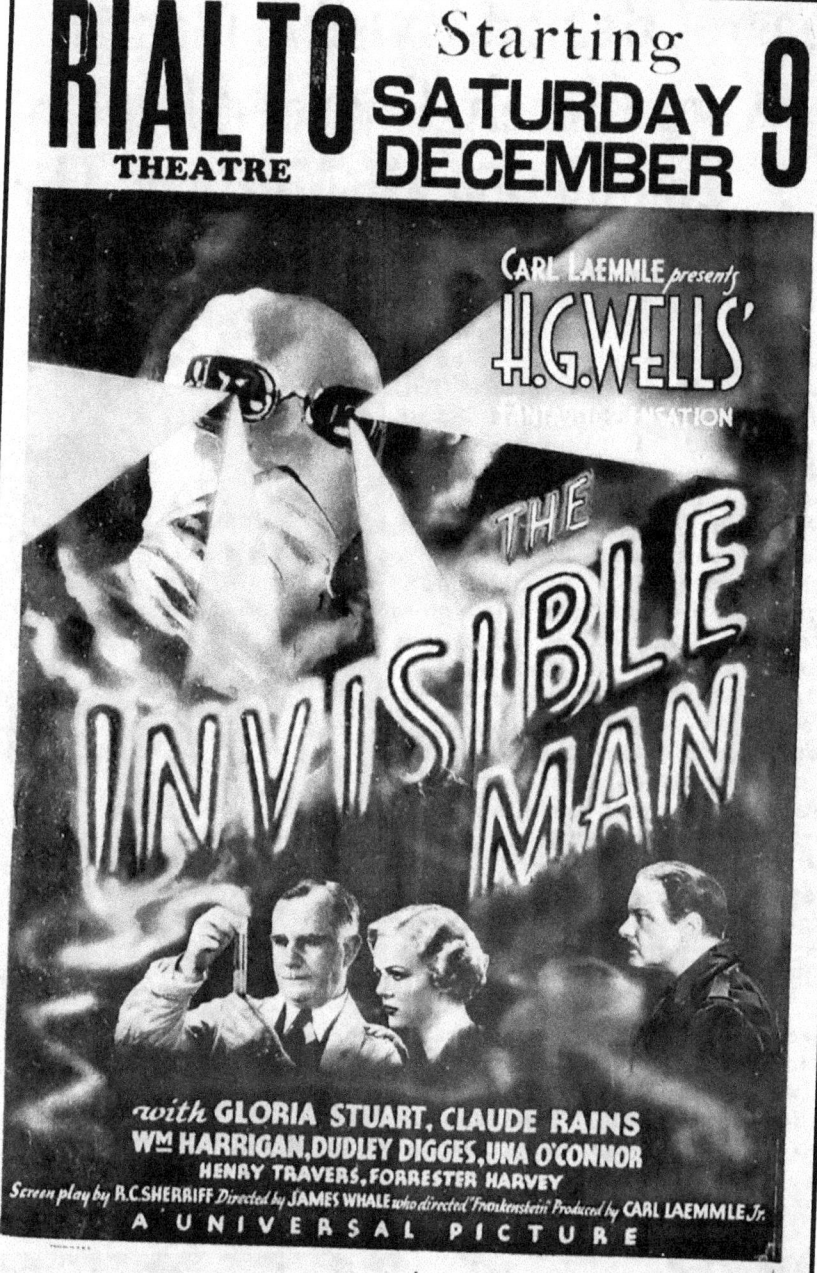

Secret Behind Invisible Man Is Kept Closely Guarded Pending Completion Of Mystery Thriller

The secret which Universal studios jealously guarded within the impenetrable walls of a forbidden sound stage for months will be revealed on the screen of the Ritz Theater next Friday and Saturday when H. G. Wells' startling "The Invisible Man" opens its long awaited engagement there.

Filmed in the utmost secrecy with "No Visitors" signs attached to locked doors, "The Invisible Man" during its production created more intriguing conjectures than any photoplay made in Hollywood in years. Until the film's recent release, only a select group of 20 people actually knew the amazing manner in which this spectacular motion picture was made, and they were under oath not to tell.

Writers, photographers, executives, were strictly barred as the cameras ground on the strangest character ever to be created by Hollywood, an unseen star! Naturally, of all places Hollywood possesses, the most easily accelerated curiosity, and rumors of every color were racing about the city of make-believe while "The Invisible Man" accomplished his spine-tingling career.

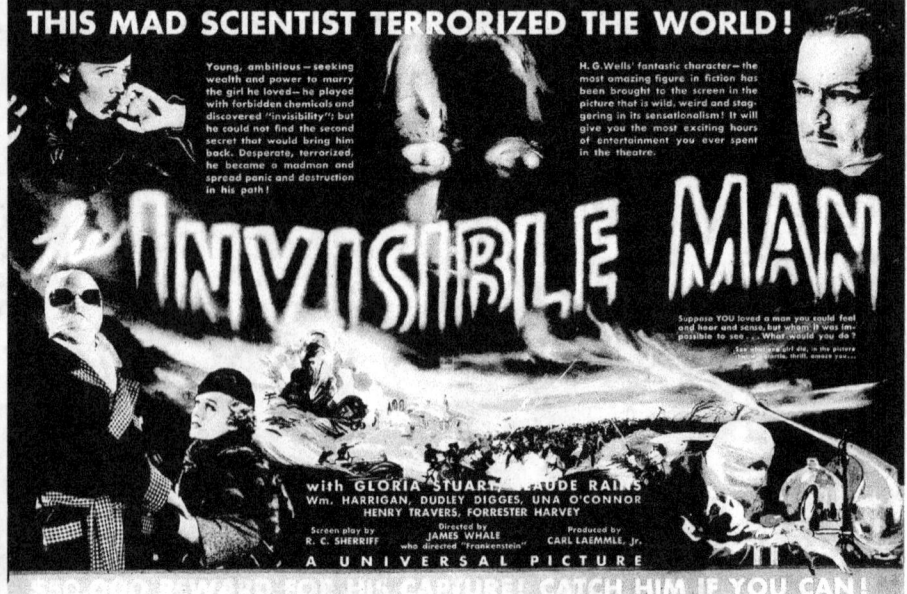

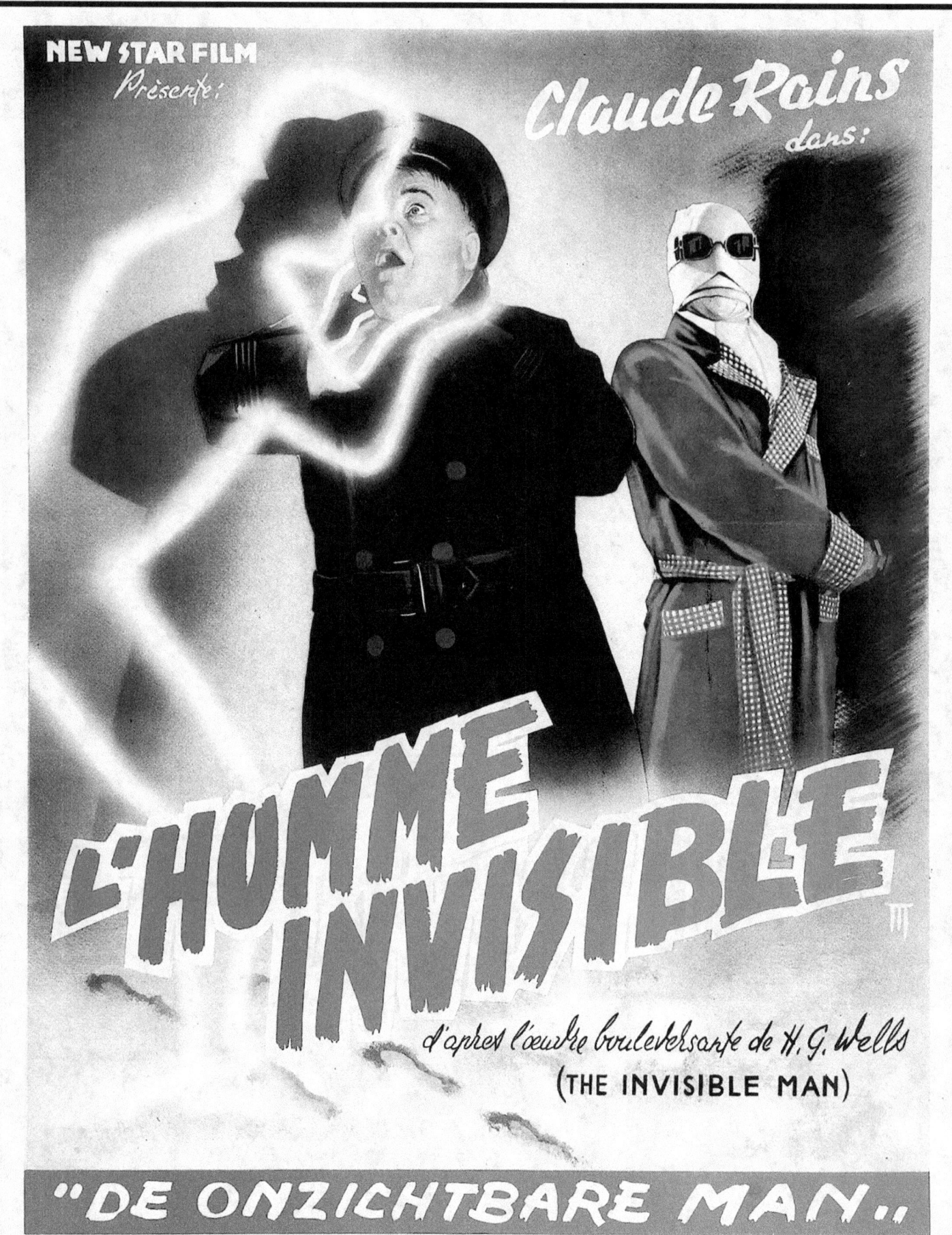

Pictures for Week Ending Nov. 24

CRITERION—"Design for Living," with Fredric March, Miriam Hopkins and Gary Cooper, opens Wednesday night.
RADIO CITY MUSIC HALL—"Little Women," with Katharine Hepburn and Douglas Montgomery.
PARAMOUNT—"Cradle Song," with Dorothea Wieck.
ROXY—"The Invisible Man," with Claude Rains and Gloria Stuart.
RIALTO—"White Woman," with Charles Laughton and Carole Lombard.
RIVOLI—"Blood Money," with George Bancroft and Judith Anderson.
ASTOR—"Eskimo."
WARNERS' STRAND—"From Headquarters," with George Brent and Margaret Lindsay.
MAYFAIR—"Midshipman Jack," with Bruce Cabot and Betty Furness.
CAPITOL—"The Prizefighter and the Lady," with Max Baer and Myrna Loy.
PALACE—"I'm No Angel," with Mae West.
HOLLYWOOD—"The World Changes," with Paul Muni and Aline MacMahon.
CAMEO—"Eat 'Em Alive."
RKO ROXY—"I'm No Angel," with Mae West.
LITTLE PICTURE HOUSE—"Moonlight and Pretzels," today; "The Devil and the Deep," tomorrow; "The Good Companions," Tuesday and Wednesday; "The Passion of Joan of Arc," Thursday.
PLAZA—"Berkeley Square," today until Wednesday; "One Sunday Afternoon," Thursday and Friday.
GLOBE—"The Private Life of Henry VIII," with Charles Laughton.
LITTLE CARNEGIE PLAYHOUSE—"Mam'zelle Nitouche," a French language film.
FIFTH AVENUE PLAYHOUSE—"Le Sang d'Un Poete," a silent French film.
ACME—"Laughter Through Tears," a Yiddish silent film.
SEVENTY-NINTH STREET THEATRE—"Lachende Erben," a German dialogue film.
YORKVILLE THEATRE — "Wiener Blut," a German language film.
FIFTY-FIFTH STREET PLAYHOUSE—"Intolerance" and "The Son of the Sheik."
LOEW'S STATE, PARADISE AND VALENCIA—"Broadway Thru a Keyhole."
LOEW'S LEXINGTON AND SEVENTY-SECOND STREET—"Broadway Thru a Keyhole," today and tomorrow; "The Kennel Murder Case" and "Broken Dreams," Tuesday until Thursday.
LOEW'S ZIEGFELD — "The Bowery," today; "Broken Dreams," tomorrow and Tuesday; "The Kennel Murder Case," Wednesday and Thursday.
LOEW'S METROPOLITAN (BROOKLYN)—"Broadway Thru a Keyhole."
PARAMOUNT (BROOKLYN) — "Cradle Song."
ALBEE (BROOKLYN) — "Only Yesterday."
FOX (BROOKLYN)—"The Mad Game."
STRAND (BROOKLYN)—"Footlight Parade."

ROXY 7th Av. & 50th St. 35c to 1 P.M. 65c To Close
Now Playing H. G. WELLS' Fantastic Sensation "The INVISIBLE MAN" Plus Big Roxy Stage Show

SHOLOM ALEICHEM'S "Laughter Through Tears"
Amer. Prem. Soviet Yiddish Comedy (Eng. Titles)
ACME THEATRE, 14th St. & Union Square.

THAT INVISIBLE ACTOR

Claude Rains Discusses His Film Role in Wells Story—Camera Magic

By ANDRE D. SENNWALD.

A HURRIED search through the better-known volumes on social behavior convinced one worried reporter that there was no precedent for meeting an invisible man. So with fingers crossed, and an ancient Spanish formula for expelling devils tucked up his sleeve, he walked into the appointed rendezvous with Claude Rains and prepared to be bamboozled.

Having witnessed Mr. Rains's repertoire of practical jokes in "The Invisible Man," you rather expected to have your nose tweaked and your ears yanked, the while a pleasant voice at your shoulder wished you a very good morning. A distressing need for accuracy makes it necessary to report that nothing like that happened. Mr. Rains came in at the door with a loud and tangible guffaw and announced that if the cinema kept throwing money at him he planned to buy a flock of sheep for his farm in New Jersey.

On the esoteric side, the British actor is a disappointment. Far from being impressed by the unholy events he was a party to in his first motion picture appearance, he thinks it was all rather a lark. He is not disturbed at the somewhat unconventional fact that his new cinema public, after dutifully attending "The Invisible Man," still has little idea of what he looks like.

"I daresay it was the best thing they could do with this face," he observed. "Now if they could keep it invisible, I might get by in the cinema."

It was while he was engaged in the play "Peace Palace" that Mr. Rains took the first tentative steps along the unhallowed path which led him into the principal rôle of the H. G. Wells shocker. His screen test consisted of a brief scene from "The Invisible Man," the scene where Jack Griffin explains to Dr. Kemp his maniacal scheme for bringing the whole world under his sway. The actor had no idea then that he would appear in that film.

He was still in the dark when he arrived in Hollywood and met his friend, James Whale, the director. Mr. Whale sent him over to the studio laboratory to "have a cast made." That should have been a warning, Mr. Rains admitted.

"The laboratory had an odd look," he said. "There were all sorts of casts about, in papier-mâché, clay and plaster. Men in white coats walked around without noise. 'Have you ever done this before?' one of them asked me. 'No,' I answered, getting apprehensive. 'Well, we'll get you a shirt. It's a dirty business,' he said. 'Did you have a clean shave this morning?' he wanted to know. I said, rather indignantly, you know, that I had. 'Well, we'll get you some vaseline for your face then,' he said.

"They made a cast and nailed me in it. Just my head stuck out. They smeared me with vaseline and then stood off and threw plaster at my head. I thought I was going to die. It was a most alarming operation. Really, I'm afraid I behaved rather badly. I went back again the next day and saw masks and half-masks of my head all over the place."

The mask fitted over his head and face and he had a little pipe in his mouth to breathe by. When he was photographed in the mask against a specially prepared background, he became invisible. On his hands and feet, under the gloves and shoes, he wore bandages which produced the same effect of invisibility before the camera.

"You see, they really photographed me straight and then took me through the pink, green and blue rooms, or whatever they are, in the laboratories, and made me disappear. Each night I saw the day's rushes and could see what they were doing to me. Sometimes they didn't get total invisibility. At night, in the projection room, I would come out opaque, or just the outline of my figure would be visible. But after the film went through the laboratory I just disappeared. On the whole, I think you can blame the laboratory for removing me from sight, although the special backgrounds, the masks and the bandages had a lot to do with it too."

Having gone that far in exposing the cinema black arts to the light of day, he thought he might as well come right out and tell all.

"It must be terribly secret, though," he said. "You mustn't breathe a word about this."

In those scenes where the invisible man was totally invisible Mr. Rains simply had the day off and the technicians went ahead without him. Those are the scenes where he toys with his bewildered pursuers, knocking off hats, riding a bicycle down the street, causing andirons, cigarettes and pieces of furniture to wander about under their own power.

"All that was done with wires," he explained. "If you stood close you could see the wires; if you stood near the camera you couldn't. I sat about for hours watching them do it, and I never had such a lark in my life.

"It was a tremendous lot of fun and I found it terribly interesting. I was always on the set an hour or so before they really wanted me. That's not the usual thing out there, you know. The players are so anxious to get away that they dash off without bothering to take off the make-up."

1934

The Black Cat

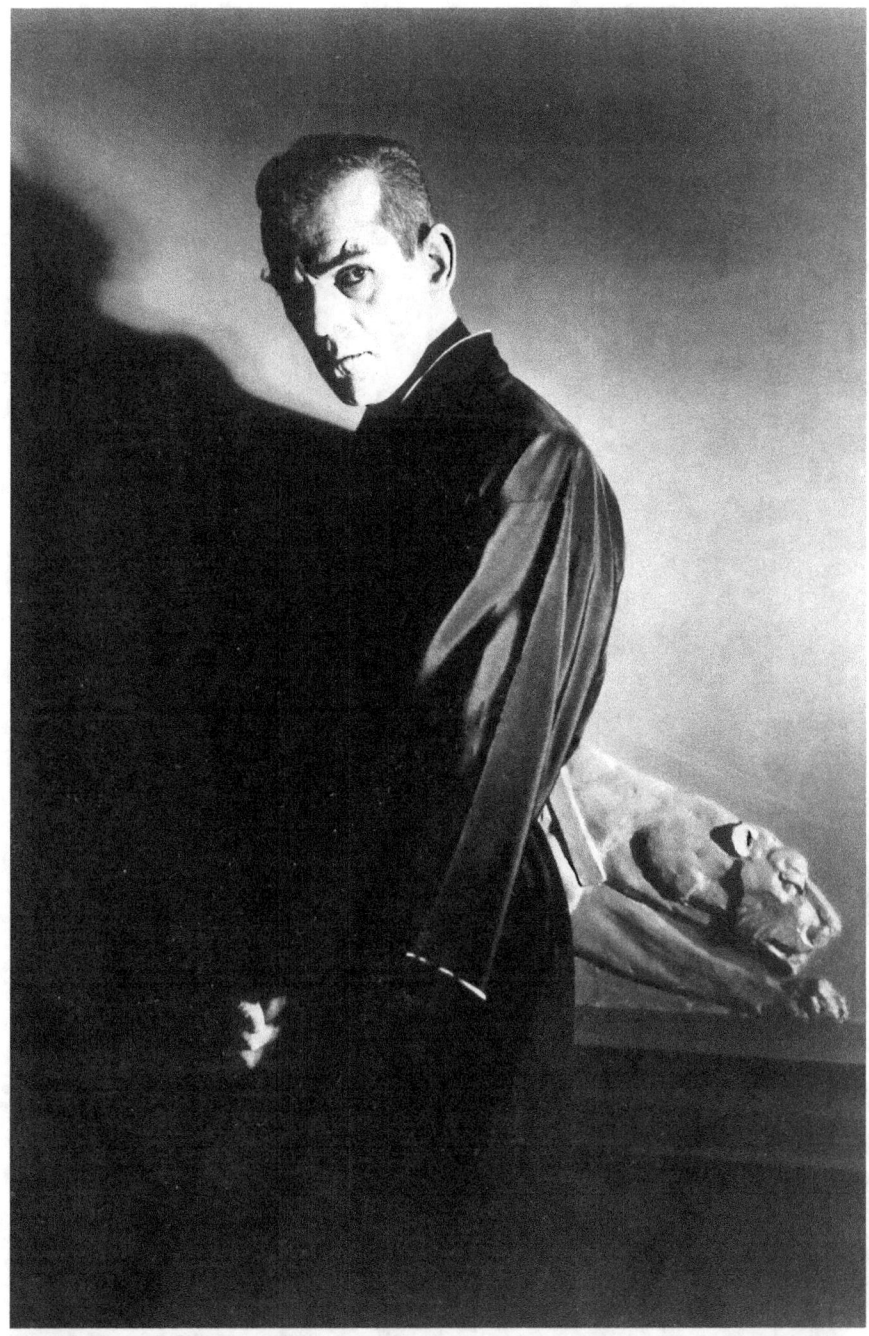

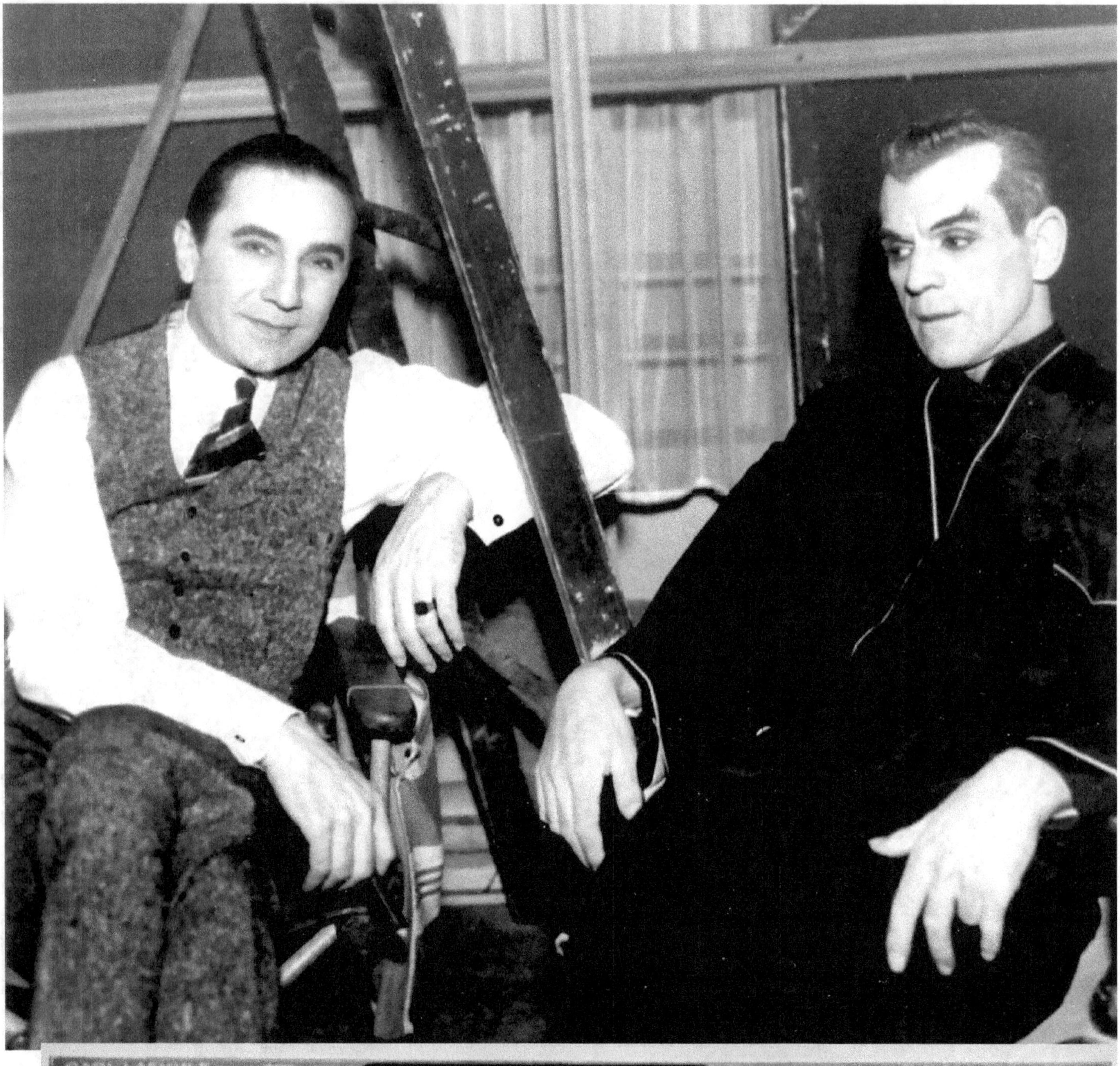

CARL LAEMMLE
KARLOFF
BELA LUGOSI
EDGAR ALLAN POE'S
"BLACK CAT"
A UNIVERSAL PICTURE

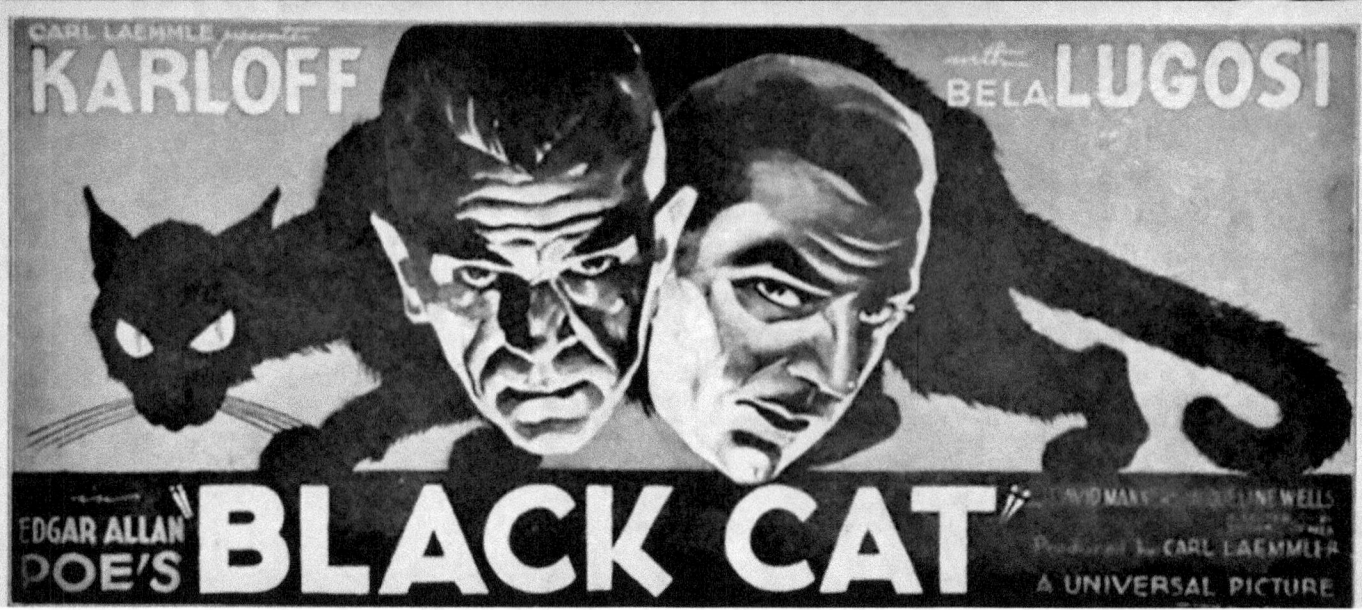

The Roxy announces its bookings for the next three weeks. Next Friday the feature will be "The Black Cat," adapted from the E. A. P. horror story. Boris Karloff and Bela Lugosi are the chief bogey men in it. "Now I'll Tell, by Mrs. Arnold Rothstein," the Fox Film version of the book by the wife of the notorious gambler, succeeds "The Black Cat."

HURRY! ONLY TWO MORE DAYS

Queen

You'll see things you never will forget!

BORIS KARLOFF and BELA LUGOSI in a story suggested by EDGAR ALLAN POE

WED.—THUR.—FRI.
SPENCER TRACY
"NOW I'LL TELL"

COMING NEXT SAT.
WHEELER AND WOOLSEY
"HIPS HIPS HOORAY"

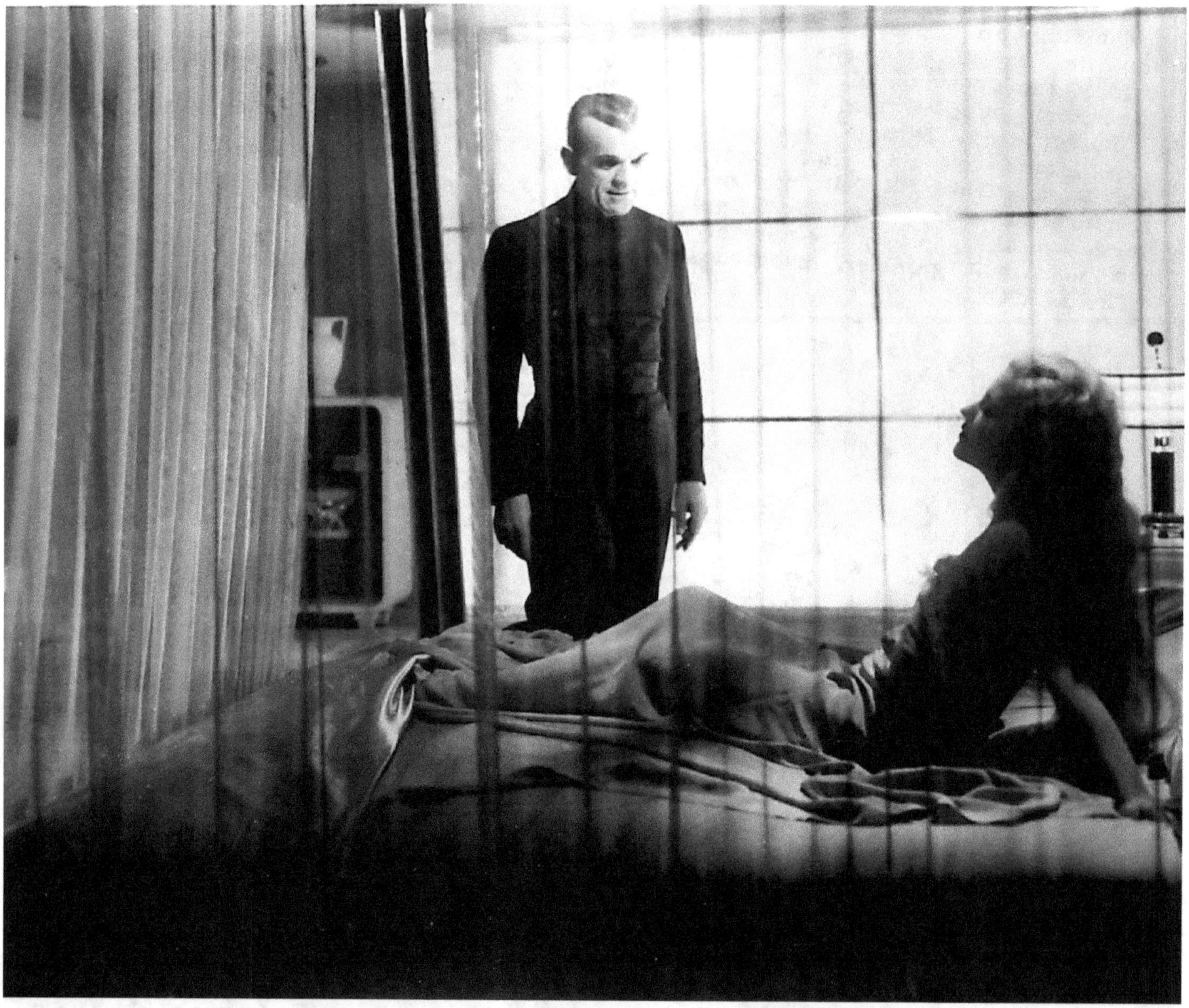

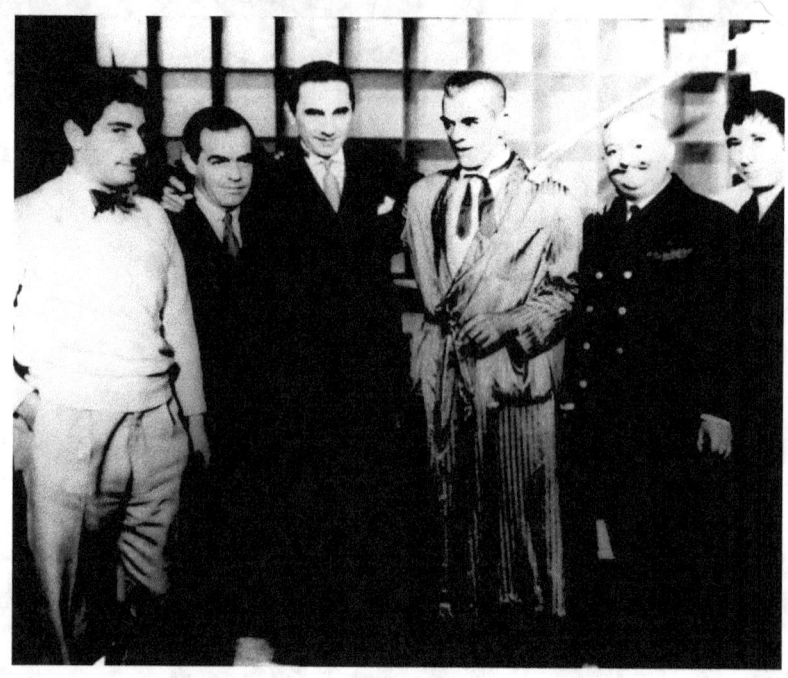

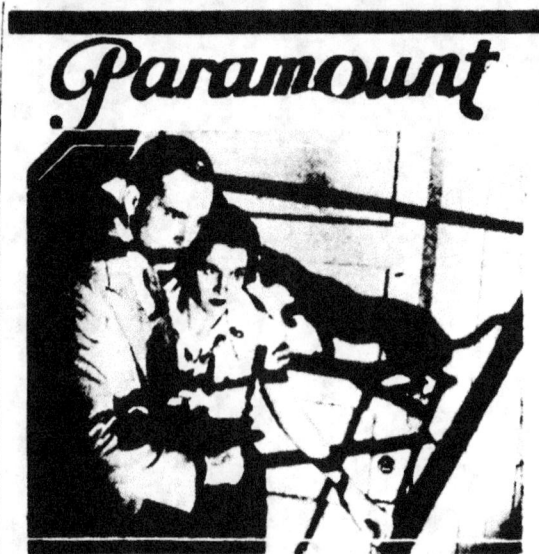

Paramount
David Manners and Jacqueline Wells in "The Black Cat" with BORIS KARLOFF and BELA LUGOSI, coming to the Paramount Monday and Tuesday.

'THE BLACK CAT' ALTHOUGH NOT POE, HAS CHILLS

Roxie Opus Pure Hollywood Contrived to Give Bogey Men Chance to Strut Stuff

By WOOD SOANES

EDGAR ALLAN POE'S "The Black Cat," if I remember my classics at all, concerned a man with a horror of dusky felines who was led by this hatred to slay his wife and wall her up in his cellar, only to be finally exposed by one of the furry pets he so disliked.

I bring the matter up in this review of "The Black Cat," which opened at the Roxie yesterday, merely to point out that Poe has provided nothing but a title for this opus, which is pure Hollywood contrived to give Bela Lugosi and Boris Karloff, its chief bogey man, a chance to strut their stuff.

This should not be taken to mean that "The Black Cat" has not its share of chills. On the contrary those who are the least bit impressionable should be sent into minor hysterics by the goings on in the eerie castle of Mr. Poelzig, the Satan worshiper, after Dr. Verdegast, his ancient enemy, arrived for a social call.

It seems that Poelzig and Verdegast were more or less friendly during the World War, but Verdegast was presented by his pseudo-friend with a very fine example of the double cross. Not only did Poelzig, an engineer, manage to kill some 10,000 men, but he shunted Dr. Verdegast into a prison camp and then appropriated his wife and daughter.

LOBBY — PERFECT OPPORTUNITY FOR SHOWMANSHIP! FLASH A SMASH FRONT!

GIANT BLACK CAT AND VIVID CUT-OUTS WILL STOP CROWDS!

Let passers-by know what you are showing. Build up a big front as illustrated—it need not be expensive. A giant compo board cat can be cut out as shown and placed over your entire box-office, reaching up to your overhead signs. Above entrance doors feature photos of Karloff and Lugosi with catch lines as shown. If possible, arrange for these heads to be situated in front of a shadow box, which will conceal pin-point spot lights focused behind the eyes of the stars, give a weird effect.

For box-office, use heads of the minor players and also a placard reading as follows: "Beware of goose pimples, shivers, chills, scares—'BLACK CAT' will give you all of these, and if you can't take it, do not see this picture, but if you are a real thrill-lover, here is the sensation of a lifetime."

Take advantage of the poster cut-outs as illustrated and also the many fine accessories which are illustrated in other parts of this press book. Make your front a flash. You never had a finer chance than this for tremendous showmanship on a picture.

STUNTS WITH YOUR POSTER CUT-OUTS

There are several excellent opportunities to work with cut-outs on this picture, inasmuch as the posters are filled with action, and the black cat is used as a predominating motif in the art work. The 3 sheet, for example, can be silhouetted, the cat moved up two or three feet, its eyes cut out and a pin-point spotlight focused on the figures below. The six-sheet can be handled in an equally effective way.

COSTUMES FOR USHERS

The illustrations show a costume suitable for your ushers, doorman or barker. Made of black sateen in small, medium and large sizes. Price, only $3.75 each.

Order direct from Valley Forge Flag Company, Spring City, Pa.

KARLOFF AND LUGOSI IN "THE BLACK CAT"

AND now, it's super-horror!

It had to come, along with super productions and super-casts and super-supers.

Carl Laemmle, Jr., pilot of Universal production destinies, announces that he has just signed a contract with Bela Lugosi, the menacing, sinister Count Dracula of one of the first of the "horror" picture series, "Dracula." Lugosi was outstanding as a long dead man who changed into a wolf, a wraith of mist or a vampire at will—and made everybody else vampires.

Lugosi will be teamed with Karloff, the gruesome, malformed monster of "Frankenstein," which holds a box-office record for "chillers" to date. Their vehicle will be "The Black Cat," described as a screenplay which will make the audience crawl under the seats. That master of mystery—probably the greatest writer of super-natural stories produced in America—Edgar Allen Poe, was the author of the original story.

Between Karloff, Lugosi, Poe and the cat, Universal executives are promising to present something which will make "The Invisible Man" appear a gentle homebody, and the fiend who lurked in "The Old Dark House" someone you'd like to know socially. Edgar Ulmer will direct. Peter Ruric is writing the screen play. Production will start on February 24.

Lugosi has been active on the New York stage as well as in pictures since "Dracula." He is terminating a personal appearance and vaudeville tour to play in "The Black Cat."

"The Black Cat" is about ready to spring before the Universal cameras. Suggested by one of Edgar Allan Poe's more chilling stories, it will present Boris Karloff and Bela Lugosi as the chief hair-raisers. The other players will be David Manners, Jacqueline Wells, Lucille Lund and Anna Duncan. Miss Duncan is the cousin of the late renowned Isadora. In "The Black Cat" she will dance something called the Appassionata.

THE UNIVERSAL WEEKLY SHOWMANSHIP SECTION

A DIGEST OF THE BEST EXPLOITATION IDEAS OF THE WEEK

POE'S "BLACK CAT" ANOTHER EXPLOITATION NATURAL FROM "U"

A NIFTY 3 SHEET

There was never but one "Frankenstein"... and that was Boris Karloff.

There was never but one screen Dracula... and that was Bela Lugosi.

There was never but one man who could bring the weird shadows from the unreal with vivid and startling reality... and that was Edgar Allan Poe.

NOW... Universal Pictures has combined this trio in one smashing production, "The Black Cat."

Here is a picture into which showmen can sink their teeth!

"Frankenstein," "Dracula," plus Edgar Alan Poe! Here is something to sell... and from a thousand angles. Realizing the tremendous possibilities in this picture Universal is producing a line of posters and accessories that will make it easy for every showman to capitalize at the box office to the fullest extent.

Cut-outs, shadow effects, special lightings in the theatre and lobby and advance stage or screen exploitation are all in the kit of tricks for this picture. Eerie shadow-box effects, special "off-stage" sound effects while trailer is running... all have important parts in pre-selling this attraction and getting early word-of-mouth propaganda whetting the public appetite for another out of the ordinary and different picture. Play up the catchline... "Things you never saw before... or even ever dreamed of..."

This is a picture to look forward to with great expectations. Plan your exploitation well ahead so as to take advantage of every angle offered in this great exploitation natural.

Fred Perry, Manager, Capitol Theatre, Binghamton, N. Y. promoted six busses from the local Greyhound Lines for his showing of "CROSS COUNTRY CRUISE." Picture shows one of the busses with the banners used. Girls were passengers on special parade trip that attracted considerable attention.

This 3 sheet is a striking example of the unusual showmanship you will find in all accessories for "The Black Cat"—A weird, eerie poster in greens, yellows, red and blues—it presents a great opportunity to the livewire manager. Cut-outs, shadow boxes, and lobby easels are just a few of the ideas that it suggests. Go after this shocker with everything you've got and you should come home with a big fat slice of the bacon! Just wait until you see the hanger—and the streamer and the smash 24 sheet. Boy! What a swell time's in store for us on this one!—More later.

183

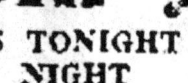

WICHITA DAILY TIMES

MIDNIGHT SHOW AT MAJESTIC

"The Black Cat" to be shown at a midnight prevue Saturday night at 11:30 o'clock brings together the screen's two master horror stars, "Frankenstein" Karloff and "Dracula" Bela Lugosi. And to give these stars the proper setting for their spine chilling work this picture is based on Edgar Allan Poe's thriller, "The Black Cat."

In "The Black Cat" Karloff and Lugosi will thrill you as never before. They will tickle you pink with goose pimples and give you the most delightful jitters of your life.

The story concerns the meeting of two old friends (Karloff and Lugosi) and the captivity of newlyweds (Jacqueline Wells and David Manners) in the home of Karloff. When Lugosi learns that his wife is dead and that Karloff is holding his daughter (Lucile Lunde) captive the two become engaged in the most terrorizing battle ever screened. Manners and Miss Wells finally escape while these two are in the midst of their battle.

Lincoln

LAST TIMES TONIGHT
BARGAIN NIGHT
"THE LINEUP"
With William Gargan and
Marion Nixon
2-reel Musical, News
1-reel—
"MOLASSES and JANUARY"

SUNDAY — MONDAY
DON'T MISS . . .
The Super-Mystery Thriller
With
Boris Karloff and Bela Lugosi

"The Black Cat"
2-Reel Comedy - Goofytone News
2 Cartoons and News
Continuous Show
Starting 1:15 P. M.

Bela Lugosi, the big shiver and shudder man, is making unpleasant faces from the screen of the Roxy this week in "The Black Cat." Although he is one of America's favorite ghouls, Mr. Lugosi's most bizarre activity in private life is a merry habit of calling up his friends on the telephone at 3 A. M. and serenading them with the ballads of his native Budapest. He first saw the light of day in Lugos, Hungary, in 1884. There is no record that he snarled. His father, who was both a baron and a banker, sent the boy to the Academy of Theatrical Art in Budapest. At 20 he made his stage début as Romeo in a Magyar version of "Romeo and Juliet." In 1925 he came to New York and contrived to memorize his lines in English without having the faintest idea of what they meant. Subsequently he studied the language and appeared on Broadway in "Arabesque" and "Open House," among others. Up to that time in his career no one had noticed anything especially werewolfish about Mr. Lugosi. It was the title rôle in "Dracula" that brought his terroristic talents to the fore. He went to Hollywood with the screen version of the popular horror play and remained for a number of other films. Mr. Lugosi was a first lieutenant in the Hungarian infantry during the war, is an inveterate gambler and owns a lyric baritone.

During the course of "The Black Cat" there are dashes of Satan worship, some torture-chamber stuff, a number of horror scenes and frequent episodes in which Lugosi and Karloff try to frighten each other by making funny faces and wiggling their Adams' apples. I think the honors went to Lugosi, because Karloff, after all, does lisp.

Anyway "The Black Cat" is all good, clean fun, something designed to give the heebie jeebies to those who like to have their spines flutter in the theater. And when the excitement, if any, subsided there were Ted Healy's stooges participating in something called "Roman Waters," a bit of madness constructed for laughing purposes.

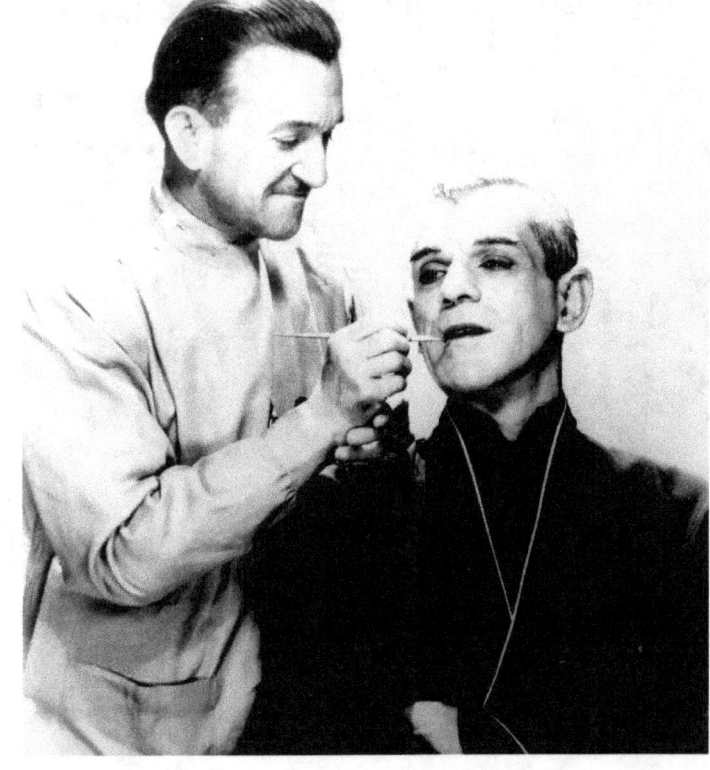

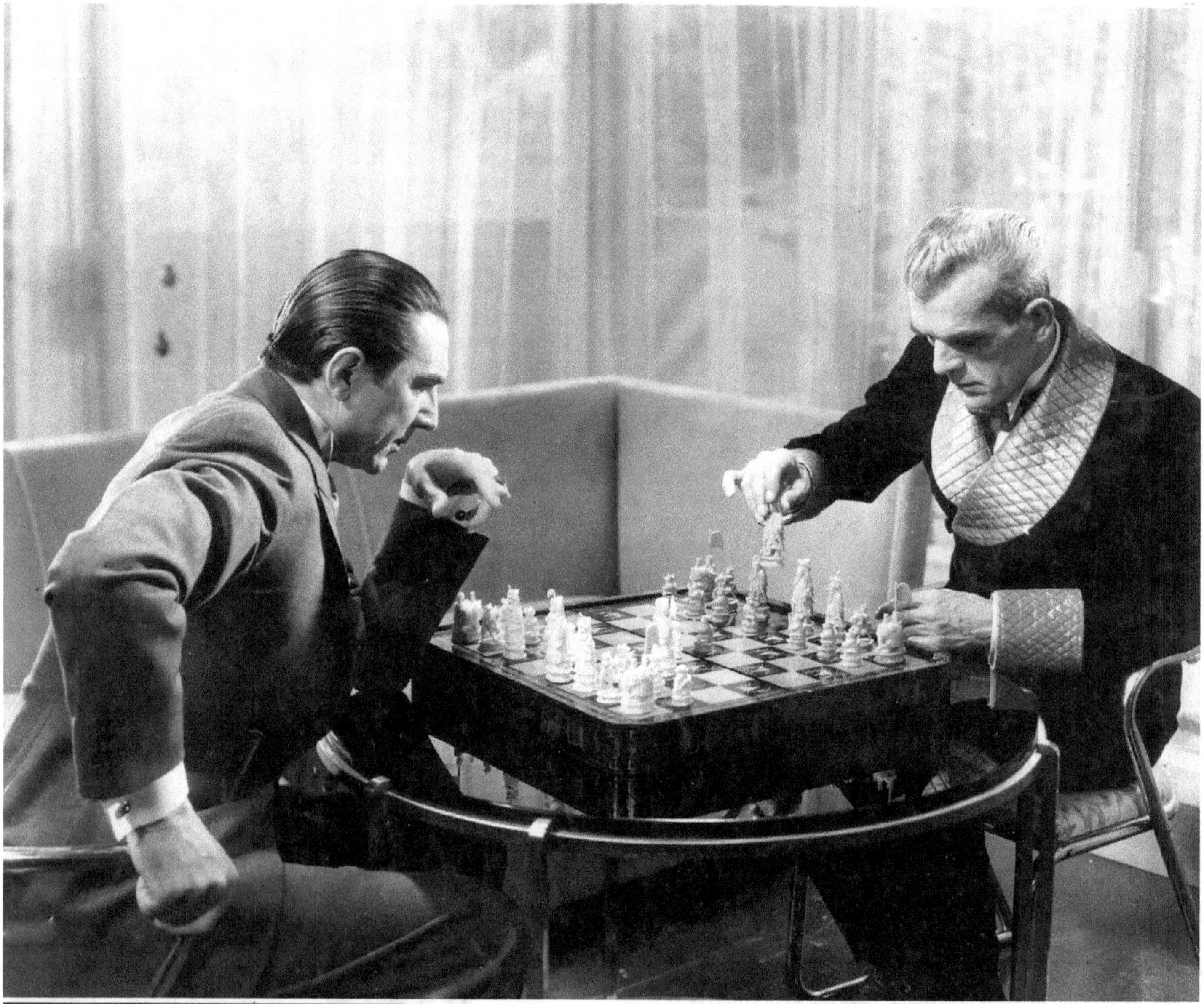

1934
U.S.A.
DRAME
LE CHAT NOIR
THE BLACK CAT
RÉALISATEUR
Edgar G. Ulmer
popcultureparadise.

KARLOFF AND BELA LUGOSI in
EDGAR ALLAN POE'S "BLACK CAT"
"FRANKENSTEIN"
KARLOFF
"DRACULA"
LUGOSI
"BLACK CAT"
KARLOFF
LUGOSI
EDGAR ALLAN POE'S
"BLACK CAT"
BEWARE!
KARLOFF
BLACK CAT
BELA LUGOSI

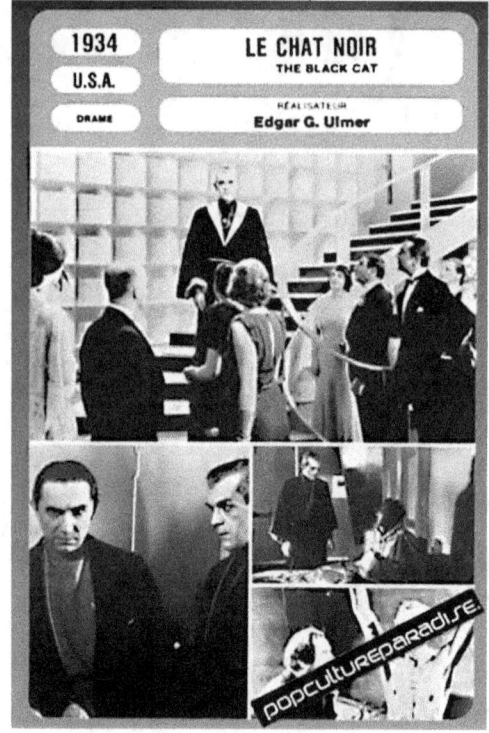

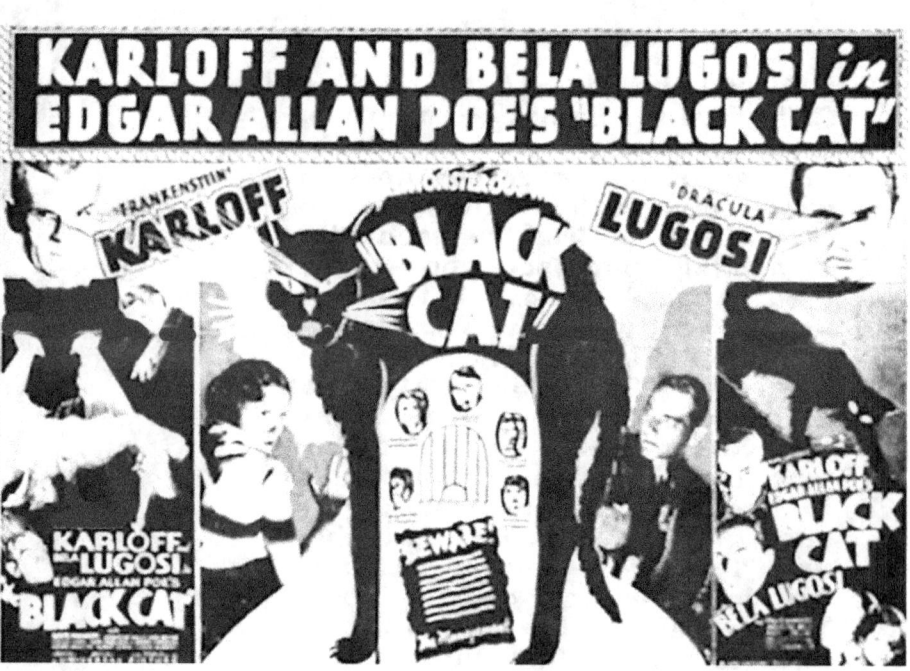

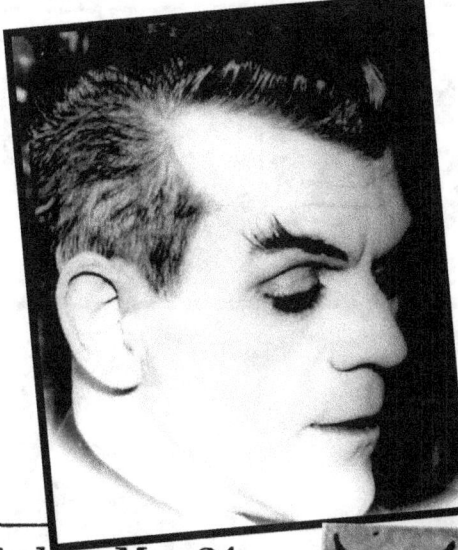

Pictures for Week Ending May 24.

CAPITOL—"Sadie McKee," with Joan Crawford and Franchot Tone.
RADIO CITY MUSIC HALL—"Stingaree," with Richard Dix and Irene Dunne.
PARAMOUNT—"Little Miss Marker," with Adolphe Menjou and Shirley Temple.
ROXY—"The Black Cat," with Boris Karloff and Bela Lugosi.
RIVOLI—"Murder at the Vanities," with Carl Brisson and Kitty Carlisle.
WARNERS' STRAND—"He Was Her Man," with James Cagney and Joan Blondell.
GAIETY—"Beyond Bengal."
RIALTO—"The Crime Doctor," with Otto Kruger; "Hollywood Party" opens Thursday.
GLOBE—"War's End," a compilation of World War films.
MAYFAIR—"Murder in Trinidad," with Nigel Bruce and Heather Angel.
WESTMINSTER CINEMA—"Friday the 13th," with Frank Lawton and Jessie Matthews.
ASTOR—"The House of Rothschild," with George Arliss and Loretta Young.
RKO PALACE—"Change of Heart," with Janet Gaynor and Charles Farrell.
RKO CENTER—"20th Century," today until Tuesday; "Finishing School," Wednesday until Friday.
LITTLE CARNEGIE PLAYHOUSE—"It Happened One Night," with Clark Gable and Claudette Colbert.
PLAZA—"This Man Is Mine," today and tomorrow; "The Trumpet Blows," Tuesday and Wednesday; "Catherine the Great," Thursday and Friday.
LITTLE PICTURE HOUSE—"The Blue Light," today and tomorrow; "The Constant Nymph," Tuesday and Wednesday; "This Is the Night," Thursday.
FIFTY-FIFTH STREET PLAYHOUSE—"Romance in Budapest," a Hungarian musical film.
ACME—"Marionettes," a Russian language film.
SEVENTY-NINTH STREET THEATRE—"Ein Toller Einfall," a German dialogue film.
TEATRO VARIEDADES—"Amor Audaz," a Spanish language film.
LOEW'S STATE, PARADISE AND VALENCIA—"Manhattan Melodrama."
LOEW'S LEXINGTON—"Manhattan Melodrama," today and tomorrow; "Looking for Trouble" and "In Love With Life," Tuesday until Thursday.
LOEW'S SIEGFELD—"Tarzan and His Mate," today and tomorrow; "Looking for Trouble" and "In Love With Life," Tuesday until Thursday.
LOEW'S METROPOLITAN (BROOKLYN)—"Sadie McKee."
FOX (BROOKLYN)—"Success at Any Price."
RKO ALBEE (BROOKLYN)—"Change of Heart."
STRAND (BROOKLYN)—"Journal of a Crime" and "A Very Honorable Guy."

Midnite Show
SATURDAY NITE 11:30
All Seats 35¢

Weird Thrills Await You!
You'll See Things You Never Will Forget!

KARLOFF and Bela LUGOSI
The Monster of "Frankenstein" and the Monster of "Dracula" Together

The BLACK CAT

With David Manners, Jacqueline Wells, Lucille Lund, Henry Armetta.

MAJESTIC

"Remember the Night." ... Kurt Siodmak and Eric Taylor will write the scenario for "Friday the Thirteenth" for Boris Karloff and Bela Lugosi, at Universal. ... "Jeeper's

1935

Bride of Frankenstein
Mark of the Vampire (in Vol. 2)
Werewolf of London
The Raven
Mad Love (in Vol. 2)
The Black Room (in Vol. 2)
The Crime of Dr. Crespi (in Vol. 2)

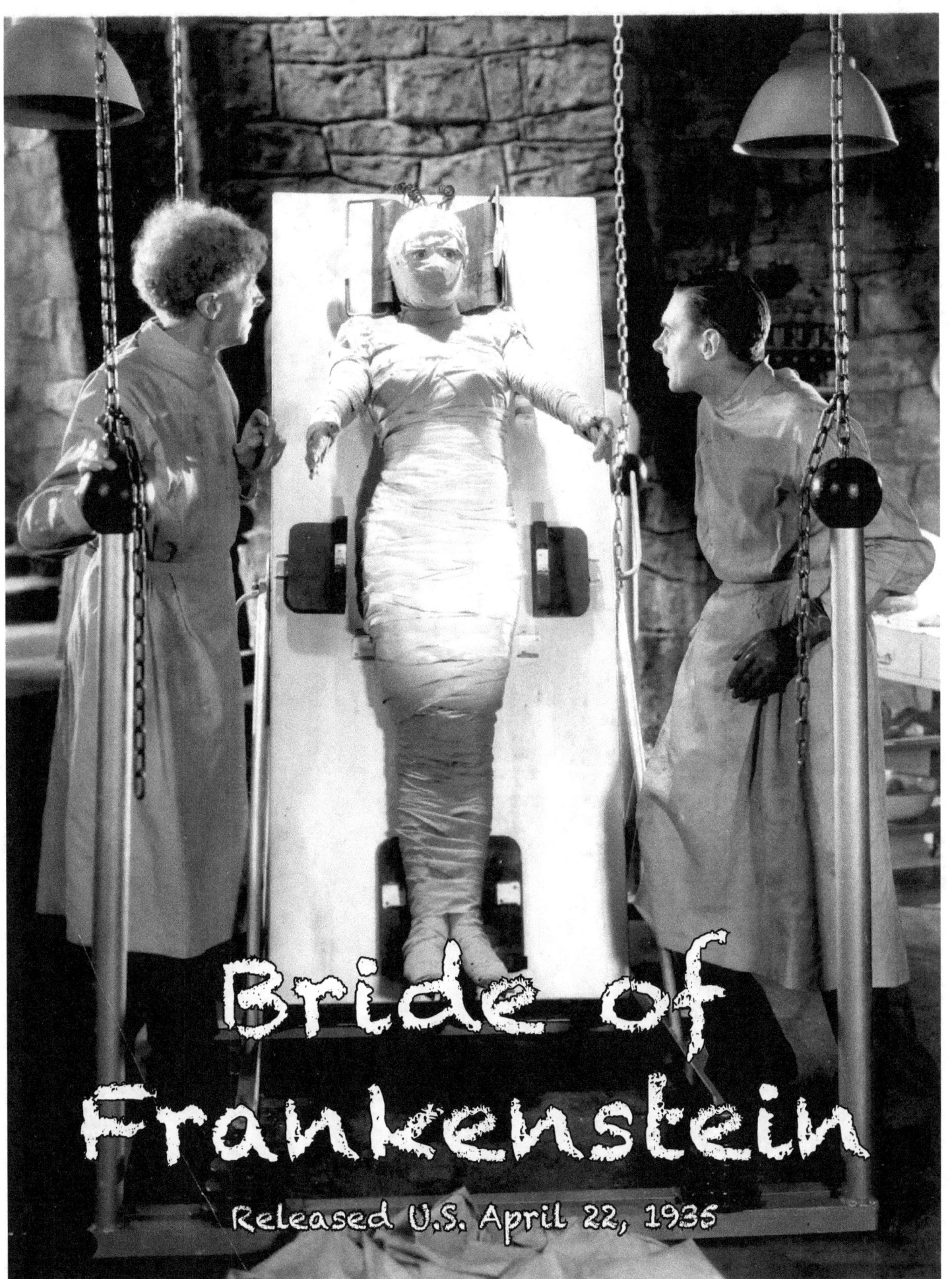

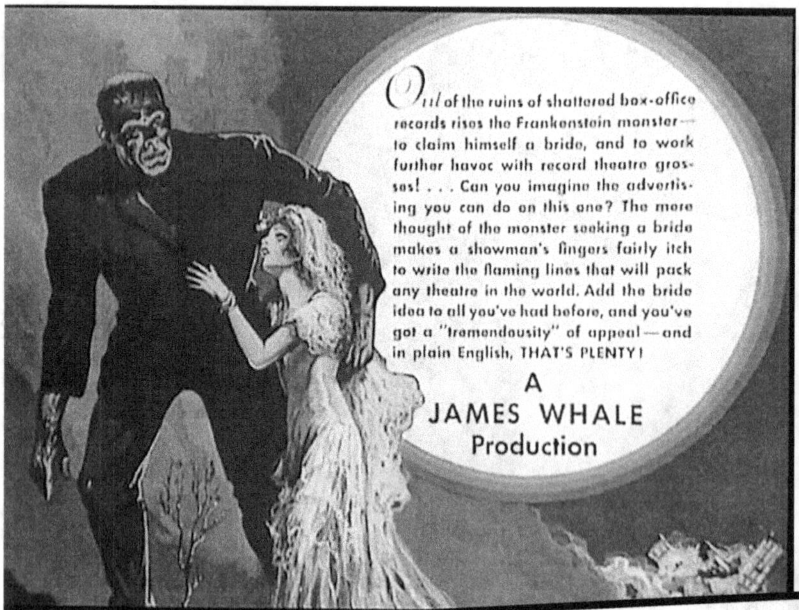
Out of the ruins of shattered box-office records rises the Frankenstein monster—to claim himself a bride, and to work further havoc with record theatre grosses! . . . Can you imagine the advertising you can do on this one? The mere thought of the monster seeking a bride makes a showman's fingers fairly itch to write the flaming lines that will pack any theatre in the world. Add the bride idea to all you've had before, and you've got a "tremendousity" of appeal—and in plain English, THAT'S PLENTY!
A
JAMES WHALE
Production

Sunday—Monday
SATURDAY MIDNITE
PREVIEW 11:30 P. M.
KARLOFF
IN
THE Bride of
FRANKENSTEIN
A UNIVERSAL PICTURE

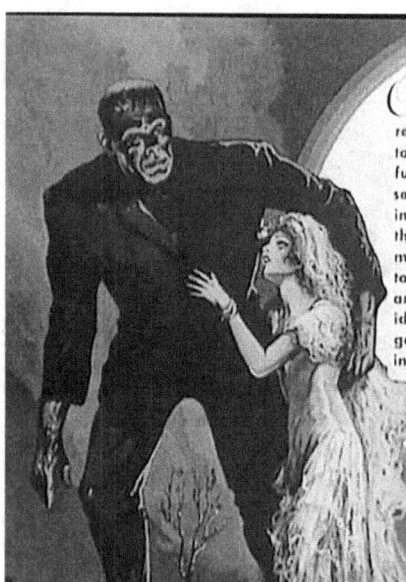

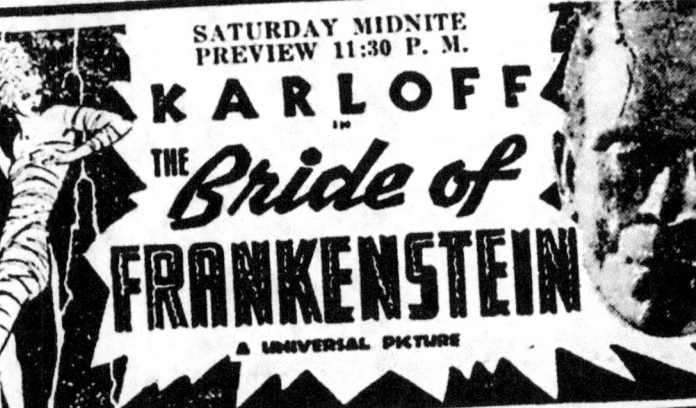

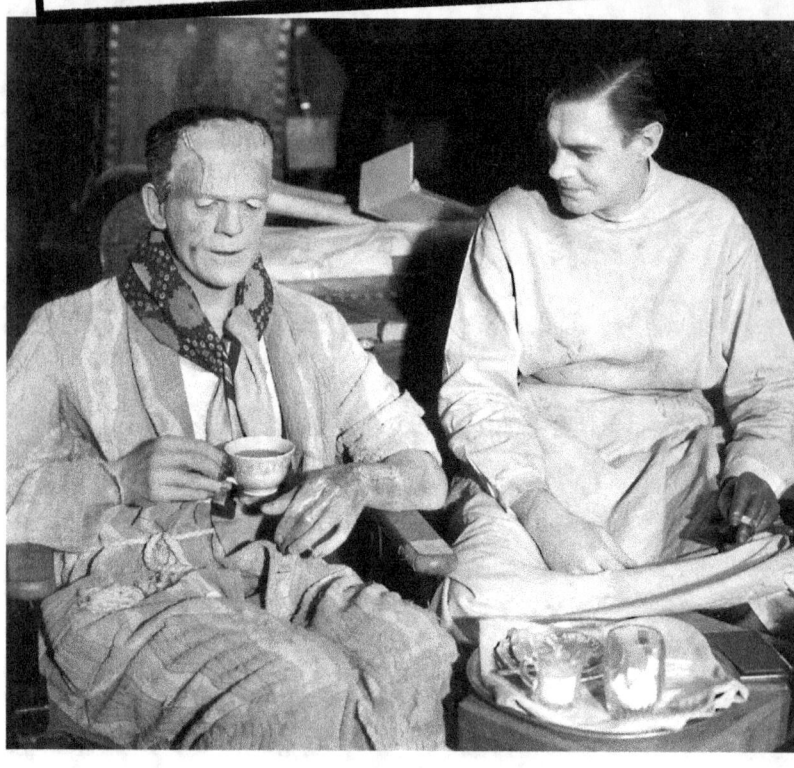

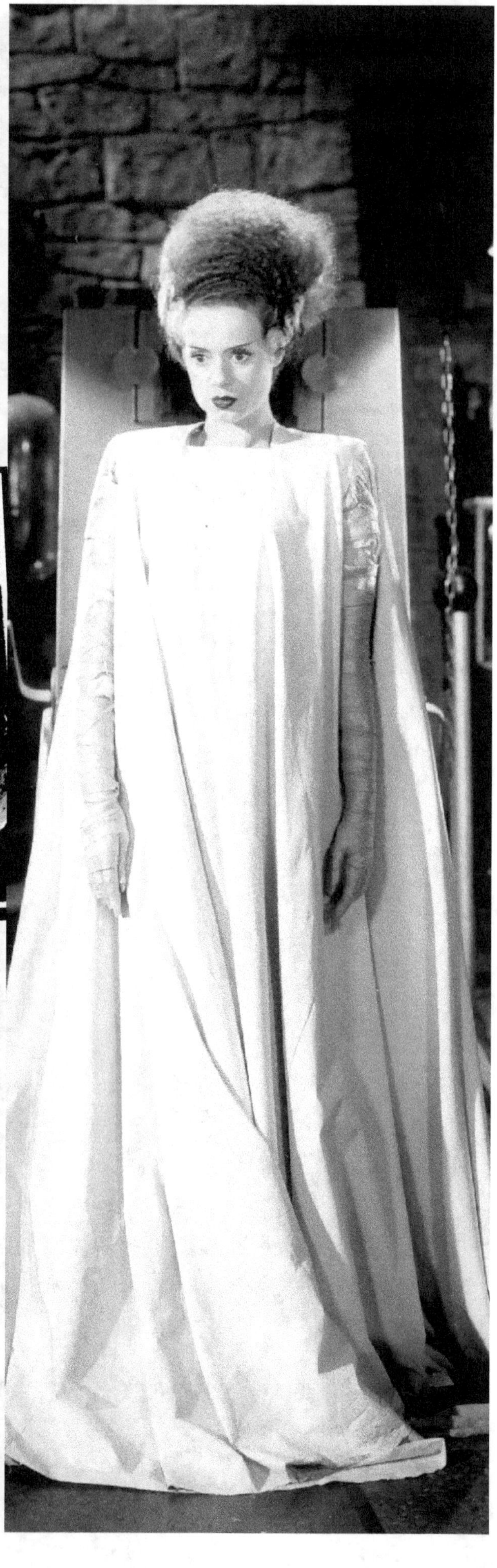

FRANKENSTEIN
MONSTER COMES BACK!

"The Monster" is at large again!

Karloff, the grotesque creature of the original "Frankenstein," a murderous giant constructed from parts of dead bodies and brought to life at the height of a crashing electrical storm, comes to the Lyric theatre next Thursday, Friday and Saturday in "The Bride of Frankenstein," a sequel to the first picture.

In this strange drama, produced for Universal by Carl Laemmle Jr., the Monster is seen in further adventures of such a hair-raising nature that the picture is said to furnish the very ultimate in ghastly thrills. At the conclusion of "Frankenstein," it will be remembered, the Monster was apparently destroyed in a burning mill but the opening scenes of "The Bride of Frankenstein" show how he escaped death and returned to throw the entire countryside into a state of terror.

Henry Frankenstein, the half mad scientist who created the Monster, finds himself forced to continue his experiments with the evil Dr. Pretorius, already successful in the creation of tiny living human beings who lack only size to make them even more perfect figures than the Monster himself.

Meanwhile, the terrifying creature continues his murderous career, until he is befriended by a hermit who teaches him to talk but again lapses into savagery and takes to the hills. From this point the excitement increases, culminating when the mad scientists collaborate on the creation of a mate for the lumbering giant. Then follows what is said to be the most amazing climax in the history of the screen.

Bride of Frankenstein," and the cast supporting Karloff includes Colin Clive, Valerie Hobson, Ernest Thesiger, Elsa Lanchester, Una O'Connor, Dwight Frye and many other motion picture favorites.

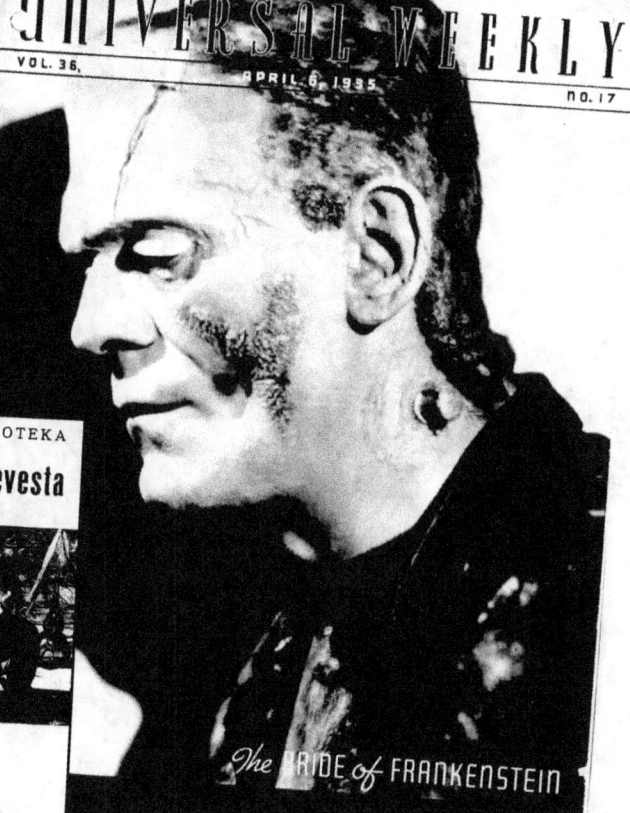

**PALACE SHOWS
"BRIDE OF FRANKENSTEIN"**

Boris Karloff, the nightmare specialist, gives movie audiences new thrills in the latest mystery drama "Bride of Frankenstein," playing through Monday at the Palace on the same bill with "Party Wire." Jean Arthur gives probably her best performance to date in the latter film.

THE FRANKENSTEIN MONSTER LIVES AGAIN — AND WANTS TO LOVE!

KARLOFF in "THE BRIDE OF FRANKENSTEIN"

LYCEUM
STARTING THURSDAY

Sunday — Monday

SATURDAY MIDNITE PREVIEW 11:30 P.M.

KARLOFF in "Bride of Frankenstein"

A UNIVERSAL PICTURE

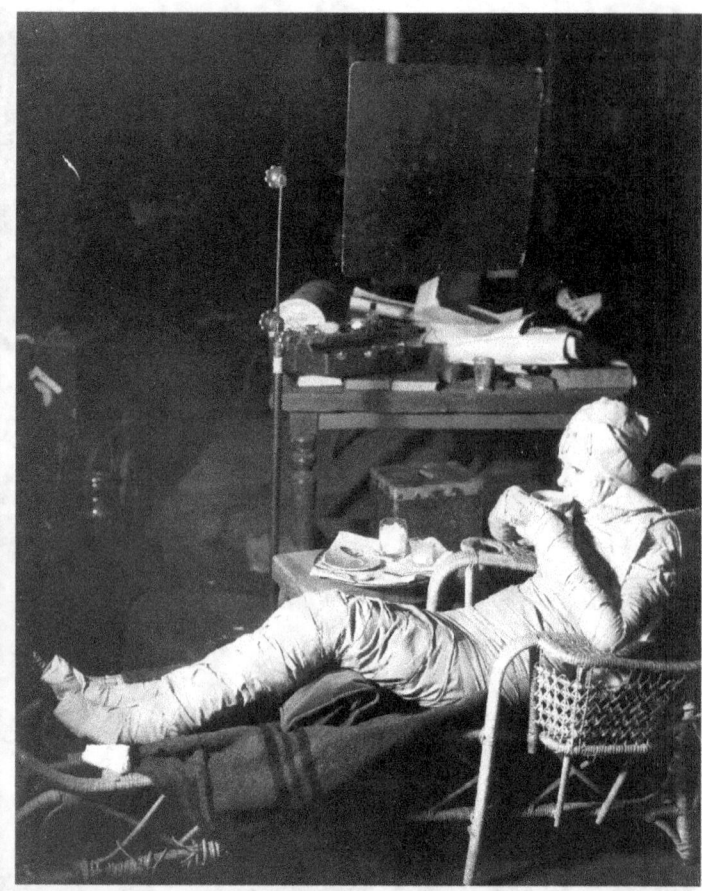

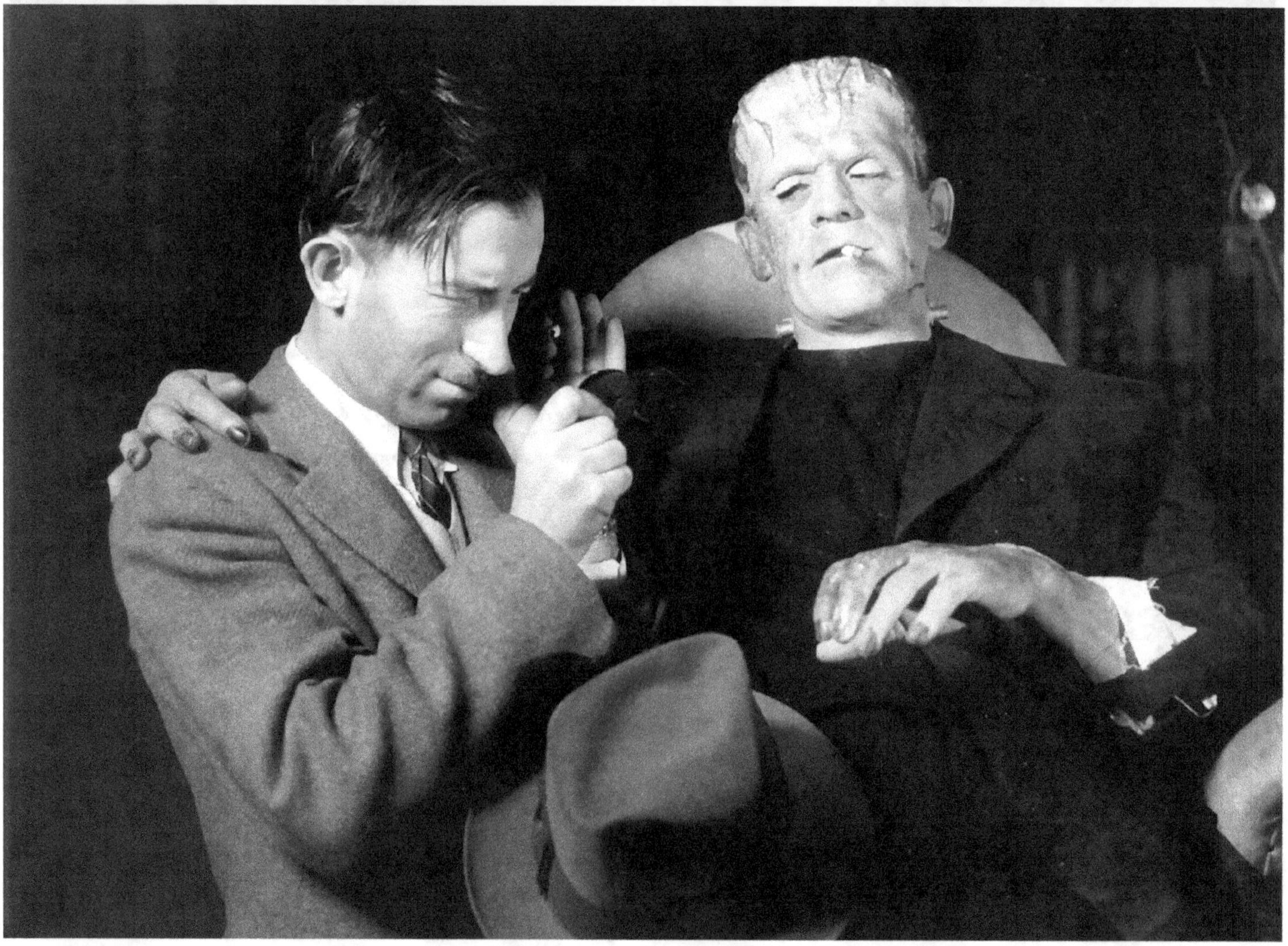

MAKE THE WHOLE TOWN SHRIEK WITH THESE!

This is where UNIVERSAL CREATED "THE BRIDE OF FRANKENSTEIN" for YOU!

the master production by masters of mystery!

CARL LAEMMLE presents the most sensational production in the history of Universal!

KARLOFF
in
"THE BRIDE OF FRANKENSTEIN"
with
COLIN CLIVE · VALERIE HOBSON
ELSA LANCHESTER
Una O'Connor · Ernest Thesiger · E. E. Clive
Produced by CARL LAEMMLE, JR.
Directed by JAMES WHALE
Screenplay by William Hurlbut and John L. Balderston

The Cast

THE MONSTER	KARLOFF
HENRY FRANKENSTEIN	Colin Clive
ELIZABETH	Valerie Hobson
THE MATE	Elsa Lanchester
MARY SHELLEY	Elsa Lanchester
DR. PRETORIOUS	Ernest Thesiger
THE HERMIT	O. P. Heggie
KARL	Dwight Frye
BURGOMASTER	E. E. Clive
MINNIE	Una O'Connor
SHEPHERDESS	Anne Darling
PERCY SHELLEY	Douglas Walton
LORD BYRON	Gavin Gordon
RUDY	Neil Fitzgerald
HANS	Reginald Barlow
HIS WIFE	Mary Gordon
UNCLE GLUTZ	Gunnis Davis
AUNTIE GLUTZ	Tempe Piggott
LUDWIG	Ted Billings
BUTLER	Lucien Prival

ALSO Harry Northrup, Grace Cunard, Joseph North, Rollo Lloyd, D'Arcy Corrigan, Jack Curtis, Helen Gibson, Frank Terry, Walter Brennan, John Carradine.

Monster Returns to Screen Life

"The Bride of Frankenstein" Opens Week at Uptown Theater.

"The Monster" is a large again! Karloff, the grotesque creature of the original "Frankenstein," a murderous giant constructed from part of dead bodies and brought to life at the height of a crashing electrical storm, comes Sunday to the Uptown theater in "The Bride of Frankenstein," a sequel to the first picture.

In this strange drama, produced for Universal by Carl Laemmle Jr., the Monster is seen in further adventures of such a hair-raising nature that the picture is said to furnish the very ultimate in ghastly thrills. At the conclusion of "Frankenstein," it will be remembered, the Monster was apparently destroyed in a burning mill but the opening scenes of "The Bride of Frankenstein" show how he escaped death and returned to throw the entire countryside into a state of terror.

Henry Frankenstein, the half-mad scientist, who created the Monster, finds himself forced to continue his experiments with the evil Dr. Pretorius, already successful in the creation of tiny living human beings who lack only size to make them even more perfect figures than the Monster himself.

Meanwhile the terrifying creature continues his murderous career, until he is befriended by a hermit who teaches him to talk but again lapses into savagery and takes to the hills. From this point the excitement increases, culminating when the mad scientists collaborate on the creation of a mate for the lumbering giant. Then follows what is said to be the most amazing climax in the history of the screen.

The oddest house in New England is the "Wedding Cake House" at Kennebunk, Me. Built of striking yellow brick imported from France, the structure is enclosed within an ornate framework of delicately carved wood.

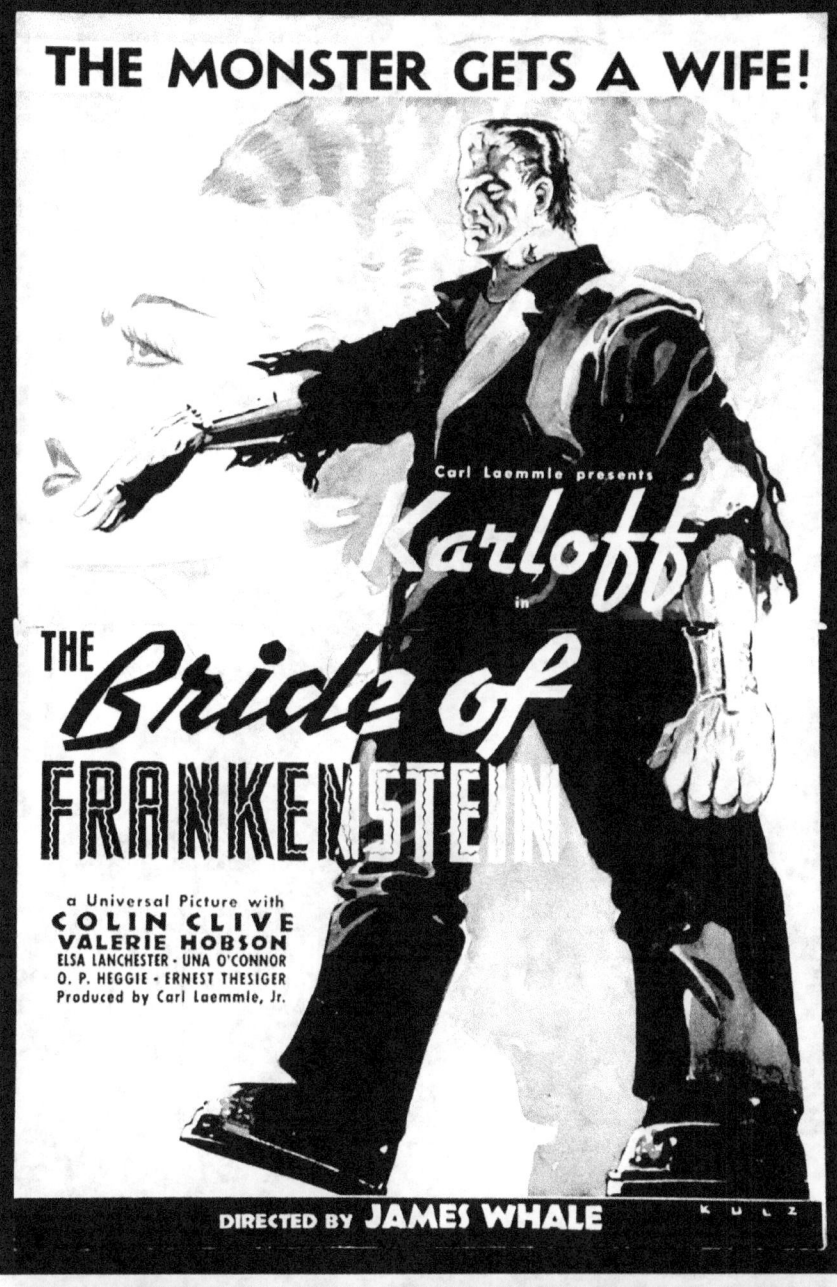

THE MONSTER DEMANDS A MATE!
Amid Lightning and Thunder—Amid Sizzling Wires and Smoking Sparks—While the Elements Burst Into A Frenzy of Wildest Bedlam—A New Monster is Let Loose Upon A Trembling World!
THE SUPER-SHOCKER of THE 20th CENTURY!
CARL LAEMMLE presents
KARLOFF
with COLIN CLIVE, VALERIE HOBSON, ELSA LANCHESTER, Una O'Connor, Ernest Thesiger, E. E. Clive...Screenplay by William Hurlbut and John Balderston
produced by CARL LAEMMLE, JR.
The BRIDE of FRANKENSTEIN
...a man monster ...a lady monster ...a monster T-H-R-I-L-L-E-R!
Warning!
NOT for the Young the Nervous the Scarey! If You Get Nightmares and Tantrums Stay Away! But If You Can Enjoy Thrills, Chills and Spine Tingling Sensations While Your Hair Stands On End . . . See This Picture
directed by JAMES WHALE
A UNIVERSAL PICTURE

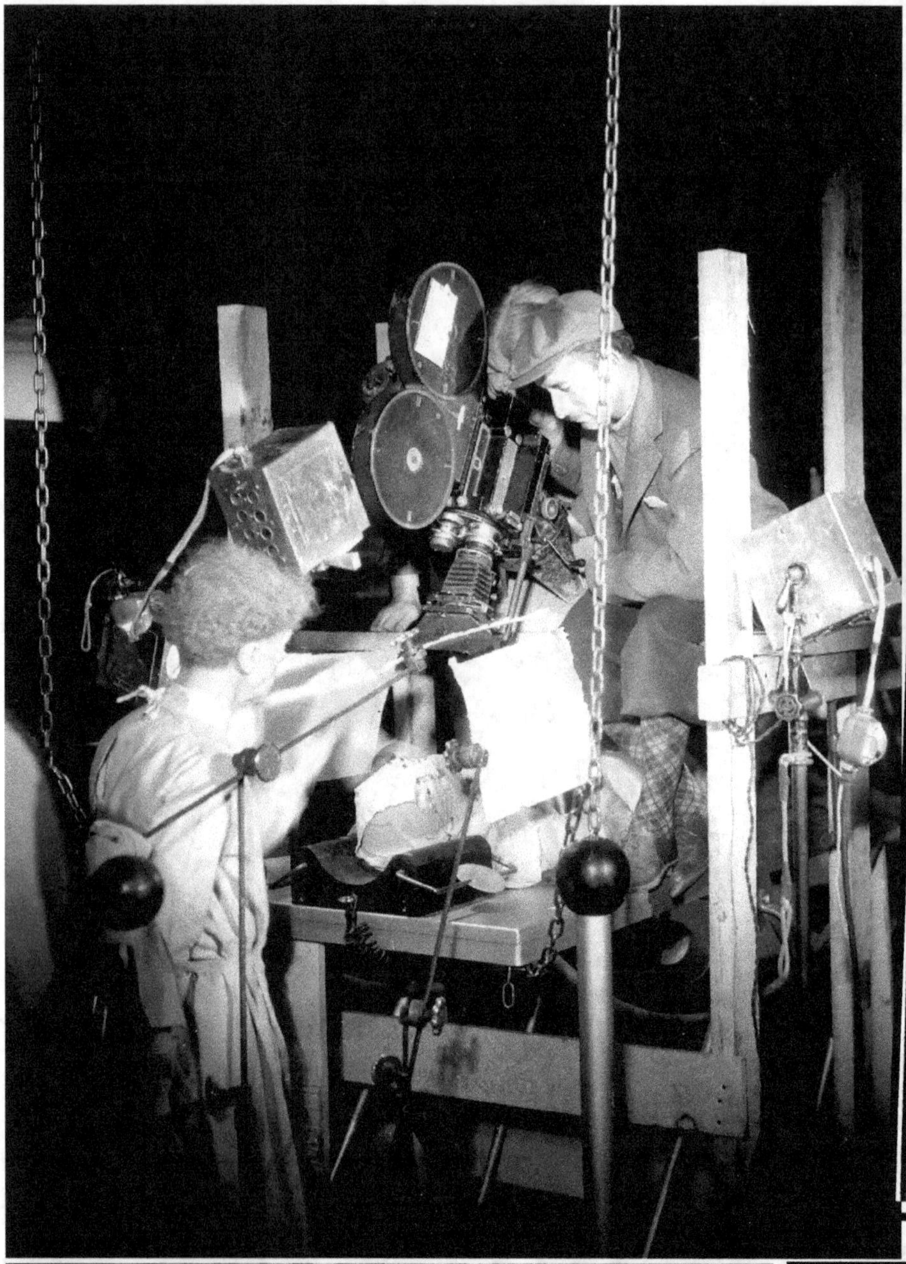

"3 ★ ★ ★ STARS"—News

ROXY
25c to 2 35c to 7
Any Day Any Seat
7th Ave. & 50th St.

The BRIDE of FRANKENSTEIN
WITH KARLOFF
• Gala Variety Revue on Stage •
Doors open 10 A.M. today

Midnite Show Tonite—All Seats 35c After 10:30 p. m.

Friday-Saturday!

—KARLOFF—

in

"The Bride Of Frankenstein"

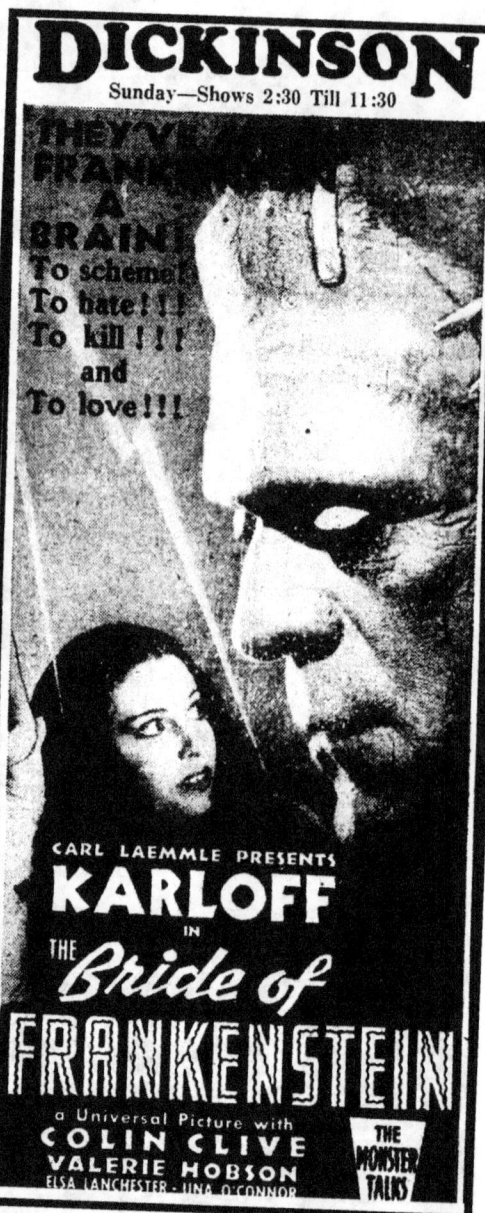

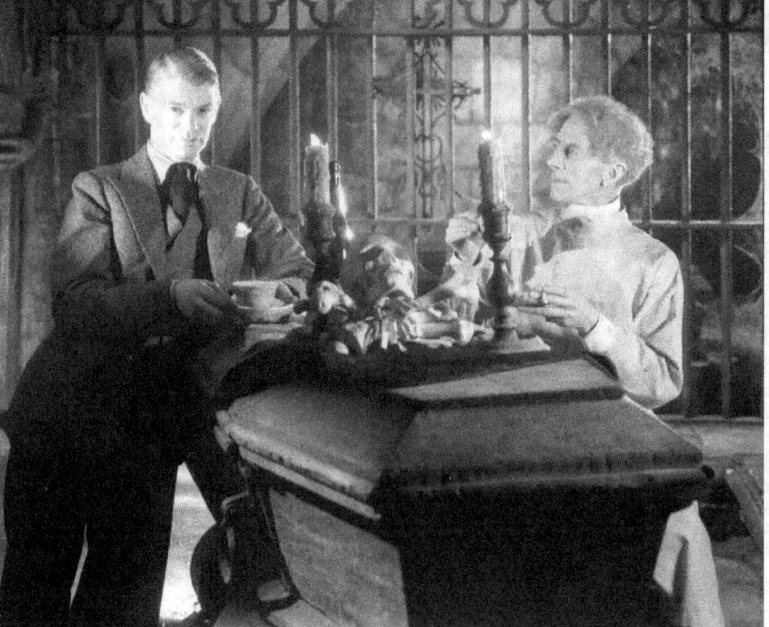

Saturday, May 4, 1935 — Our New Tele

'Frankenstein,' Super-Monster, Learns to Talk, Falls in Love In Ellanay's Horror Picture

Boris Karloff and Elsa Lanchester Teamed in Film That Out-Ranks Previous Shocker For Hair-Raising Thrills

THE hair-raising Universal story, "The Bride of Frankenstein," opened an engagement of one week yesterday at the Ellanay Theater.

It is strong fare, but a thrilling, action-filled picture which fires the imagination as few films have done, and without question sets a new high mark in the realm of the "horror picture."

The present picture is a sequel to the original "Frankenstein" of three years ago, telling of the creating by a half-mad scientist of a "Monster" in human form, built up from parts of dead bodies.

This grotesque creature embarked on a wild career of murderous destruction, with his crimes mainly prompted by bewilderment and fear.

In "The Bride of Frankenstein" he learns to talk, and becomes part of a vast excitement when a woman is similarly created at the height of a wild storm. Then follows a crashing climax which will leave any audience well-nigh breathless.

As before, Karloff is starred as "the Monster," and gives a truly remarkable characterization of the menacing, lumbering brute, savage and yet filled with misunderstood kindness.

In spite of his ruthless crimes, he is at all times an object of sympathy and pity.

Karloff's supporting cast includes Colin Clive, Valerie Hobson, O. P. Heggie, Ernest Thesiger, Elsa Lanchester, Una O'Connor, Dwight Frye and E. E. Clive.

* * *

WARNING!
This Picture Not for the Young, The Nervous—The Scarey, Or Those With Weak Hearts!

207

"BRIDE OF FRANKENSTEIN" PARAMOUNT FRIDAY-SATURDAY

The screen's strangest, most weirdly thrilling motion picture comes to town on next Friday when "The Bride of Frankenstein" opens an engagement at the Paramount theatre.

Three years ago the original "Frankenstein" started the hearts of theatre goers to pounding at the exploits of "the Monster," that grotesque creature built up from parts of dead bodies by a half-crazed scientist, and brought to life to pursue a bewildered career of murder and destruction. Now Universal has produced a hair-raising sequel to the original story, following the further adventures of the Monster and showing how a woman is constructed in the same manner and brought into the world as his companion.

WARE THEATRE - BEVERLY | **3 DAYS** THUR. FRI. SAT. STARTING **JULY 18**

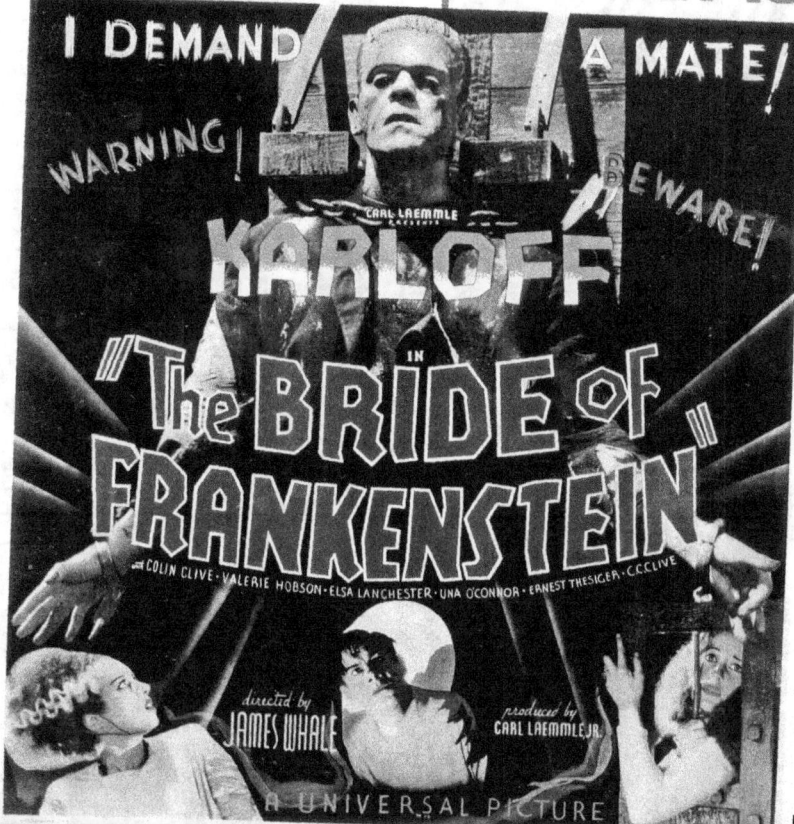

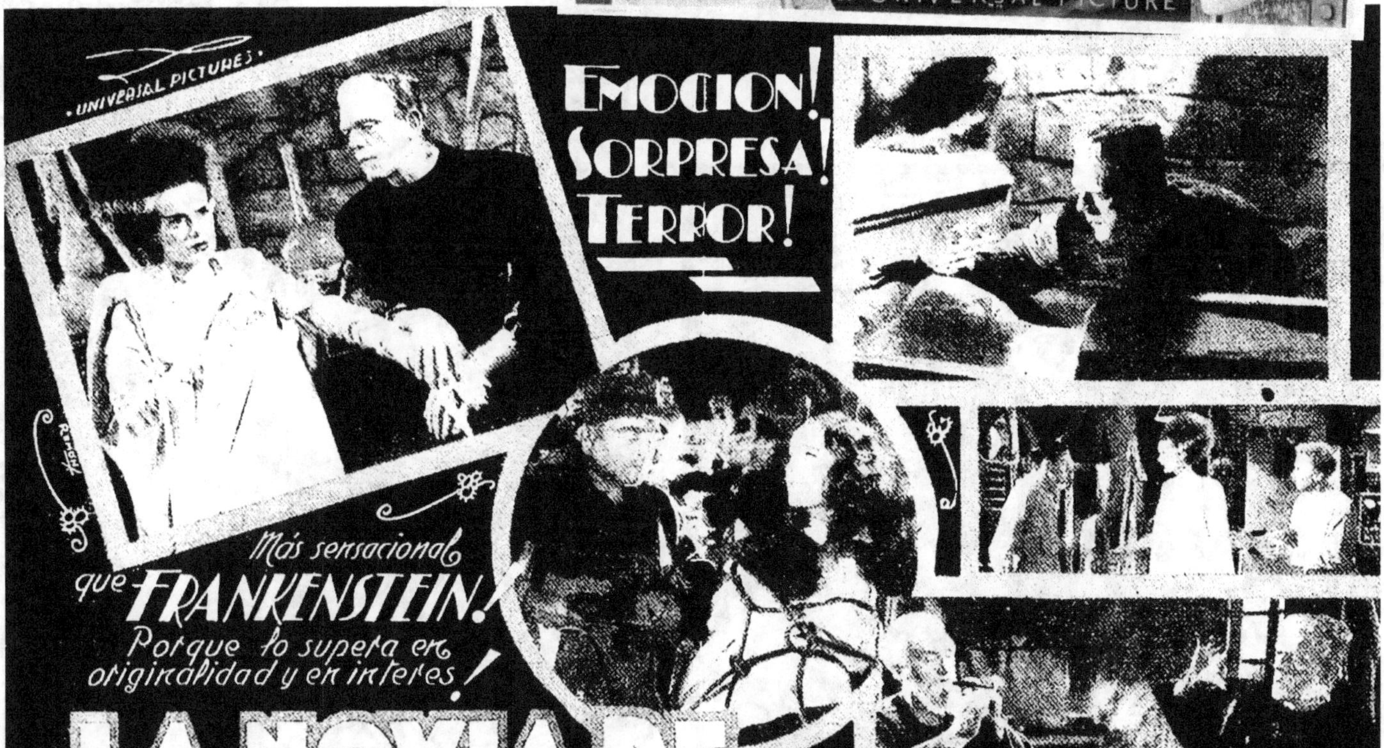

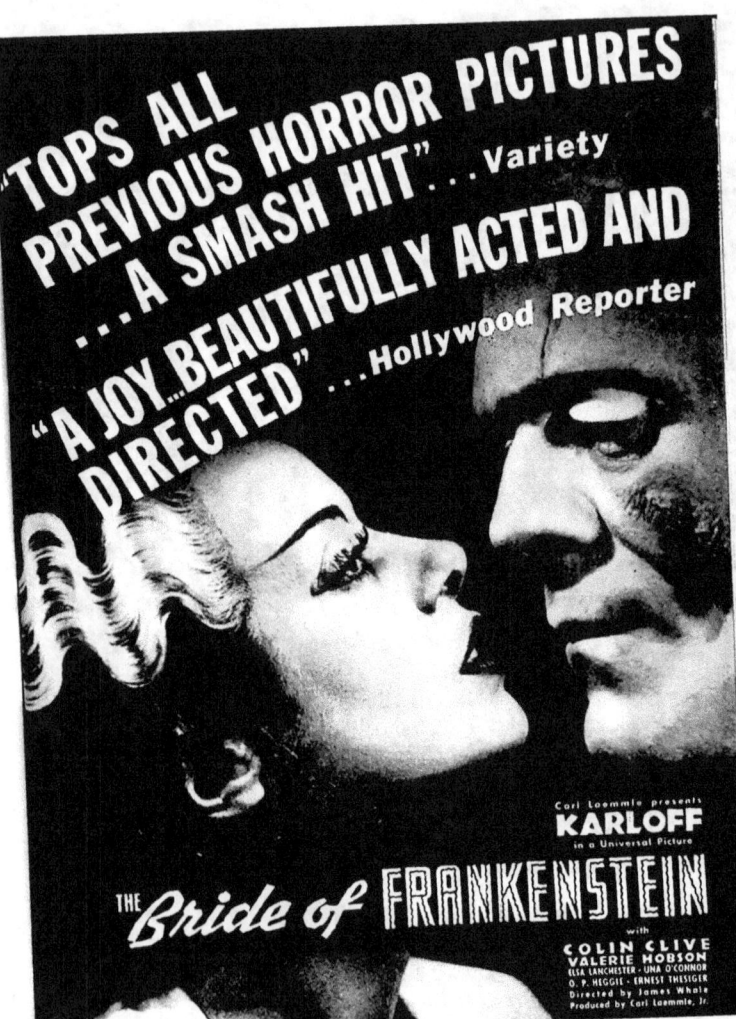

IDEAS THAT ARE Clicking!

WHEN members of the Eighth Illinois Regiment glimpsed the ILLINOIS GUARDSMAN, the regimental paper, the cover was imprinted with selling copy for "Imitation of Life." Al Blasko, manager, Metropolitan Theatre, Chicago landed the tie-up as part of his big hold-over campaign for the picture. During the run Fredi Washington, of the cast made personal appearances. A hook-up carried parts of her interview with the manager at each performance to the street, five thousand autographed Fredi Washington photographs were distributed. Movies were made of the gala opening and were shown on the screen the latter part of the run. Thirty thousand heralds were distributed two weeks in advance. Imprinted napkins were used in restaurants. Twenty-five thousand imprinted bags were distributed by stores. Twenty-five hundred stickers were pasted on taxi cab and store windows. Congratulations, Blasko, for a fine campaign!

* * *

One of the series of teaser ads used by the Roxy Theatre, New York City for "Night Life of the Gods." Watch the Showmanship Section of the Weekly for details of the big campaign.

* * *

Frank Smith and John Joseph, manager and publicity manager, Palace Theatre, Chicago, realize the importance of early reviews on a big picture. They held a preview of "The Good Fairy" for the press four days in advance. Result, smash reviews on opening day.

Bob Page, manager of the Strand Theatre, Altoona, Pa., sniped the snow piles for his campaign on "Straight From the Heart," the Baby Jane picture. He used 14 x 22 inch cards with a large heart on which was imprinted the star, title, theatre and dates. He sniped the main streets in town as well as roads leading into the city. Page also tied-up with the local department store for Baby Jane dress display using local kiddies as models. Stunt was used at store and later at theatre.

THE UNIVERSAL WEEKLY SHOWMANSHIP SECTION
A DIGEST OF THE BEST EXPLOITATION IDEAS OF THE WEEK

Hold your breath!—the Bride of Frankenstein is coming!?!

SHIVERS and shakes! Gurgles and shrieks! Frankenstein!

Not so many years ago we had a confab with a chain advertising head. "Keep that monster face out of the ads," he ordered. "Cut it out of the trailer. Wipe it off the theatre front. It'll drive away business!" "But pul-eeze, Mister," we pleaded, "that face will pull. That face will stop them in their tracks and send them scooting into the theatre." "Nonsense," he bristled. "Let us try just once," we begged. "All right, just once" he compromised.

Once was enough. "Frankenstein" is now show history. Smacko, socko, loco went the house records from border to border and coast to coast. The monster made the nation's hair stand on end. It was a face that made a fortune for the picture business!

And here's mighty grand news for showmen—the face that made a fortune is going to make another fortune for you. The monster is coming back! And he's calling for a bride! *And he GETS his bride!* A new Frankenstein wave of hysteria will engulf the land. Faces will pale and knees will wobble and hearts will stop beating when the mighty Karloff sweeps on your screen and says, "Come on folks, meet the bride!"

They're only shooting "Frankenstein" now; but NOW is the moment for you to start advertising for that SECOND fortune! NOW is the time to let the gossip columnists know that they searched far and wide for a woman who would DARE to play the role of the bride of the monster.

Tease "The Bride of Frankenstein" in your lobby, in your newspapers and even on your screen with advance production notes. The millions who made box-office history for "Frankenstein" are eagerly waiting to meet the bride!

Give the monster the works!

JOE WEIL

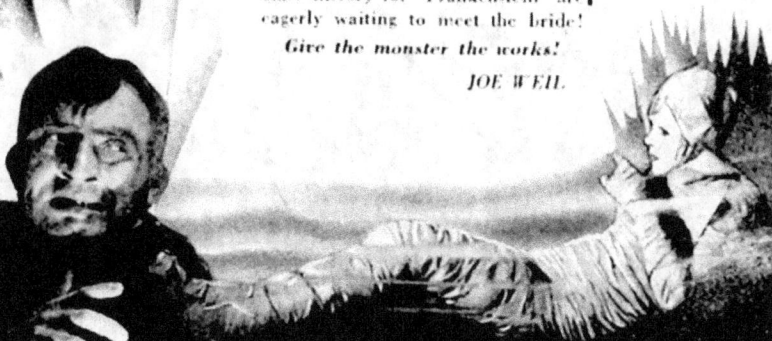

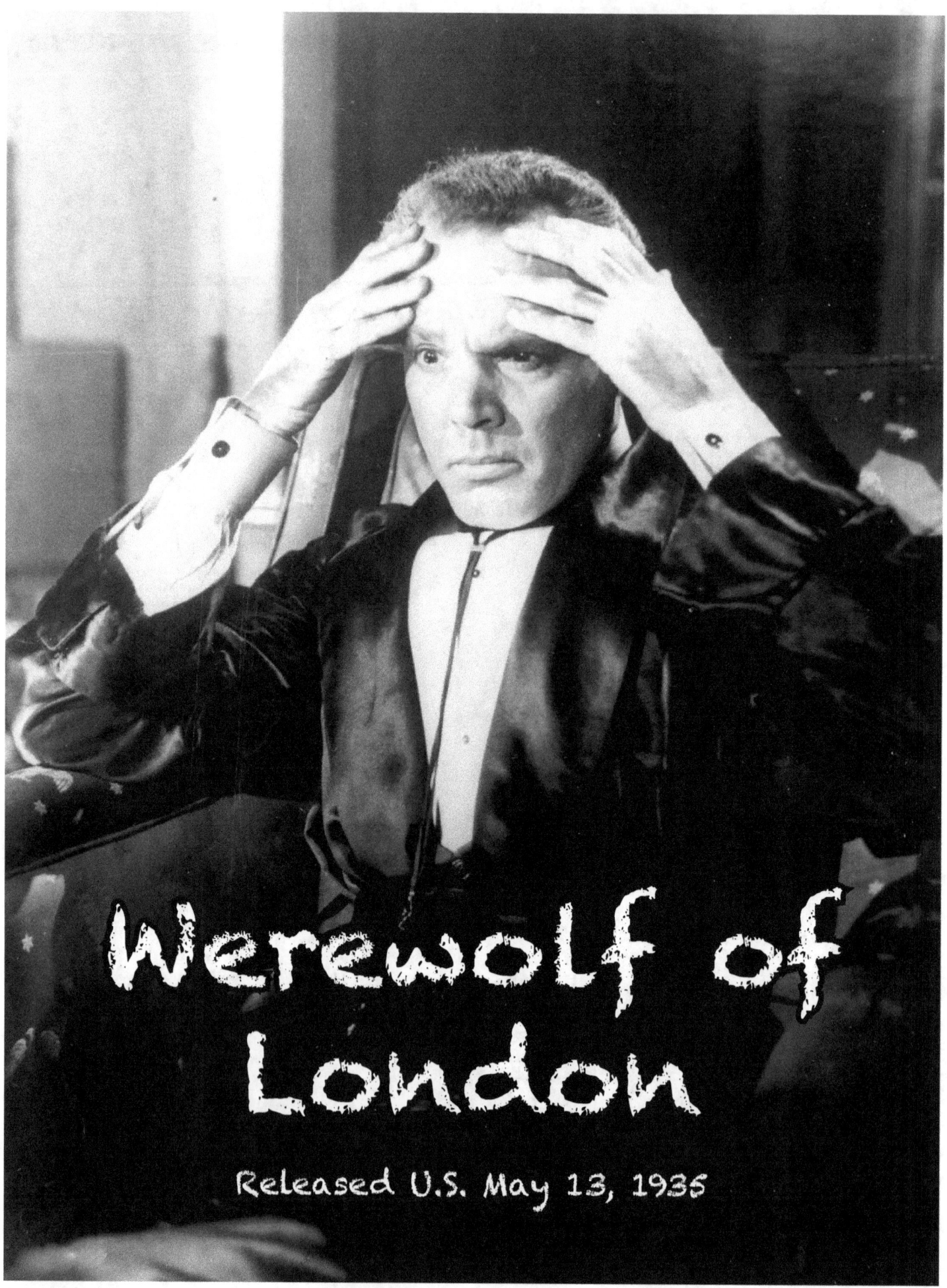

HENRY HULL AVERTS PANIC

'Tobacco Road' Star Ends Smoke Scare in Chicago Theatre.

Special to THE NEW YORK TIMES.

CHICAGO, Sept. 21.—The quick thinking of Henry Hull, star of "Tobacco Road," prevented a near riot at today's matinee performance in the Selwyn Theatre.

When thick white smoke from the eighteenth story vent of the Hotel Sherman, a block away, began eddying into the theatre, several women arose and began talking excitedly about "the fire." Soon half the audience was preparing to go.

Mr. Hull, a veteran trouper, stepped out of character and addressed the audience:

"Are you all as crazy as Jeeter? If there were a fire here, you would be notified and the theatre cleared. Stop talking and sit down."

"Okay, let the show go on," some one in the audience cried.

"That's fine," said Mr. Hull. "Where was I?"

A prompter in the audience spoke up with the cue, Mr. Hull laughed, the actors took up their parts and the audience relaxed.

The cause of the excitement was a grease fire in the basement kitchen of the Sherman.

Wife of Werewolf

Valerie Hobson has an exciting time of it in the Wigwam's film, "Werewolf of London," when her husband turns from man to wolf under a spell.

CARL LAEMMLE
presents
A SHIVERY, SHUDDERY SHOCKER THAT WILL MAKE YOUR HAIR STAND ON END!
WEREWOLF OF LONDON
with
Henry HULL - Warner OLAND
Valerie HOBSON Lester MATTHEWS
CLARK WILLIAMS
SPRING BYINGTON
LAWRENCE GRANT
Story by ROBERT HARRIS
By day a man ... by night a beast! Waking hours sacrificed to science... wicked hours dedicated to death!
Look for the marks of the werewolf! Look for the signs of the fangs! Look for the gashes left by the tell-tale claws when the werewolf prowls!
You see before you... but hardly dare believe... a terrific transformation take place... a man changing into a werewolf!
The studio that gave you "Dracula", "Invisible Man" and the "Bride of Frankenstein" now flashes before your eyes another weird, wild thriller with an amazing masterpiece of make-up that will set the country talking!
The werewolf strikes when the moon is full, and a shuddering world waits for the next victim!
DIRECTED BY STUART WALKER
produced by STANLEY BERGERMAN
A UNIVERSAL PICTURE

DRAMATIC TALKIE IS AT AMERICAN

Butte House Presenting "Werewolf of London" on Double Bill.

Men turn into wolves before your eyes, beautiful flowers eat live frogs and attempt to eat children and moonlight becomes crystallized as it strikes strange flowers in Universal's newest and spookiest film, "Werewolf of London," which opens today at the American theater, with Henry Hull and Warner Oland in the leading roles.

"Werewolf of London" is the story of an English scientist who goes to Tibet seeking the fabled "wolf flower." This is the flower, mythology tells us, which was used to prevent a man from turning into a wolf. The idea was that "Werewolf" was half man and half wolf, and if he bit a human that person was transformed into a wolf each month during the full of the moon.

This English scientist, played by Henry Hull, finds his wolf flowers, but he is also bitten by a werewolf. He returns to England with his flowers—his only safeguard against the dread horror of turning into a wolf. The flowers are stolen and Hull becomes a wolf and throws London into a furore.

"Mills of the Gods," with May Robson, Victor Jory and Fay Wray, is the other feature on the program. Latest news is also shown.

"WEREWOLF OF LONDON"
RIALTO, B'way at 42nd
25c to 2 P.M.

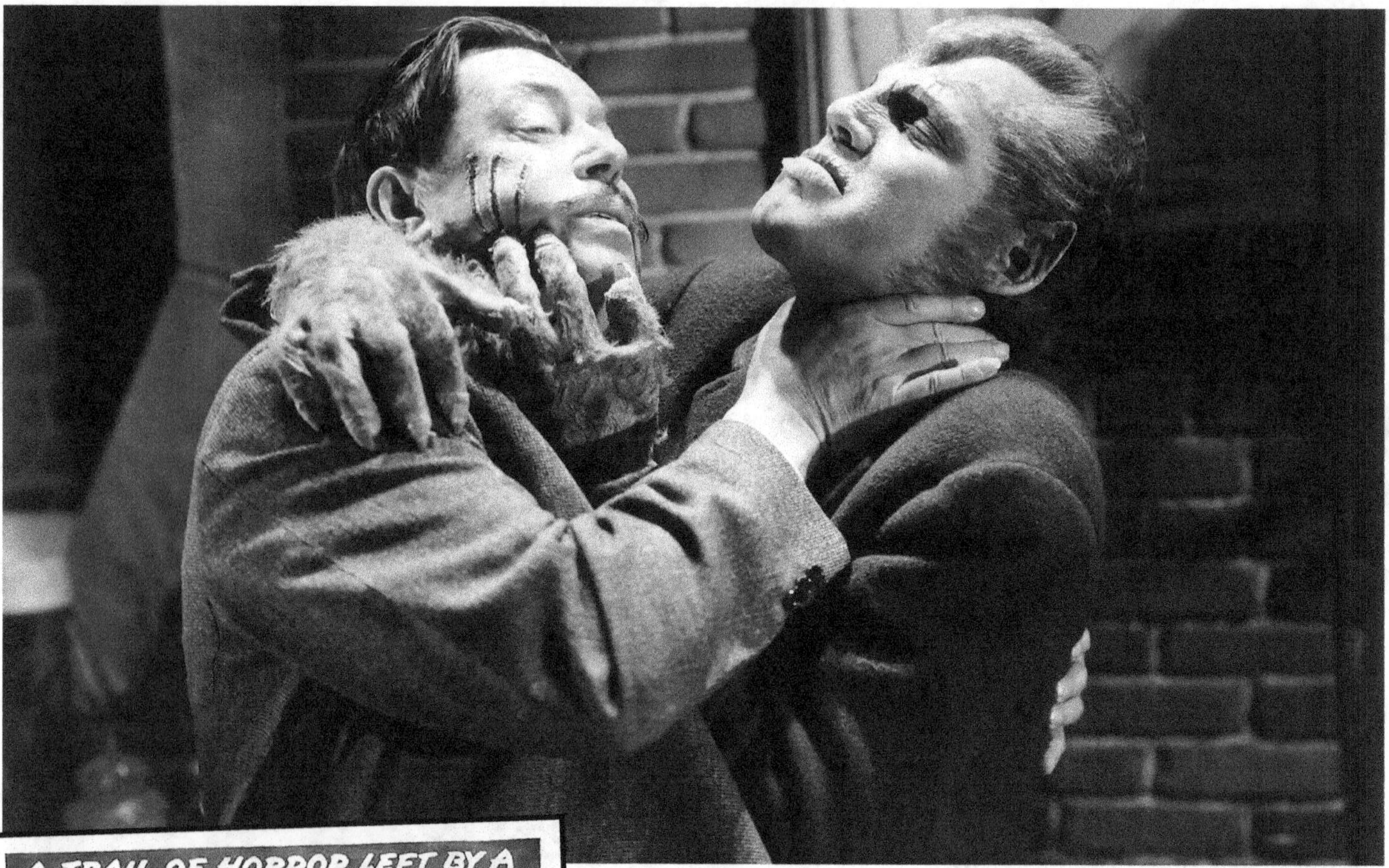

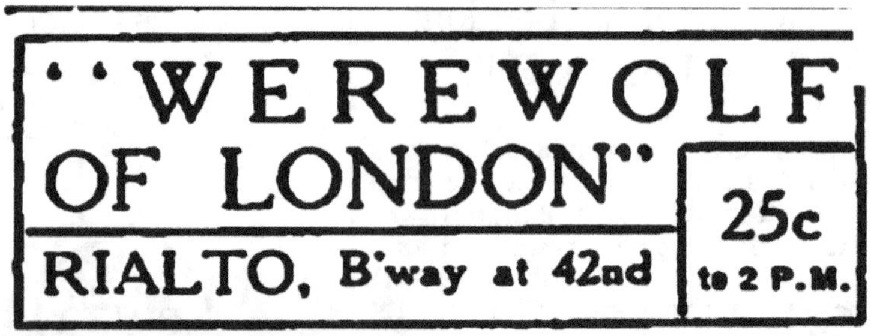

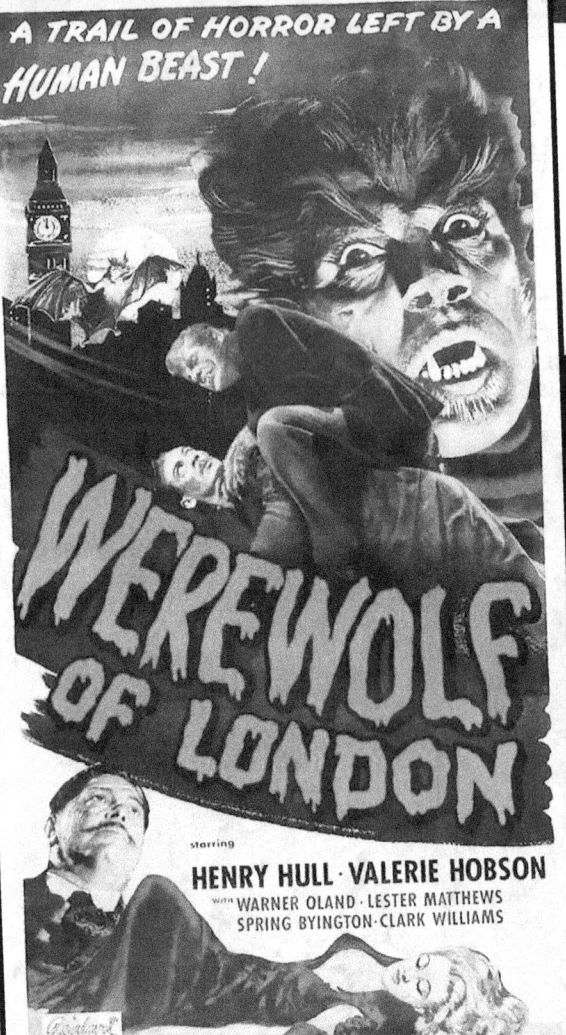

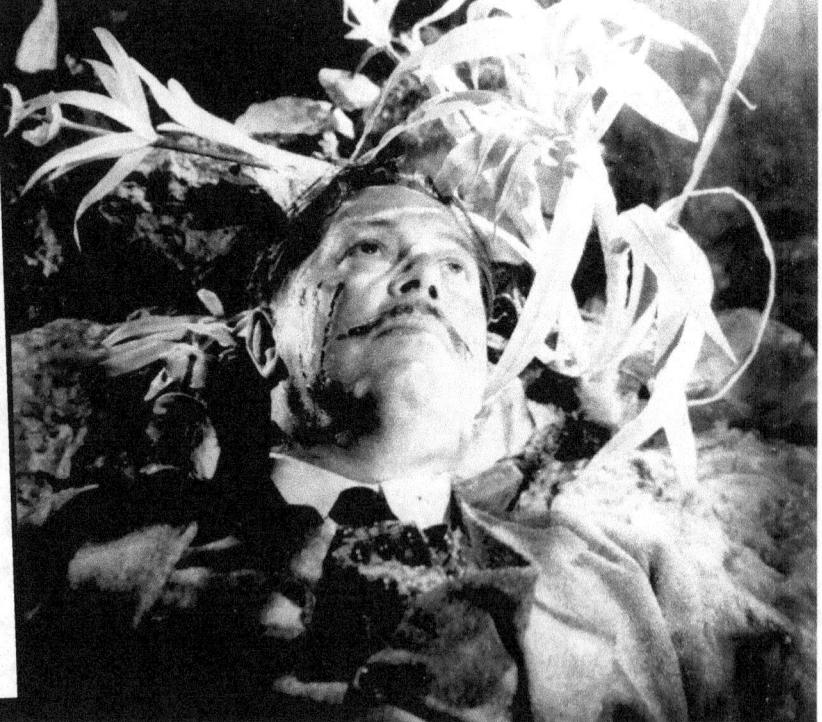

ANTLERS

Antlers open during the summer only on Friday, Saturday and Sunday. Matinee Friday at 2:45. Saturday and Sunday two matinees starting at 1 and 3 o'clock. Evening shows at 7 and 9 o'clock.

The shocker that tops them all, "The Werewolf of London," a wierd, wild, shivery, shuddery thriller, with Warner Oland and Henry Hull. Also chapter seven of "Call of the Savage," a Terryton cartoon, "What a Night" and Antlers news.

Wigwam Shows Horror Film With Oland

'Werewolf of London' Tells Story of Strange Plant And Affliction

"THE WEREWOLF OF LONDON," at the Wigwam starting today, has a double appeal to those who like both horror cinemas and Warner Oland.

D. D. Glendon, a great floriculturist, learns of a strange flower that is said to take its life from the moon. It is called the wolf-flower and is believed to be able to combat the terrible affliction of those known as werewolves. This flower grows in a weird valley far up in the fastness of the mountains in Tibet.

Taking his young secretary, Glendon goes after the wolf-flower.

As Glendon stoops to pick one, he is attacked by a vicious wolf who bites him on the arm and then slinks away. In the distance, the wolf seems to take the form of a man. In spite of his pain, Glendon manages to save the plant.

Months later, Glendon is giving a flower show in his gardens, in London. Among the doctor's strange exhibits is a plant that eats frogs. This plant catches a small boy after the manner of an octopus. Glendon frees the boy and thus meets Dr. Yogami, who is also interested in strange plants. Yogami knows that Glendon has been in search of the famous wolf-flower and tries to ascertain if he has indeed found one.

Through Yogami, Dr. Glendon discovers that someone in London is in urgent need of the wolf-flower. He has a feeling that it is Yogami, and that it is Yogami who is the were-wolf that bit him in the valley of Tibet. He cannot throw off this suspicion. He keeps his wolf-flowers under lock and key in his garden, having need of them himself to ward off the increasing signs of lycanthropy which have developed as a result of the wolf bite he suffered in Tibet. In spite of these treatments, however, Glendon is horribly frightened by the appearance of hair growing all over his body.

"DRACULA" JUST A SISSY BESIDE 'WEREWOLF OF LONDON'

A vampire is always a gentleman except when it is a lady, but a werewolf is a brute. The vampire bleeds his or her victims with the neatness of a surgeon or a blackmailer, but a werewolf is inclined to leave things a shambles. The bite of the vampire does not mean instant death, or necessarily death at all. The bite of the werewolf kills at once or infects with lycanthrophobia, the contagious werewolf disease, eventually fatal. However there is one consolation. You do not have to go to any special trouble to kill a werewolf, such as driving a stake through his heart. The ordinary rifle or revolver bullet does the trick very nicely.

All these points of difference between the vampire and werewolf will be moot subjects when "Werewolf of London," Universal's latest and reputedly best thriller comes to town at the Strand theater tonight. It will unquestionably cause discussion about "Dracula," the first of all shudder films, also, incidentally, a product of the same Universal studio. Henry Hull's portrayal of the werewolf, a man who periodically is afflicted with wolf madness, will be compared with Bela Lugosi as the vampire Count Dracula.

However, according to advance reports emanating from the Universal, the sinister Count Dracula will be considered a mere sissy when Hull's werewolf takes the screen. The makeup of the noted stage actor is said to be a more appalling affair than the one which Karloff wore as the Frankenstein monster. It took six hours daily to put on, and two hours to remove. Fangs, two inches long, which are fitted into the lower jaw, and an entire false forehead are a few simple details of this involved makeup.

While uncarthly creatures are by no means strangers to the cinema ever since "Dracula" started the fashion back in 1931, this is the first screen appearance for the werewolf. Strange as it may seem and believe it or not, there is evidence for his existence in real life too. Just as the folk lore of all countries have stories of vampires, so have they of werewolves. Science now recognizes both as pathological cases.

According to Montague Summers who has written learned books on both subjects, "werewolf" means "man-wolf," a man who thinks he is a wolf and acts like a wolf as Hull does in the film. Like the vampire the werewolf feels the urge to do his deadly work at night. Any night will do for the vampire but the victim of lycanthrophobia goes on the prowl only when the moon is full.

The vampire is a much more difficult creature to detect. There is no change in appearance when the vampire feeling overcomes him. That is why Bela Lugosi as Dracula could maintain the poised, sleek, well groomed manner of a European nobleman. With the werewolf there is said to be a change in appearance, more or less marked when the victim feels the wolf possession coming on. This happens in the case of Dr. Glendon, the character played by Hull, who shows many of the characteristics of a wolf when the moon is full. No one would mistake him for a gentleman after one look.

Vampires are defined as people supposed to be dead, "the undead," as the folk stories term them, who rise from their coffins at nightfall to prey on the living. The werewolf is strictly a living individual. If you kill him you may rest easy. He won't be back. Vampires know the trick of the Oriental magicians, called levitation, or the power to move through the air. Werewolves stick close to the ground and lope along like wolves.

Once a vampire always a vampire; there is no known cure for the disease. Werewolves are more fortunate, but not much more. There is thought to be a cure for the man wolf seizure. It is called the mariphasa lumina lupina. This is a flower which like the century plant blooms only by moonlight and is found in Tibet. Dr. Glendon, plant scientist is searching for this flower to study it when he becomes infected with lycanthrophobia from Warner Oland who has the part of an Oriental scientist, Dr. Yogami, also a sufferer.

"The Werewolf Of London" At Lincoln

"The Werewolf of London," featuring an all star cast, is showing at the Lincoln theatre tonight and Sunday. Added attractions include a comedy, cartoon, news and Chapter 11 of "Roaring West".

SCREEN NOTES.

Universal will display two of its horror films on Broadway this week. On Thursday night "The Werewolf of London," with Henry Hull, Warner Oland and Valerie Hobson, will open with a preview showing at the Rialto. A change in plans brings "The Bride of Frankenstein," with Boris Karloff, Colin Clive and Elsa Lanchester, into the Roxy on Friday instead of "Mr. Dynamite," as previously announced.

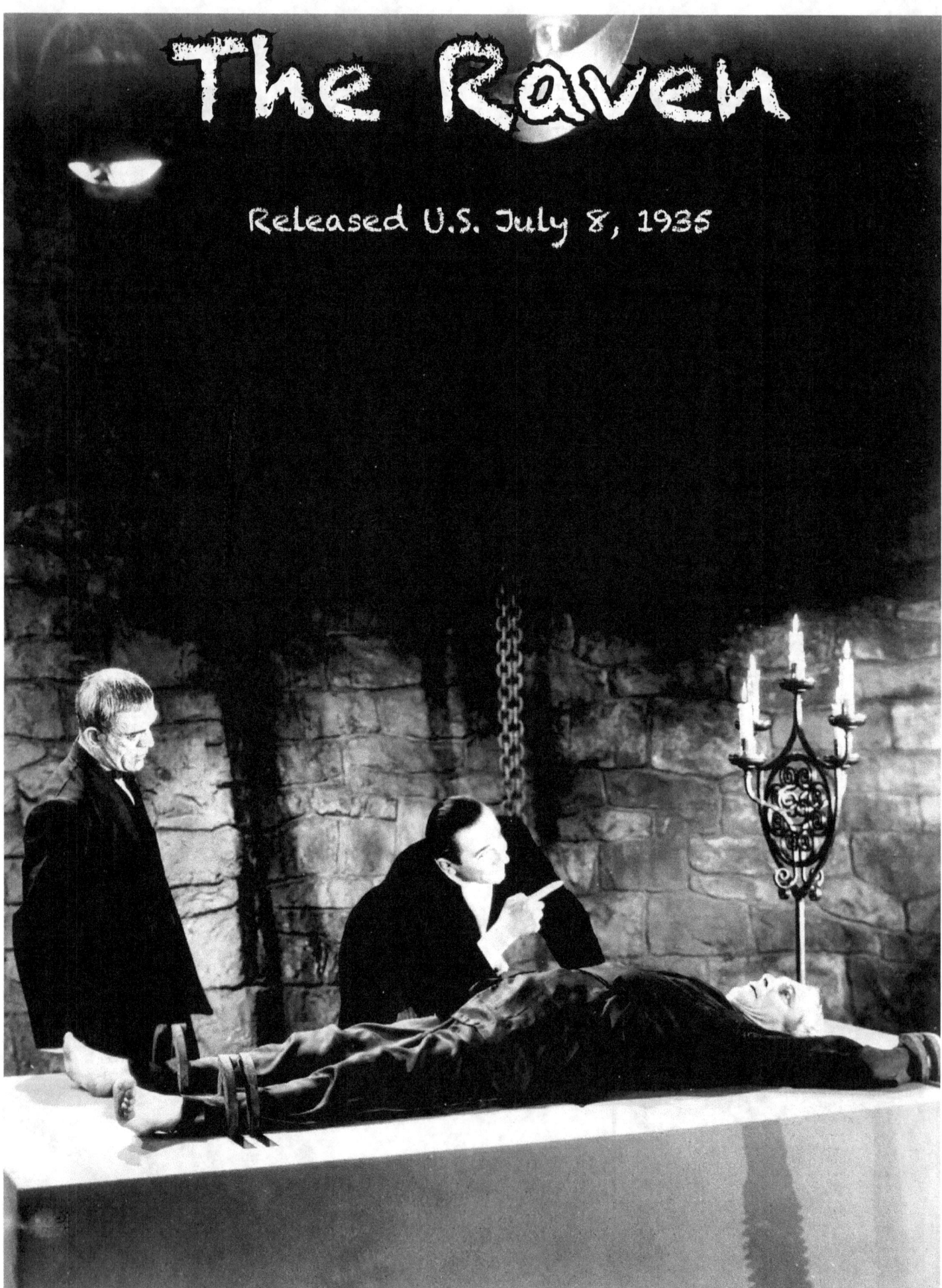

Everyone likes to be scared. All horror fans or friends will get their stomachs full of scary things if they attend a showing of "The Raven". Boris Karloff and Bela Lugosi are the film's leading characters.

Lugosi is a doctor (in "The Raven") who has a mania for Poe's stories. His mania controls his actions to such an extent that he carries the action of the tales over into his personal life. Karloff is the victim of the demented doctor. Lugosi carved Karloff's face into a horrible distorted leer and puts him at his mercy, an unwilling tool for his fiendishness.

Inez Courtney, Lester Mathews, Spencer Charters and Ian Wolf are other important actors in the show.

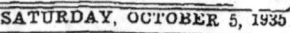

BEAUTY AND THE BEAST — Irene Ware, one of the screen's most charming screamers, and Bela Lugosi, that bad, bad man who is always going around frightening somebody. The scene is from 'The Raven' in which Lugosi's playmate is Boris Karloff.

New Horror Picture Heads Bill at Orpheum

If one can consider the monster of "Frankenstein" and the vampire of "Dracula" vieing with each other for horror honors, says advance notices, one then can anticipate the chills and thrills that are packed into Universal's "The Raven," which will be the chief picture attraction at the Orpheum Thursday.

Suggested by Edgar Allen Poe's immortal classic, this film boasts the combined master mystery talents of Boris Karloff and Bela Lugosi. These two chill chasers are co-starred in the picture, the cast of which includes Irene Ware, Lester Matthews, Samuel Hinds, Inez Courtney and many others.

The plot concerns the mental flights of a famous surgeon who is a Poe addict and who, like the great poet, is of a morbid, brooding turn of mind. "The Raven" always fascinated him, to the extent of his having a stuffed replica of this bird standing beside him on his desk. The shadow of this bird of ill omen predominates the theme of the story, which actually begins when its principal character, a notorious criminal hiding from the police, comes to the doctor to have his face changed. Promising to perform this difficult operation, the mad doctor betrays his patient and holds him in his grip until he does his bidding in a diabolic plan he has conceived. Into their lives comes a beautiful girl, over whom the raving doctor casts a spell, while her father and sweetheart attempt to save her. The story builds to heights of horror, culminating in a most amazing and thrilling climax.

A second feature on the Orpheum's new bill will be Alice Brady in "Lady Tubbs," a scintillating comedy drama with an all star supporting cast. The Orpheum's new program will be completed by a Mickey Mouse cartoon in technicolor and titled, "The Band Concert."

7th Ave. & 50th St.	KARLOFF & LUGOSI
ROXY	in "THE RAVEN"
25¢ to 2 35¢ to 7	BIG REVUE ON STAGE — HERMAN TIMBERG & Others

Universal's screen version of Edgar Allan Poe's "The Raven" will open at the Roxy on Independence Day. Boris Karloff and Bela Lugosi head the cast.

UNIVERSAL for the BIG MONEY MAKERS! Here are three!!

TRADE SHOWS
YOU MUST NOT MISS!!
EACH AT THE PRINCE EDWARD THEATRE, LONDON

TO-DAY MONDAY at 3 p.m.
CHINATOWN SQUAD

TO-NIGHT AT 8.45
ALIAS MARY DOW

TO-MORROW TUESDAY JULY 16
EVENING — AT 8.45
THE RAVEN

★★★★★ Personal appearance of **BELA LUGOSI!!**

UNIVERSAL Productions • Presented by Carl Laemmle

229

PICTURE TEAMS "HORROR" PAIR

"Don't Bet On Blondes," With Warren William, Also On Bill Which Opened Today

If you can picture the monster of "Frankenstein" and the vampire of "Dracula" vieing with each other for horror honors, you can anticipate the chills and thrills that are packed into "The Raven," which began a three-day engagement at the Iowa today.

Suggested by Edgar Allen Poe's immortal classic, this film boasts the combined master mystery talents of Boris Karloff and Bela Lugosi. These two chill chasers are co-starred. Irene Ware, Lester Matthews, Samuel Hinds and Inez Courtney are supporting players.

The plot concerns the mental flights of a famous surgeon who is a Poe addict and who, like the great poet is of a morbid, brooding turn of mind. "The Raven" always fascinated him, to the extent of having a stuffed replica of this bird standing beside him on his desk. The shadow of this bird of ill-omen predominates the theme of the story, which actually begins when its principal character, a notorious criminal hiding from the police, comes to the doctor to have his face changed.

1936

The Invisible Ray
The Walking Dead
Dracula's Daughter
Revolt of the Zombies
Devil-Doll (in Vol. 2)
The Man Who Changed His Mind (in Vol. 2)

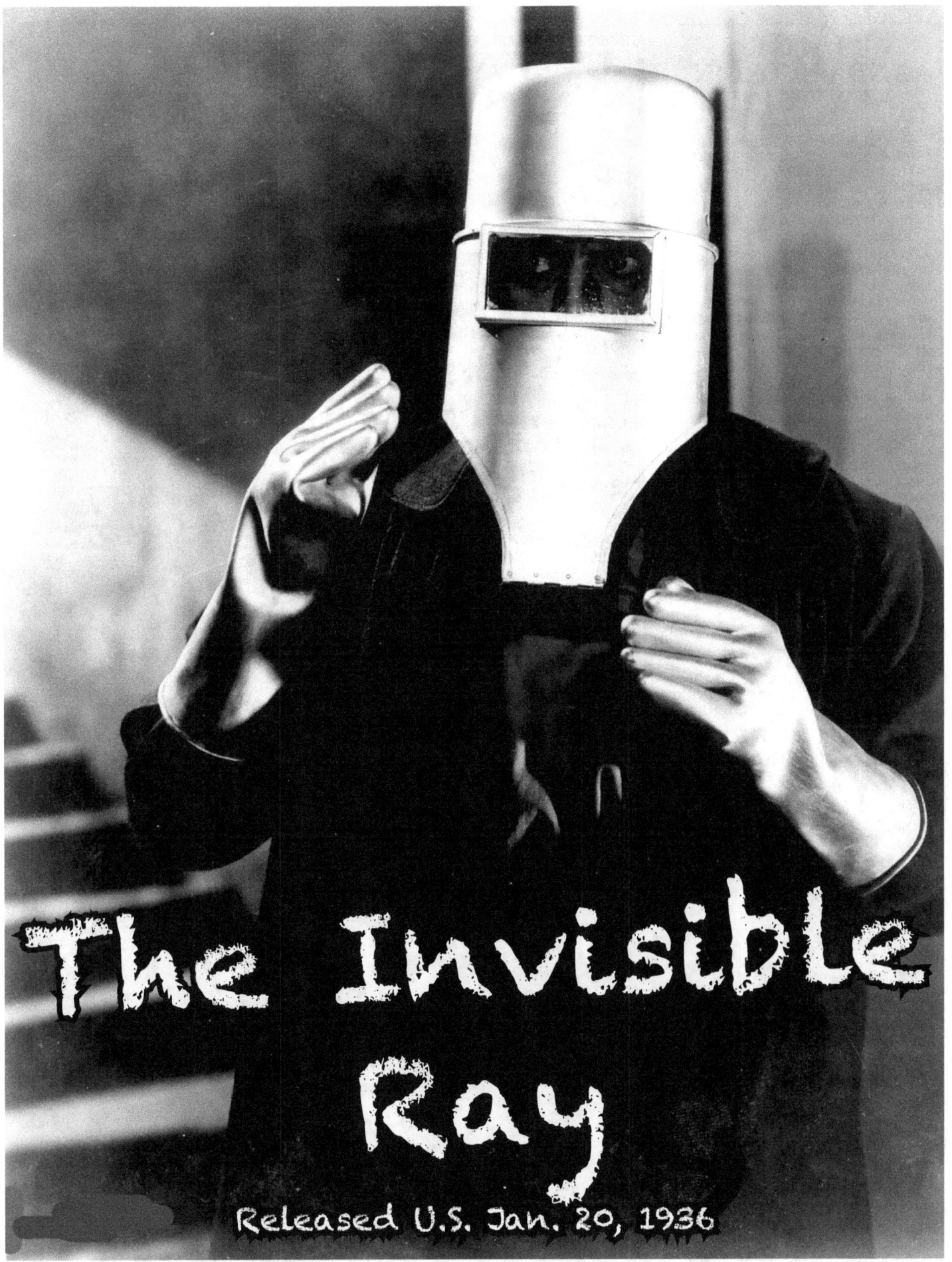

KARLOFF AND LUGOSI IN NEW THRILLER!

Never before have we shown such a spectacular and genuinely thrilling motion picture as "The Invisible Ray," the Universal drama which comes to the Orpheum theatre next Thursday, Friday and Saturday.

Karloff and Bela Lugosi, two of the screen's most sinister figures, are co-starred again in this remarkable picture, which combines mystery and startling adventure with a depiction of scientific marvels not yet actually accomplished by experimentors.

Karloff, as a "lone wolf" scientist working entirely by himself, brings down from the heavens an actual reproduction of the battle of suns and stars millions of years ago, and the great glass dome of his laboratory is filled with blinding light as prehistoric events in a starry nebula are relived. Later he discovers a substance a thousand times more powerful than radium, and looses it on his enemies before an accident finally makes him a victim of his own ruthlessness.

"The Invisible Ray" was directed by Lambert Hillyer, and the cast appearing in support of Karloff and Lugosi includes Frank Lawton, Frances Drake, Walter Kingsford, Beulah Bondi, and Violet Kemble Cooper.

Do not fail to see this gripping and remarkably colorful picture.

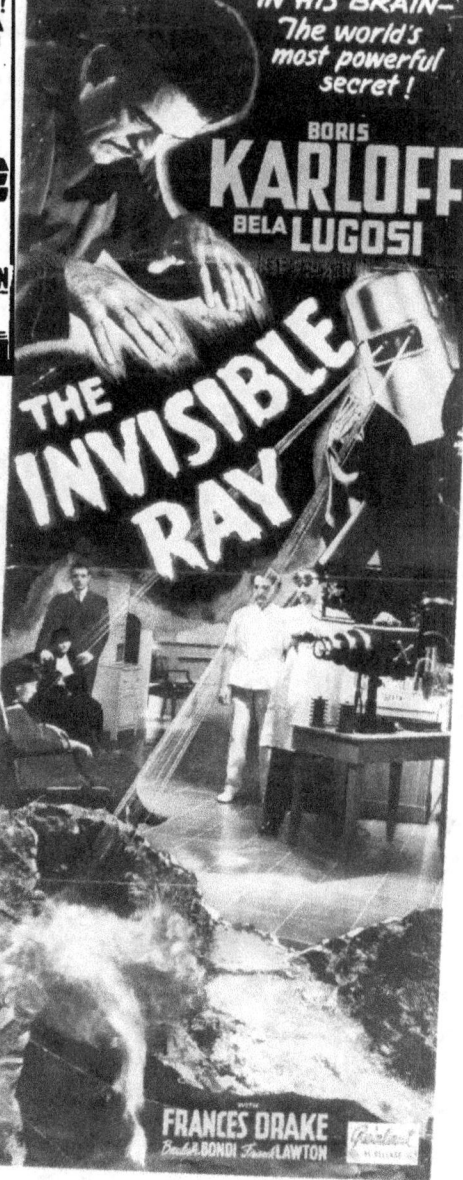

KARLOFF, LUGOSI IN DIXIE'S NEW SHOW

"THE INVISIBLE RAY" ONE OF OUTSTANDING OF YEAR'S PICTURES

Few motion pictures of the current season have proven so genuinely interesting as "The Invisible Ray," the Universal drama which opens an engagement of three days at the Dixie Theater beginning today.

Karloff and Bela Lugosi, two of the screen's most sinister individuals, are costarred in this unusual screen play, and are the focal points of a story in which they are bitter enemies. Both are scientists, but Karloff has struck out in to unexplored fields; and before the camera are seen a number of his advanced experiments which are literally awe-inspiring and startlingly picturesque. Never before has the screen shown such spectacular accomplishments in the scientific world, and all are filled with intense interest.

In the great glass dome of his laboratory Karloff produces an actual reproduction of the swirling suns and stars of the heavenly nebula Andromeda, exactly as they appeared millions of years ago. Later in the story he discovers the new element which he names Radium X, a thousand times more powerful than radium, and which he uses with deadly effect against his enemies. The climax of the story is literally hair-raising.

Others in the cast of this strange story are Frances Drake, Frank Lawton, Beulah Bondi, Walter Kingsford and Violet Kemble Cooper, while a large share of the credit for a most unusual picture must be given to Director Lambert Hillyer. From a production standpoint the film is unusual, and impressive backgrounds are shown successively in the Carpathian Mountains, in Africa and in Paris. The screen play was produced by Edmund Grainger after an original story by Howard Higgin and Douglas Hodges, with screen play by John Colton.

"The Invisible Ray" will interest you and thrill you mightily. We unhesitatingly recommend it as a picture which you will enjoy.

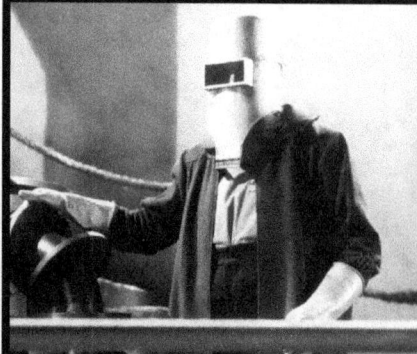

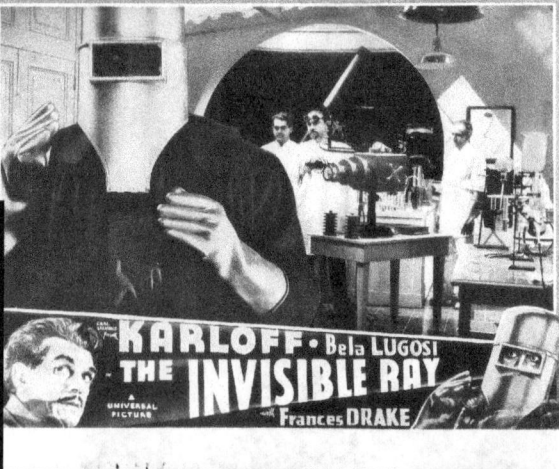

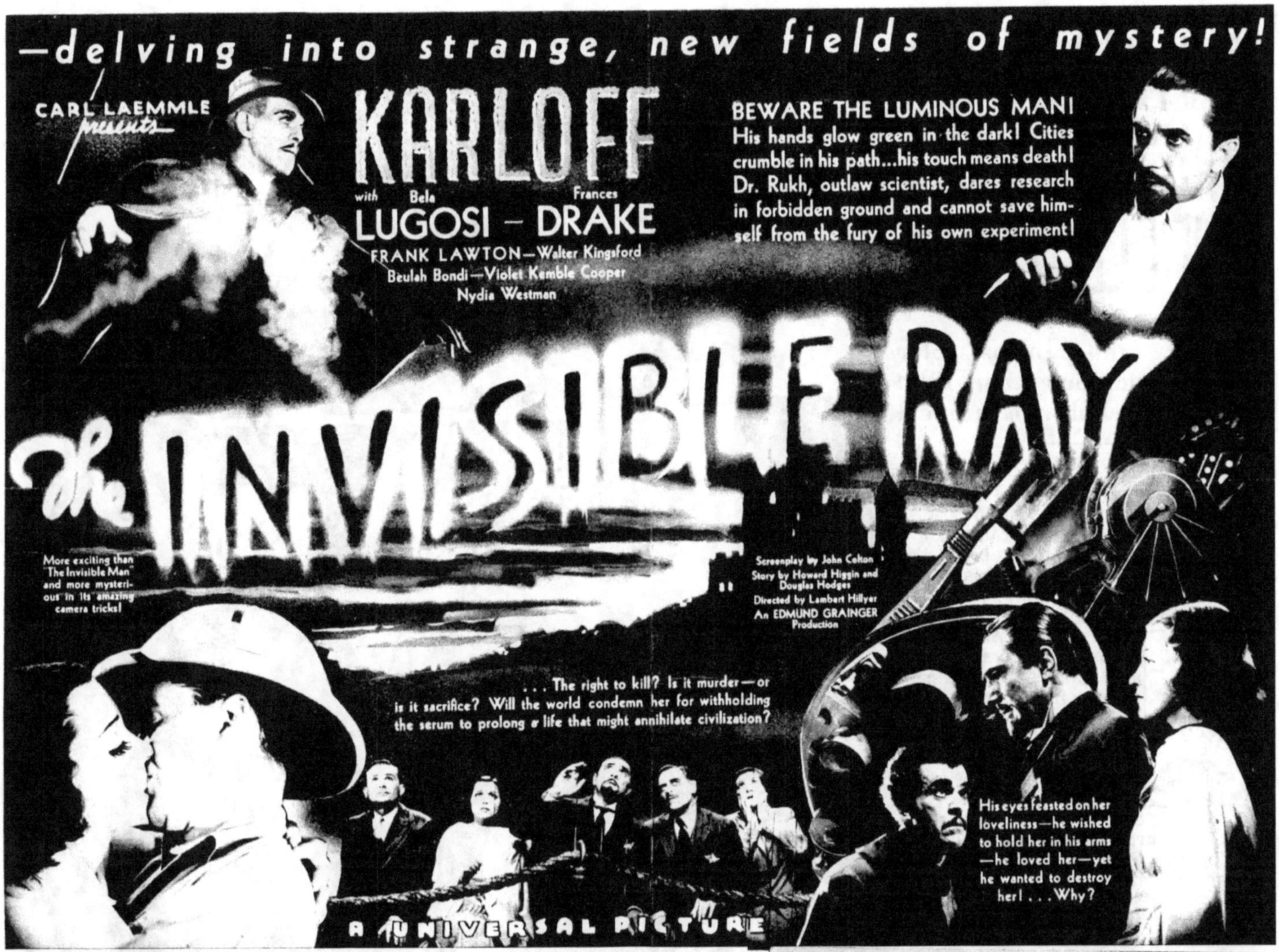
—delving into strange, new fields of mystery!
CARL LAEMMLE presents
KARLOFF
with Bela LUGOSI – Frances DRAKE
FRANK LAWTON—Walter Kingsford
Beulah Bondi—Violet Kemble Cooper
Nydia Westman
BEWARE THE LUMINOUS MAN! His hands glow green in the dark! Cities crumble in his path...his touch means death! Dr. Rukh, outlaw scientist, dares research in forbidden ground and cannot save himself from the fury of his own experiment!
The INVISIBLE RAY
More exciting than "The Invisible Man" and more mysterious in its amazing camera tricks!
Screenplay by John Colton
Story by Howard Higgin and Douglas Hodges
Directed by Lambert Hillyer
An EDMUND GRAINGER Production
. . . The right to kill? Is it murder—or is it sacrifice? Will the world condemn her for withholding the serum to prolong a life that might annihilate civilization?
His eyes feasted on her loveliness—he wished to hold her in his arms—he loved her—yet he wanted to destroy her! . . . Why?
A UNIVERSAL PICTURE

HISPANO AMERICAN FILMS S.A. presenta a
BORIS KARLOFF EN
EL PODER INVISIBLE
BELA LUGOSI
FRANCES DRAKE
FRANK LAWTON

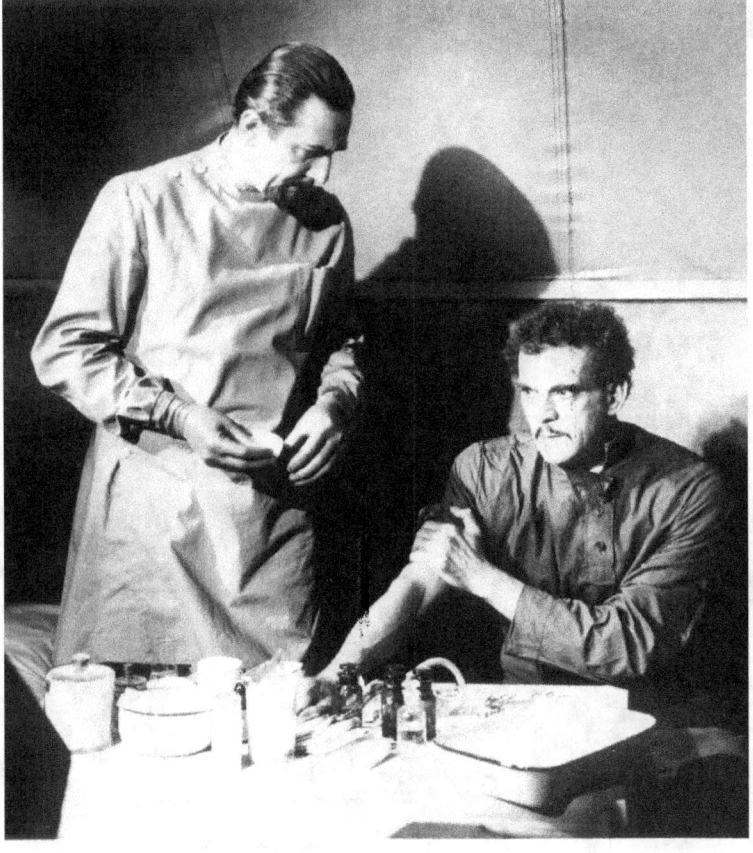

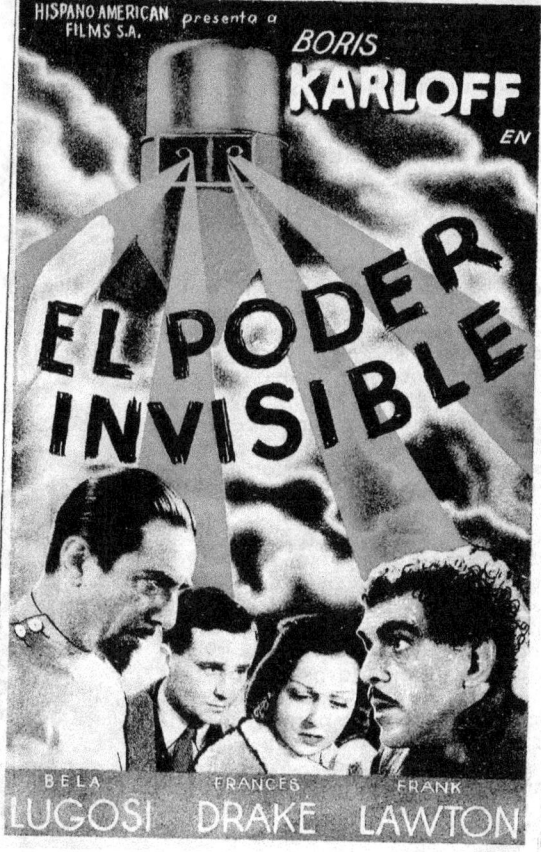

INVISIBLE RAY SHOCKING BUT NOT ELECTRICAL

Karloff and Lugosi Star In Pseudo-Scientific Film With Melodrama Appeal

By WOOD SOANES

HOLLYWOOD'S two most learned men of science, Boris Karloff and Bela Lugosi, are at each other's throats again on the screen of the Franklin this week in a little fantasy from Universal called "The Invisible Ray."

On this momentous occasion Messrs. Karloff and Lugosi find themselves in possession of some very interesting facts on the subject of astro-chemistry, whatever that may be, and being Messrs. Karloff and Lugosi they have no mind to share the honor or the loot.

"The Invisible Ray," nevertheless, is one of Universal's better films in this pseudo-scientific series and has less of the formal horror elements that served to elevate the two protagonists to cinema fame. There are shocks of course for those who shock readily, but nothing electrical.

An original story built around the two actors there is little in the film for the other players. Frank Lawton and Frances Drake amble leisurely through the romantic roles, Violet Kemble-Cooper finds time for a bizarre study of Karloff's mother, and Beulah Bondi is an amusing English lady explorer.

✩ ✩ ✩

Although it attains no melodramatic heights, "The Invisible Ray" contains some interesting photography and should have a certain amount of juvenile appeal as well as holding the attention of older melodramatic fans. Its companion picture also goes into the thrill market for a polite excusion.

"Guard That Girl" has to do with a late millionaire's will and the efforts of his relatives to chisel in on the swag. In order to circumvent such evil shenanigans, her lawyer hires not only guards but a girl to impersonate the heiress, at which time the fun, so to speak, begins.

Frances Drake turns in the best performance, in a small role, with Elizabeth Risdon displaying dramatic competence as the aunt. Robert Allen, Florence Rice, Ward Bond, Nana Bryant and several others have commonplace roles and play them that way.

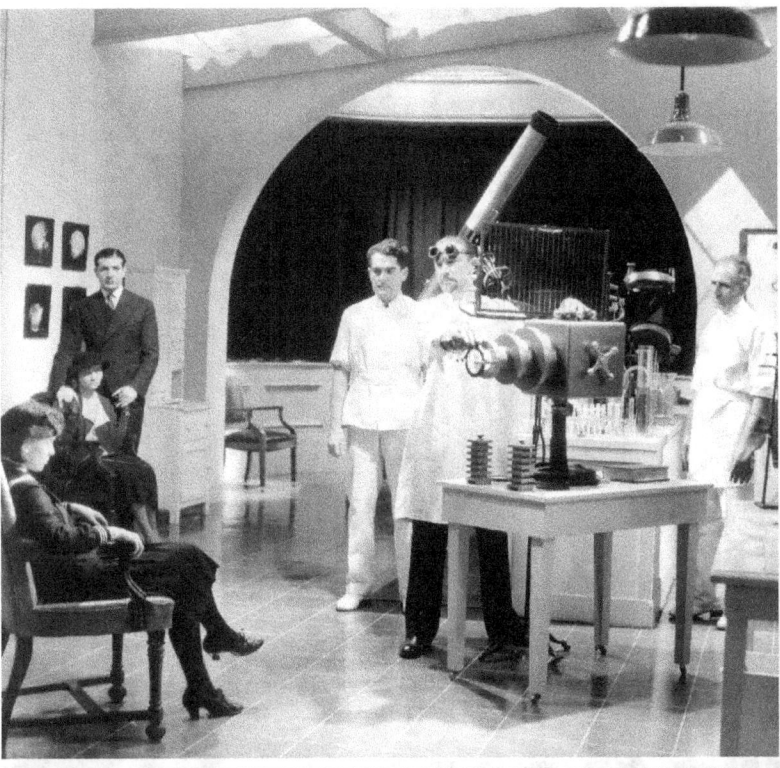

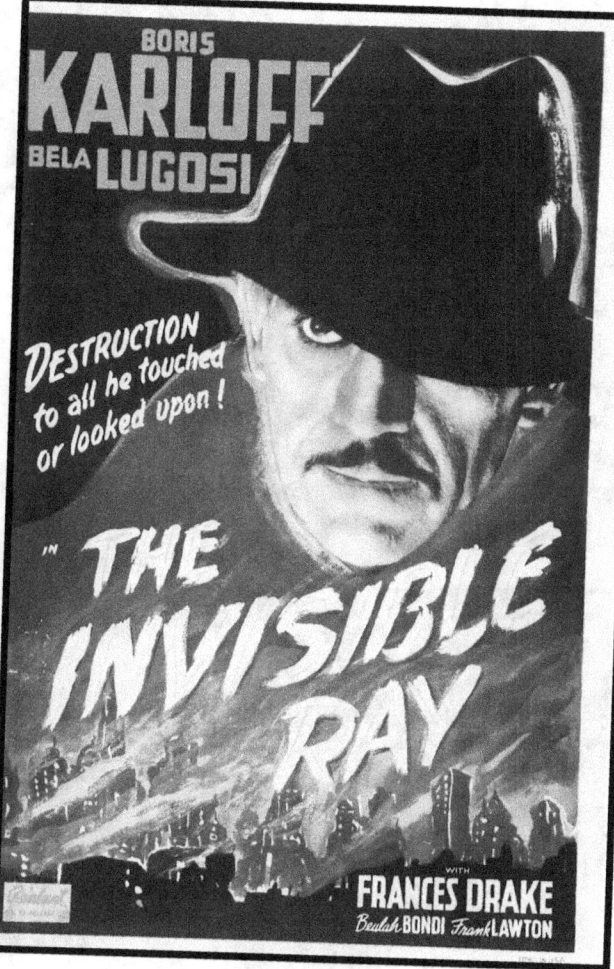

"INVISIBLE RAY" IS OAKS FEATURE FILM

Photographic effects never before attempted were accomplished successfully during the filming of "The Invisible Ray," the tense drama of science now playing at the Oaks Theater along with "Guard That Girl," with Florence Rice and Robert Allan.

Boris Karloff and Bela Lugosi are starred in "The Invisible Ray," and in the story Karloff is poisoned by Radium X, a newly discovered substance a thousand times more powerful than radium, causing his face and hands to become luminous in the dark. After weeks of experimenting studio camera men headed by John Foulton, evolved a method of transferring this effect to the screen; and in the picture the hands and face of the unfortunate man are seen to glow with a surging, unearthly brilliance.

In "Guard That Girl," Robert Allan has the unpleasant task of trying to figure out from where the next death-dealing arrow will fly. It is a baffling mystery which moves at a fast pace and until the last scene in the climax leaves one in doubt as to the guilty party, it is declared.

An added color cartoon and the news events complete the bill which will run through tomorrow night.

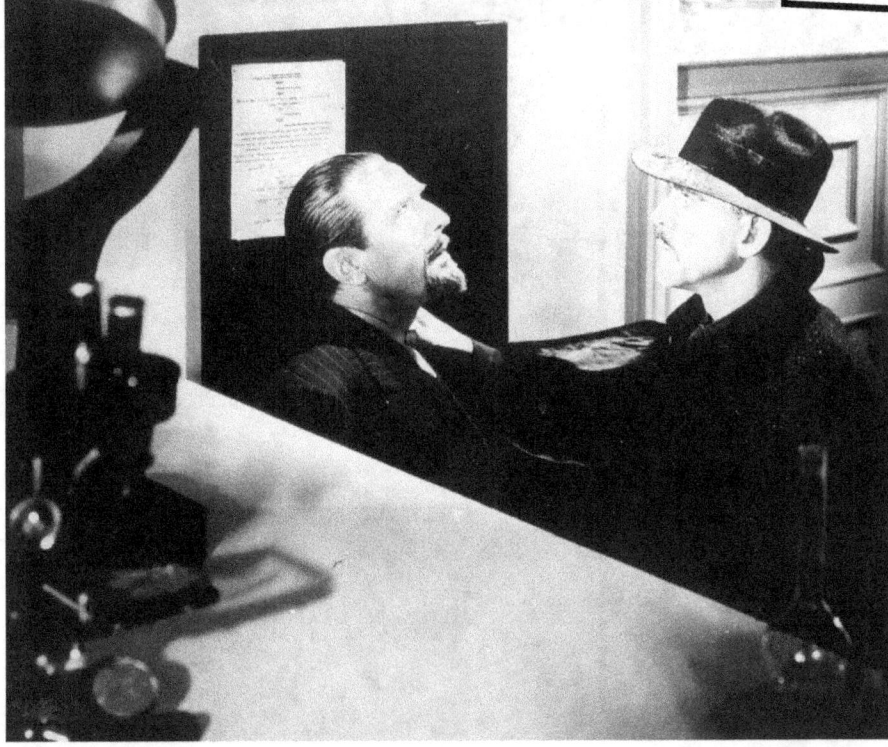

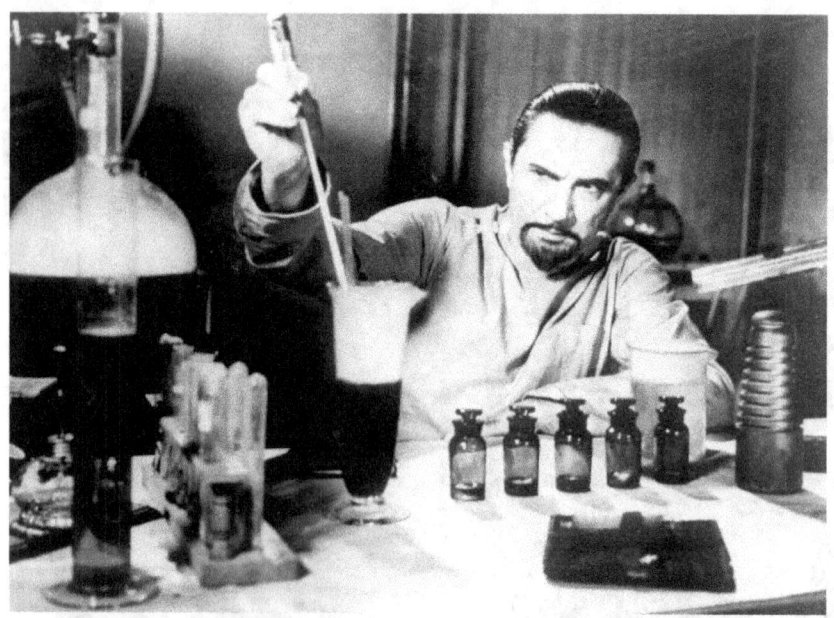

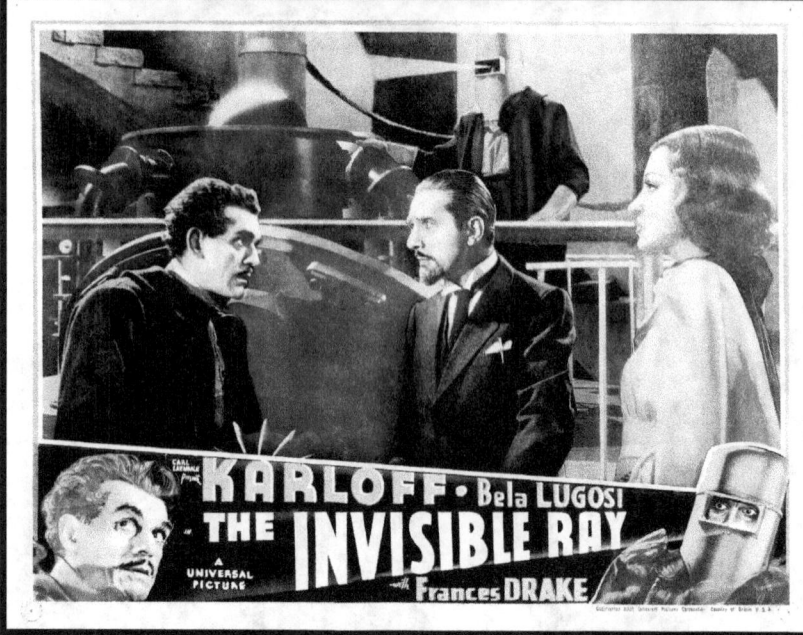

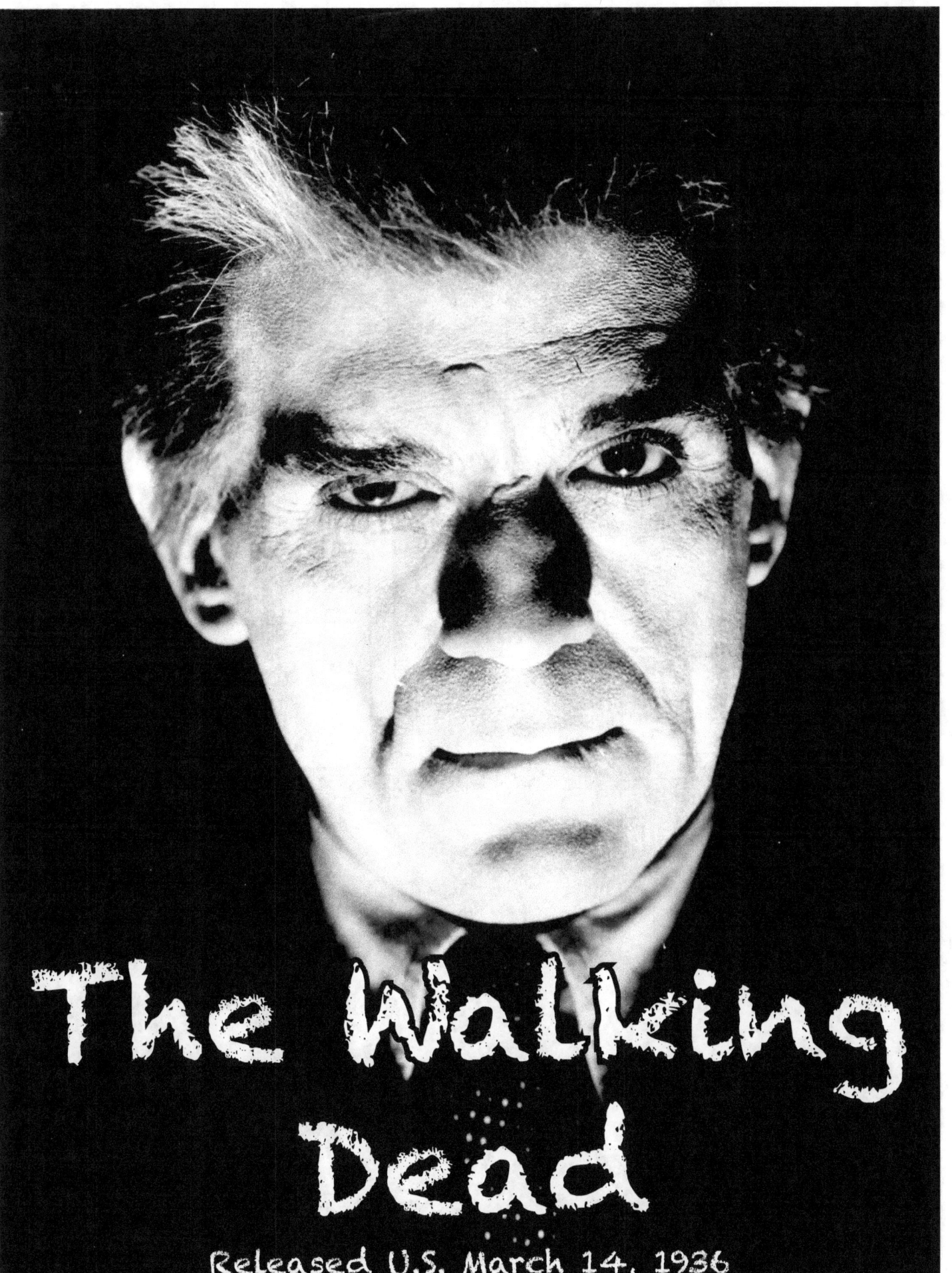

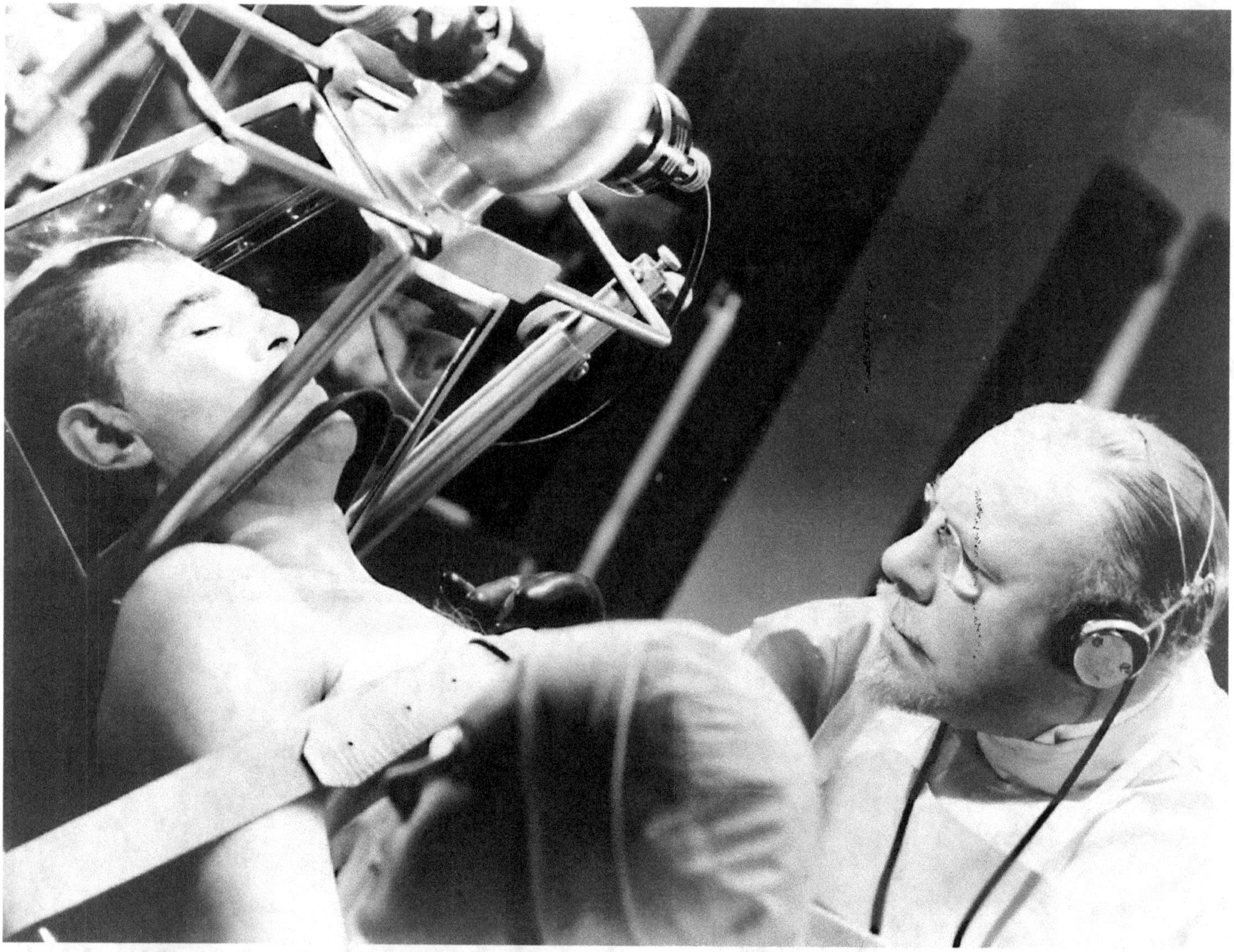

STRAND B'WAY & 47TH

Pop. Prices—Midnight Shows

BORIS KARLOFF

in "The WALKING DEAD"

Mat-inee **10c** | Eve 7-9 **20c**

NEW TUES. & WED.

COMING THURS & FRI.

BORIS KARLOFF

—in—

"The Walking Dead"

WARNING! If you have a weak heart **DO NOT** attempt to see this picture.

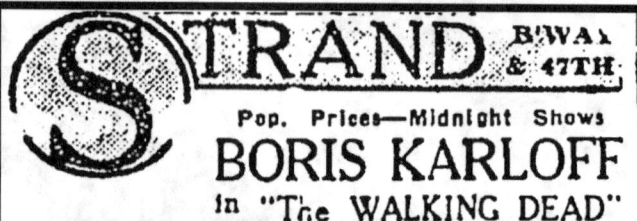

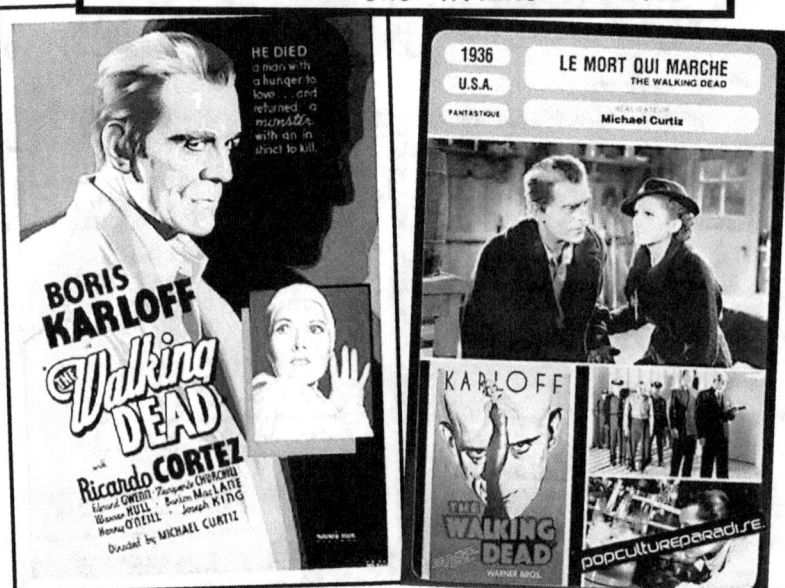

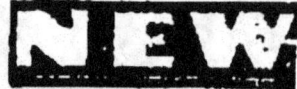

THE SCREEN CALENDAR

ASTOR—Don't Gamble With Love: Ann Sothern.
CAMEO—Three Women, a Russian film.*
CAPITOL—Wife vs. Secretary: Jean Harlow, Clark Gable, Myrna Loy.
CENTER—Voice of Bugle Ann; Love on a Bet, opens Wednesday.
CINEMA DE PARIS—Le Bonheur: Charles Boyer.
55TH ST. PLAYHOUSE—Liebelei: Magda Schneider, Paul Hoerbiger.
LOEW'S STATE—Rose Marie: Jeanette MacDonald, Nelson Eddy.†
MUSIC HALL—Follow the Fleet: Fred Astaire, Ginger Rogers.*
PALACE—The Story of Louis Pasteur and It Had to Happen.†
PARAMOUNT—Trail of the Lonesome Pine: Sylvia Sidney.*
RIALTO—Garden Murder Case: Edmund Lowe, Virginia Bruce.
RIVOLI—Modern Times: Charlie Chaplin, Paulette Goddard.*
ROXY—Rhodes: Walter Huston, Oscar Homolka.
STRAND—The Walking Dead: Boris Karloff, Marguerite Churchill.
WORLD THEATRE—The Wedding March, an Italian film.

REVIVALS.

ACME—Builders of Socialism, a Russian film.
8TH ST. PLAYHOUSE—Next Time We Love, today and tomorrow; Strike Me Pink, Tuesday and Wednesday; The Thin Man, Thursday and Friday; Ceiling Zero, starts Saturday.
LENOX PICTURE HOUSE—Stormy: Noah Beery Jr., today only.
LITTLE CARNEGIE—The Guardsman: Lynn Fontanne, Alfred Lunt.
PLAZA—Professional Soldier, today and tomorrow; Next Time We Love, Tuesday and Wednesday; Strike Me Pink, Thursday and Friday.

*Holdover. †Second run.

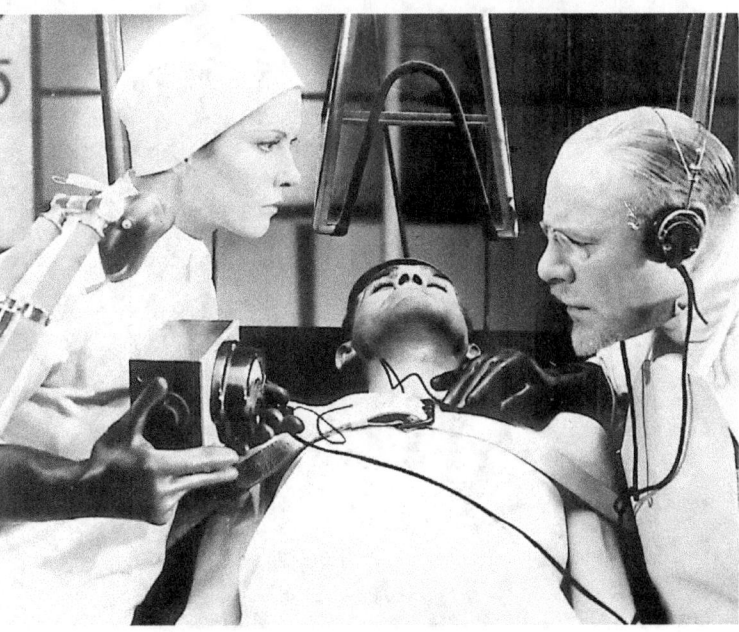

AMERICAN
CORNING, IOWA
Friday
BARGAIN SHOW
Adults 16c - Students 11c
Children 10c
BORIS KARLOFF
—in—
"THE WALKING DEAD"
NOTE—On this bill we will also run the 1st Chapter of "FLASH GORDON"
Saturday
GENE AUTRY
"SAGEBRUSH TROUBADOR"
Plus 1st Chapter
'FLASH GORDON'
Comedy—
"Slide, Nellie, Slide"
— Cartoon —

HE DIED A MAN
with a hunger to love
AND RETURNED A MONSTER
with an instinct to kill!
See a famous scientist bring back an electrocuted convict from beyond the grave... to wipe out the killers who had railroaded him to the 'Chair'!
SEE BORIS
KARLOFF
THE WALKING DEAD
A WARNER BROS. PICTURE WITH RICARDO CORTEZ
EDMUND GWENN • MARGUERITE CHURCHILL • WARREN HULL • BARTON MacLANE
Directed by MICHAEL CURTIZ

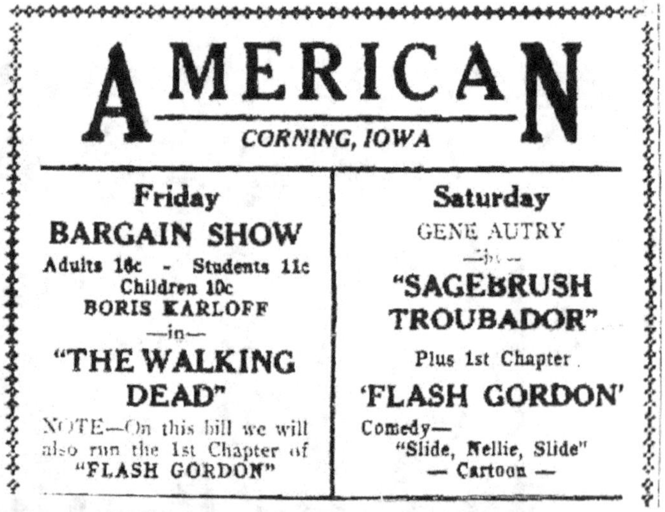

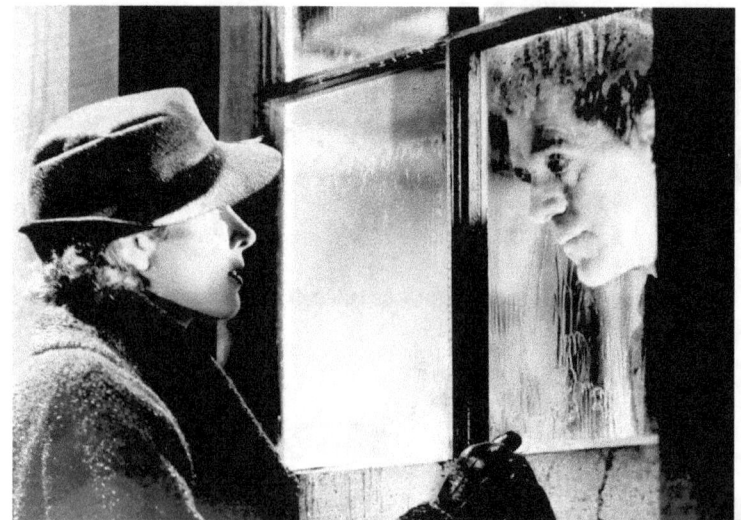

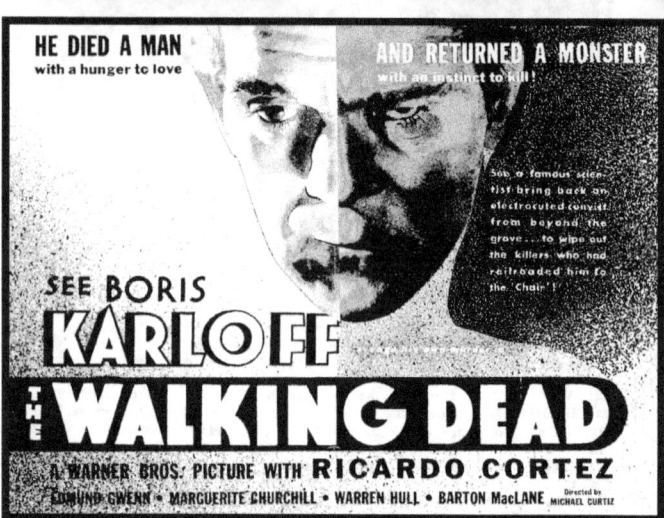

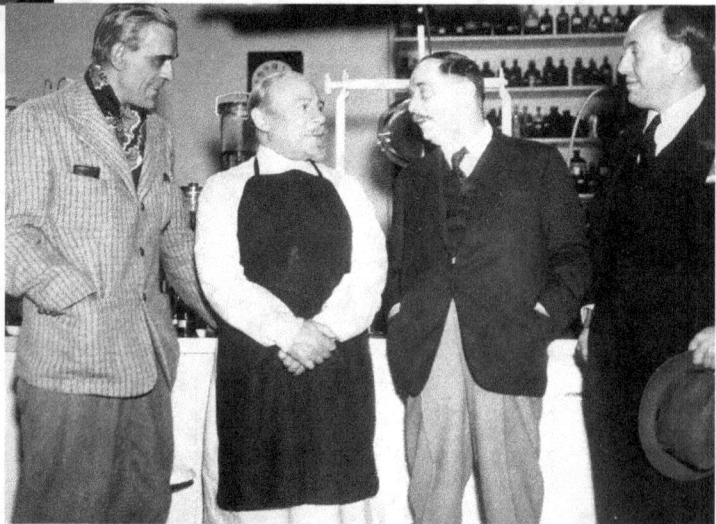

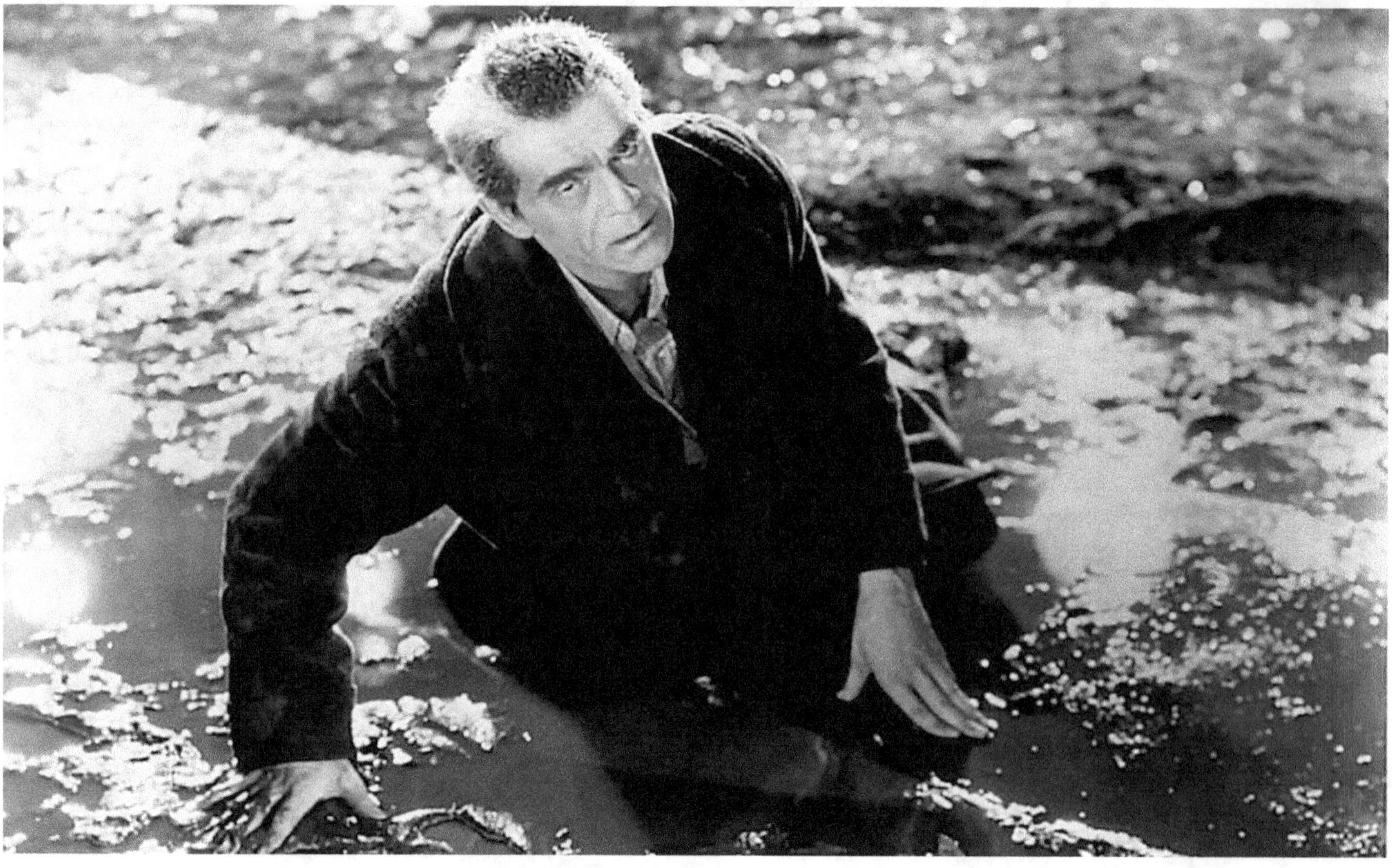

Dracula's Daughter

Released U.S. May 11, 1936

Thrills And Chills In Sigma's Feature Film

Dracula is dead but "Dracula's Daughter" is roaming across the screen at the Sigma theatre in search for human blood. Gloria Holden plays the role of the red lipped, white faced, tall and beautiful daughter of the gentleman known as Dracula. A cast of well known chillers including Otto Kruger, Irving Pichel, Edward Van Sloan and Lily Malyon support the lovely lady with a lust for human blood. Others in the cast are Marguerite Churchill, Claude Allister, Nan Gray, Halliwell Hobbes, E. E. Clive, Billy Bevan and Christian Rub.

The picture opens with the scene showing the cremation of the dead Dracula. The vampire has had a stake driven thru his heart. This supposedly ends all of his vampirish activities. His daughter stands silently by watching the activities. She hopes that the cremation of the vampire will release her in all ways that she may be connected with that cold blooded legion.

To escape of sights that would remind her of her father the daughter goes to London. There the curse of her heritage tells and the lust for blood becomes strong within her. Then one night when the streets of London are soupy with fog the vampire walks. Dracula's daughter seeks human prey on the streets of London. Her servant, another one of the vampires, brings a beautiful girl to the home. Dracula's daughter tells the girl that she merely wants to paint a portrait of her. The next day they find the girl unconscious in the street. On her neck are two tiny marks—the mark of the vampires. In the meantime the man who killed Dracula has been arrested for homicide, or rather vampiricide.

Once a person has been attacked by a vampire they are more susceptible to the attacks at other times. The friends of the girl try to protect her from the vampires. Then comes another dark and foggy night and once again the vampires walk. A thrilling climax brings an unusual ending to this chiller.

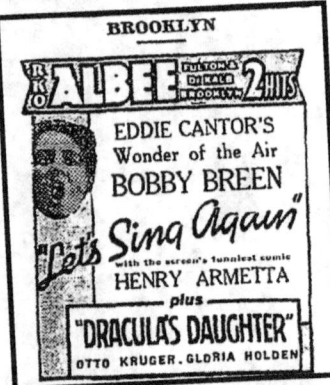

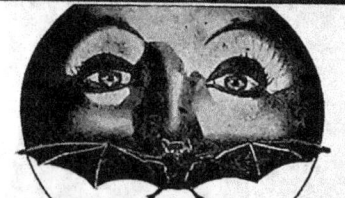

Her Eyes Spelled Doom!

Her Kiss Spelled Death!

HER HEART ACHED FOR LOVE... WHILE HER BRAIN SEETHED WITH THE DREAD URGE OF THE VAMPIRE TO—

KILL! KILL! KILL!

DRACULA'S DAUGHTER

With
**OTTO KRUGER
GLORIA HOLDEN
IRVING PICHEL**
Marg. Churchill

MORE WEIRD THAN "FRANKENSTEIN"
MORE THRILLING THAN "DRACULA"

WE DARE YOU
TO WALK ALONE AGAIN THROUGH THE BLACKNESS OF NIGHT AFTER YOU HAVE SEEN THIS PICTURE!

VAMPIRES & VOODOO!
Werewolves & Witchcraft!
MURDER & MADNESS!
SHE'S WEIRD!!

"Dracula's Daughter," the Universal film at the Star Theatre Sunday, is a case of romance versus necromancy, with the accent on the neck, as far as the vampire's appetites are concerned.

Every adult knows what romance is. For the benefit of the uninitiated, it is a growing attachment between a girl and a man under the influence of moonlight, roses and music. An excellent example is the romance between the two characters portrayed by Otto Kruger and Marguerite Churchill in "Dracula's Daughter" on the screen.

Kruger has the role of a scientist who tries to cure the vampire of her playful little tricks. Miss Churchill is seen as the sweetheart whose romantic ideas lead her into jealousy and into the vampire lady's mysterious parlor. Which is much more ominous a chamber than the spider's best room of classic fame.

Necromancy is the black art practiced by Dracula's Daughter. It is her magic of invoking evil through the hold she has on human beings because of her hypnotic influence. She has inherited her vampire's desire from Dracula, who craved human blood. This sorceress asks the scientist to help her escape from the curse of heritage. Gloria Holden interprets the compellingly fascinating personality.

When she gets some romantic ideas herself and tries to win him away from his sweetheart, then comes the tug of war. It becomes a battle between a girl and a superwoman over the possession of a man.

The situation is solved only when the climax of the photoplay has been reached. Lambert Hillyer directed the tensely dramatic narrative. Other players prominent in the cast include Edward Van Sloan, Irving Pichel and Hedda Hopper.

She gives you that
WEIRD FEELING
DRACULA'S
DAUGHTER
WITH
OTTO
KRUGER · GLORIA
HOLDEN
MARGUERITE CHURCHILL
EDWARD VAN SLOAN · IRVING PICHEL
NAN GRAY · Story suggested by OLIVER JEFFRIES
A Realart RE-RELEASE

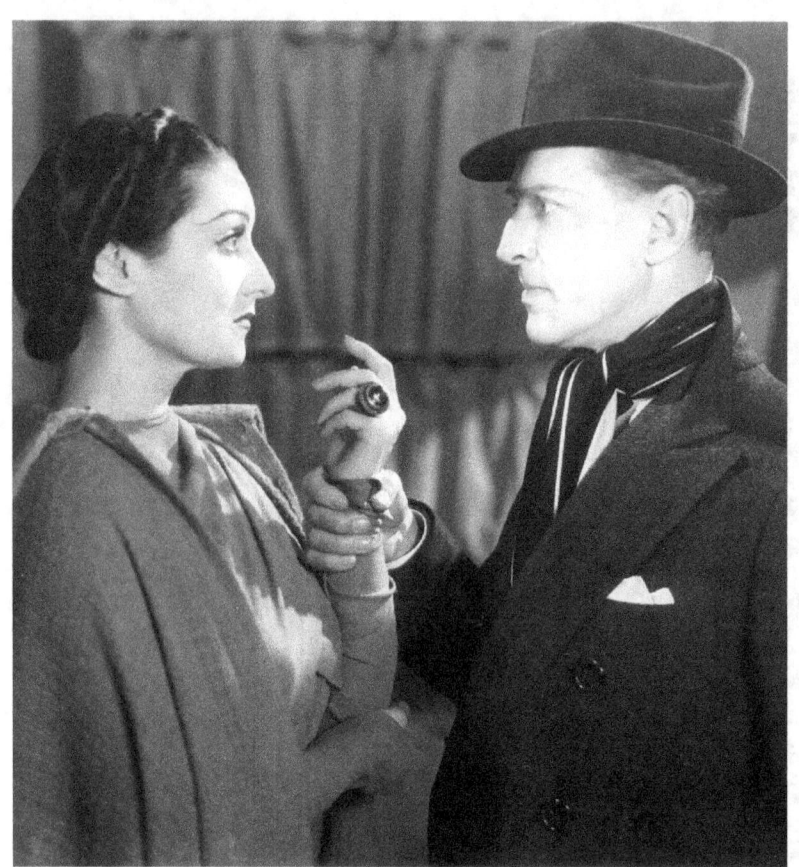

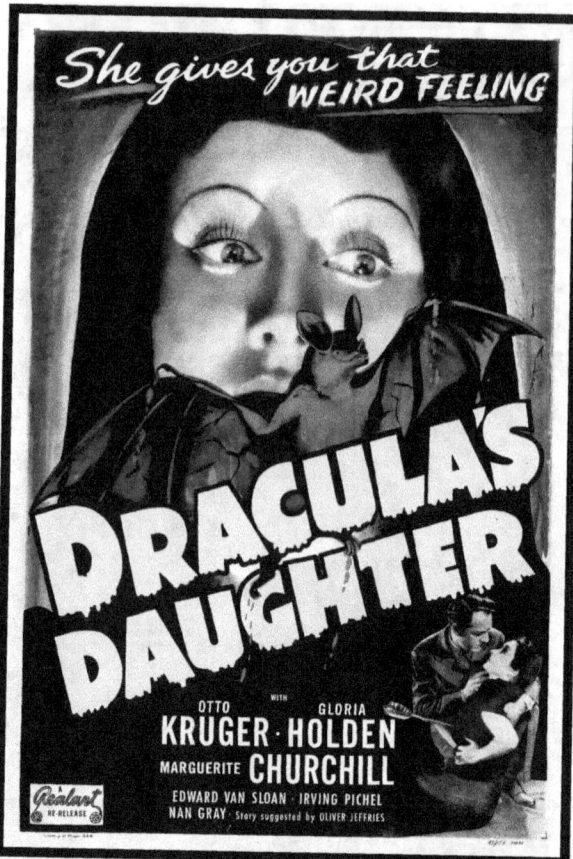

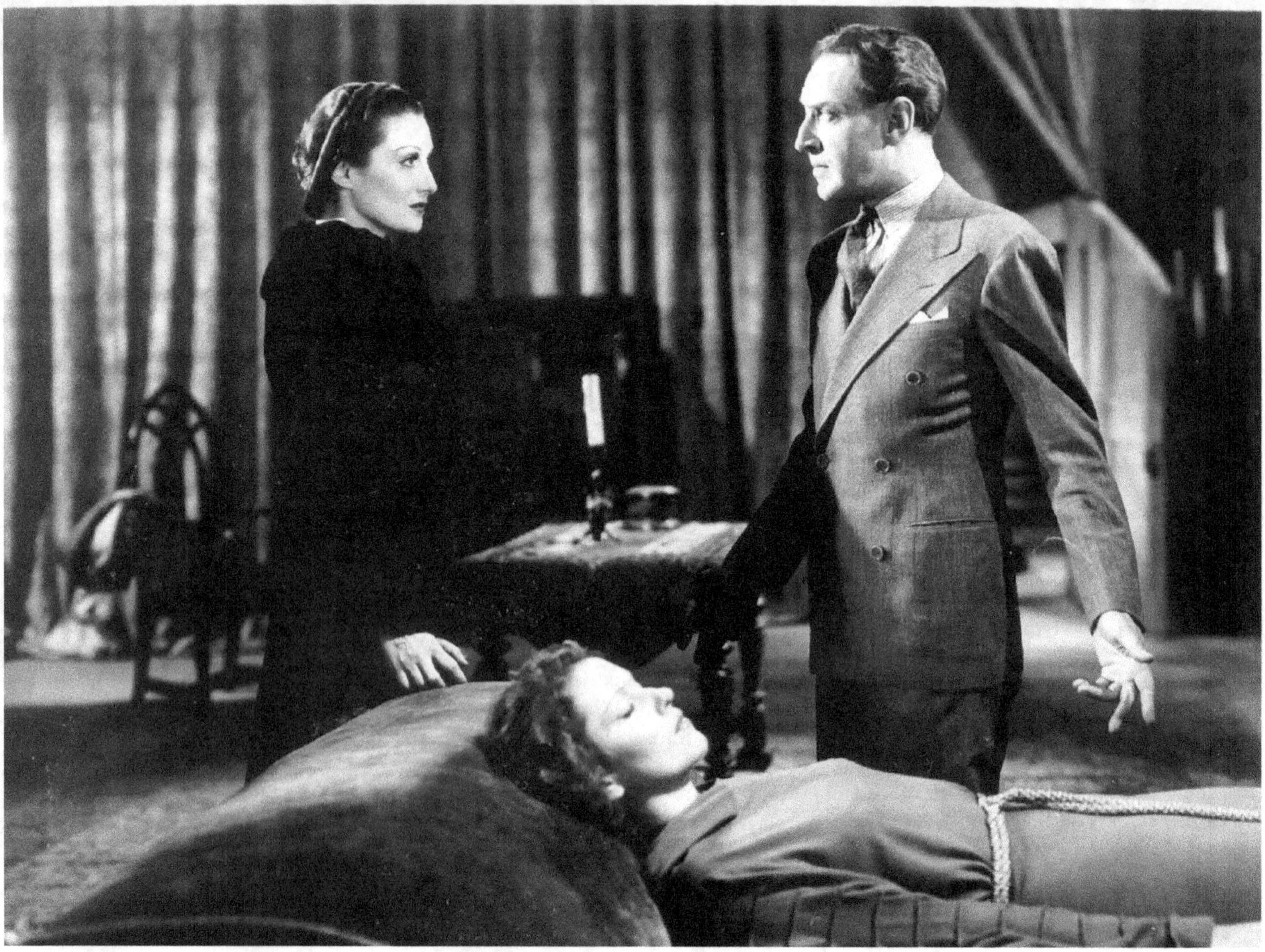

Friday, October 1, 1937

Holden's Work In 'Zola' May End 'Horror Cycle'

By ROBBIN COONS

HOLLYWOOD—One of the best performances in that performance-studded film, "The Life of Emile Zola" is that of Gloria Holden. I didn't realize this until I met Gloria Holden in person. Now I know she's an actress, and one of the most interesting in these parts.

Miss Holden played the role of Madame Zola, necessarily a shadowy character since Paul Muni is starred alone and the picture is Zola's story, not his wife's. In the film Madame Zola is little more than a background figure of sympathy and quiet understanding.

In life Gloria Holden is a vivid young person of unusual beauty, humor and intelligence. She has the blackest hair in town, and a bright smile that lights up interesting tawny eyes.

Went Into Debt

It may have been the eyes that made somebody think she would be the perfect "Dracula's Daughter." She played that one and well, but it is what is behind the eyes that is directing her present course in pictures.

You hear about actors "starving for their art." Gloria Holden didn't exactly starve, but she took a financial beating and is ready to take another, if need be, to do only what she wants to do in pictures.

She's an English girl, came to this country as a child, gravitated to the theater naturally. She had been in hit plays on Broadway before she came to Hollywood, was tested, and found herself happily with a "seven-year contract."

"I took it seriously," she smiles, "that seven-year contract. I also took an apartment, sent for my furniture, and went into debt. Then they wanted me to do another 'Dracula's Daughter' — this time something about a leopard woman."

So Gloria found herself, not wishing to devote her life to horror movies, jobless in Hollywood. She had plenty of offers, but not of parts she cared to play. She held on, by renting her apartment and taking a hotel room, for nearly six months.

"I could always sell my furniture, some jewelry I had, some fine orientals, and get back to New York," she says, "but I wanted to wait as long as possible. I was ready to go when 'Zola' came. They told me it wouldn't be much of a part, but I said I'd be happy to do it even if only the back of my head showed. For the chance to play in scenes with Paul Muni—you see, I want to be as superb a character actress as he is an actor—I'd have taken the part if they warned me all my scenes would be cut!"

As it happens, enough of her work remains to make a distinct impression—and Muni himself told her she deserved better roles. Whether the plaudits will bring immediate assignments of the kind she wants she still doesn't know. But on her earnings from "Zola" she is prepared to wait and see.

For her spirit, I hope she wins.

GLORIA HOLDEN
Tires of "Dracula" Roles

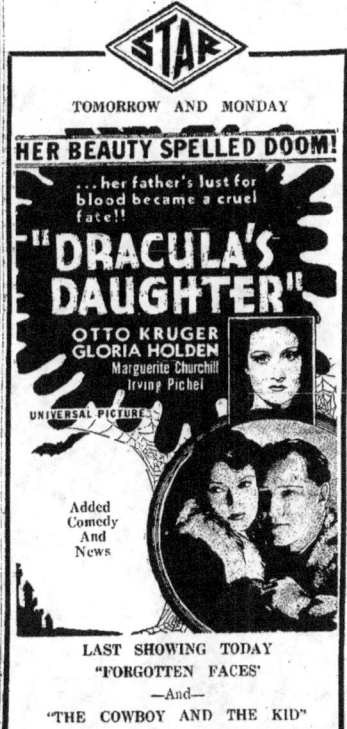

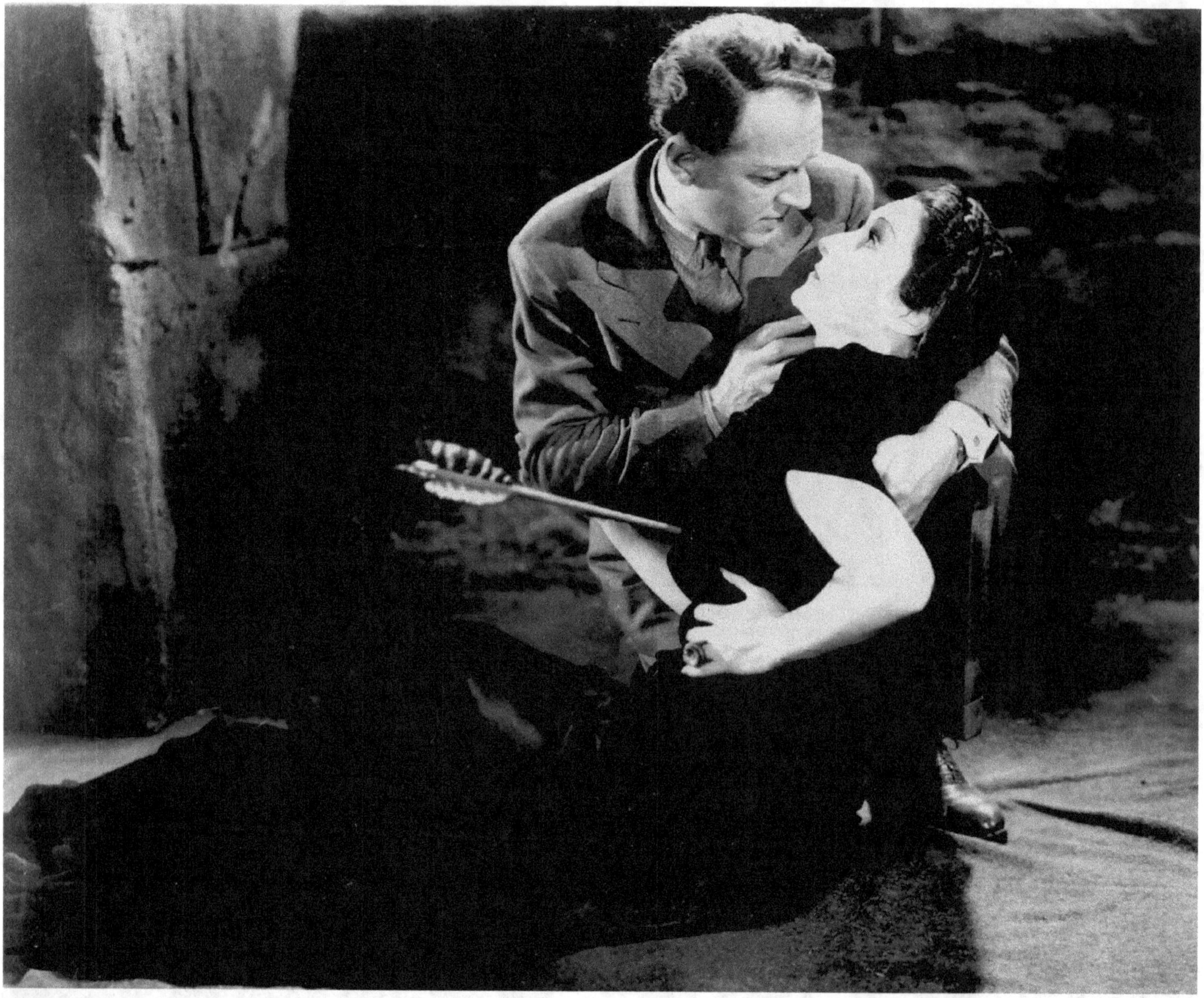

SHIVER SENSATION OF THE SEASON
DRACULA'S DAUGHTER
WITH
OTTO KRUGER · GLORIA HOLDEN · MARGUERITE CHURCHILL
IRVING PICHEL · HEDDA HOPPER
EDWARD VAN SLOAN · NAN GRAY
DISTRIBUTED BY

TEXAS
NOW
ACTION!
THRILLS!
ROMANCE!
Women obeyed her commands . . . Men feared her strange power . . . More sensational than her unforgettable father!
"DRACULA'S DAUGHTER"
with
OTTO KRUGER
GLORIA HOLDEN
Marguerite Churchill
SILLY SYMPHONY
Color Cartoon
COMEDY
PARAMOUNT NEWS
TUESDAY—ONE DAY ONLY!
TOM BROWN · MARION NIXON
"SWEEPSTAKE ANNIE"
WERA ENGELS
INEZ COURTNEY

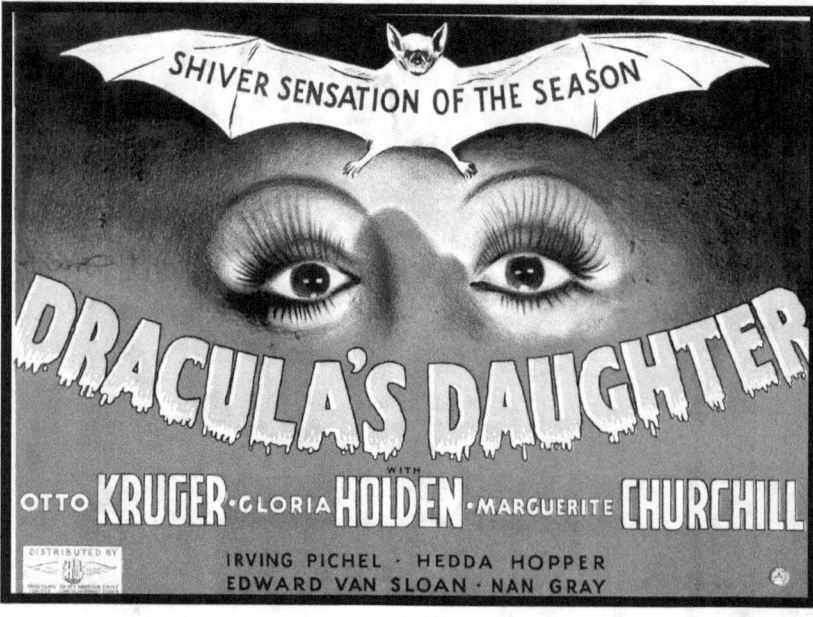

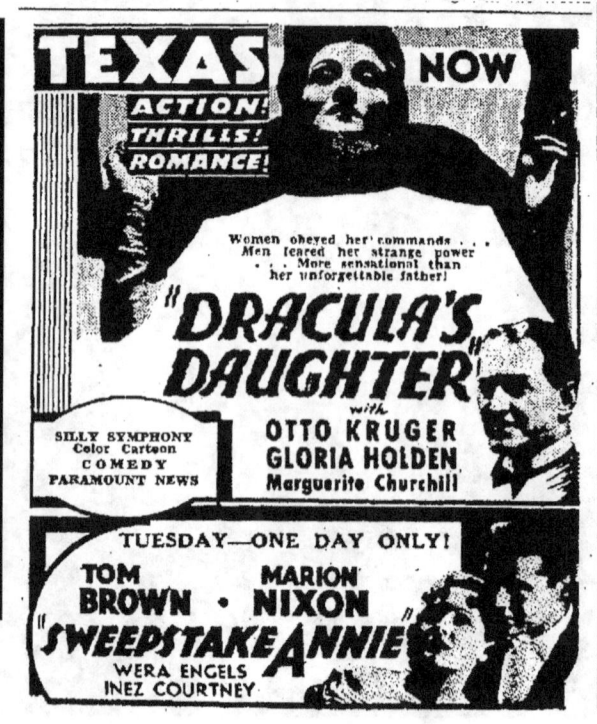

Revolt of the Zombies

Released U.S. June 4, 1936

Revolt of the Zombies—Singularly unexciting melodrama which confuses hypnotics with zombies and otherwise fails to justify its title's promise. With Dorothy Stone, Dean Jagger and Robert Noland. At the Rialto.

CATCHLINES

Weirdest love story in two thousand years.
Zombies! Not dead! Not Alive!

He took the power of an ancient mystic race and used it to create an army of robots.

Passionate romance in a mighty city which passed away when its rulers lost the power to make Zombies!

500,000 people, soulless but alive, piling mighty blocks of granite to build a city which passed away two thousand years ago!

Filmed in ancient Angkor... the world's mystic city... built by robots... in ruins because they lost the power to make Zombies... fascinating and passionate romance of today with the hidden mystic secrets of yesterday.

Mighty Angkor! Ancient land of mystery... Place of Zombies... Not dead — not alive — but touched by the finger of death... a fascinating romance.

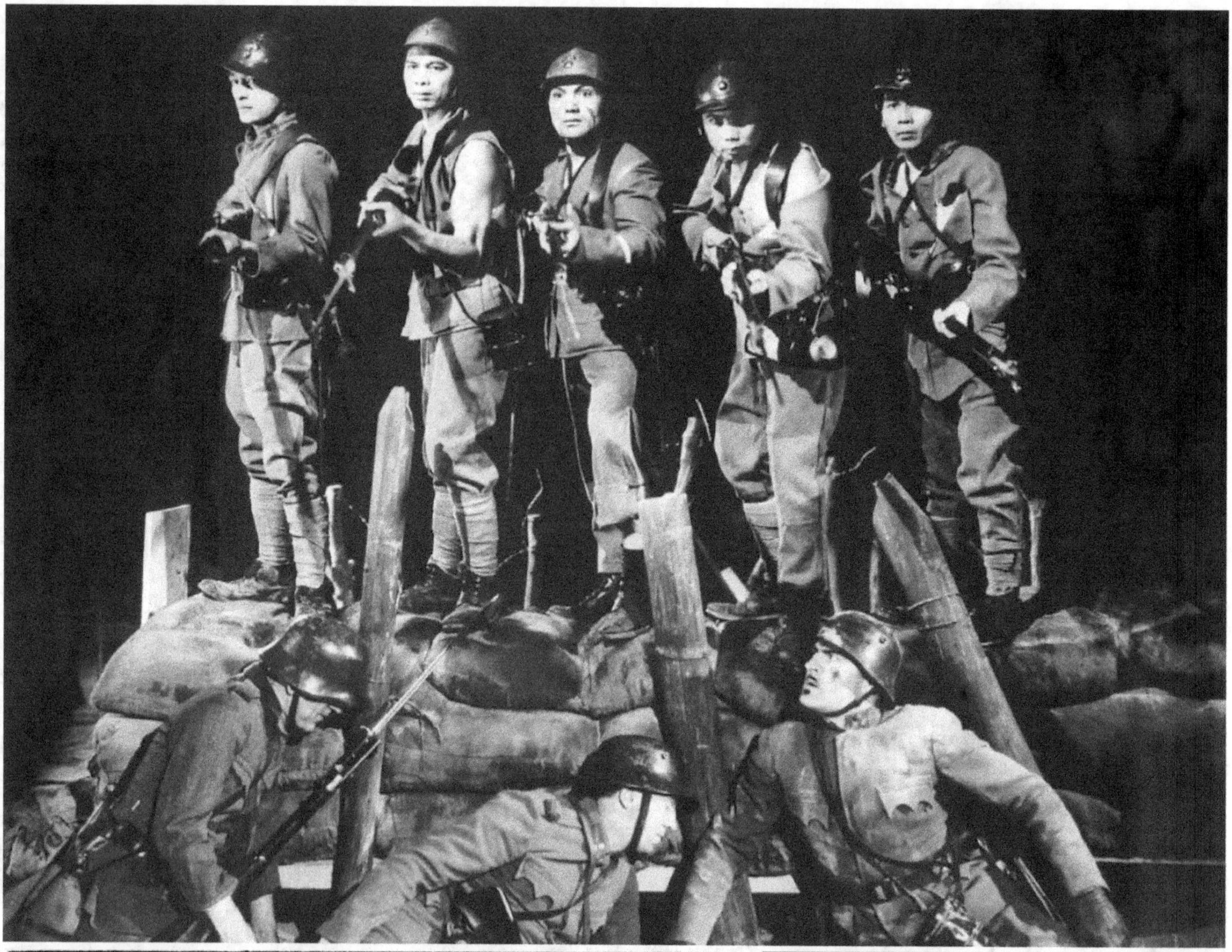

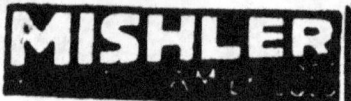

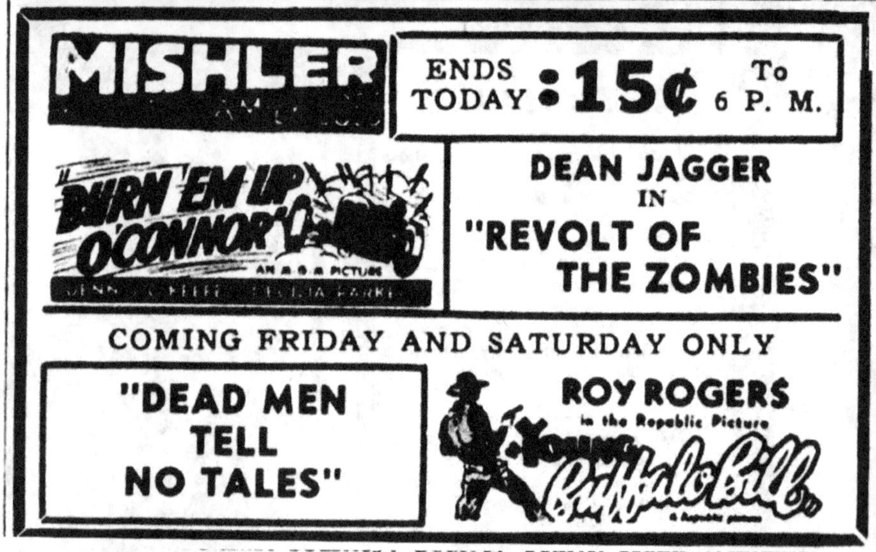
MISHLER
ENDS TODAY : 15¢ To 6 P. M.
"BURN 'EM UP O'CONNOR"
AN M-G-M PICTURE
DEAN JAGGER IN "REVOLT OF THE ZOMBIES"
COMING FRIDAY AND SATURDAY ONLY
"DEAD MEN TELL NO TALES"
ROY ROGERS in the Republic Picture
Young Buffalo Bill
A Republic picture

The Living Dead march again... TORTURING! TERRORIZING!
"REVOLT OF THE ZOMBIES"

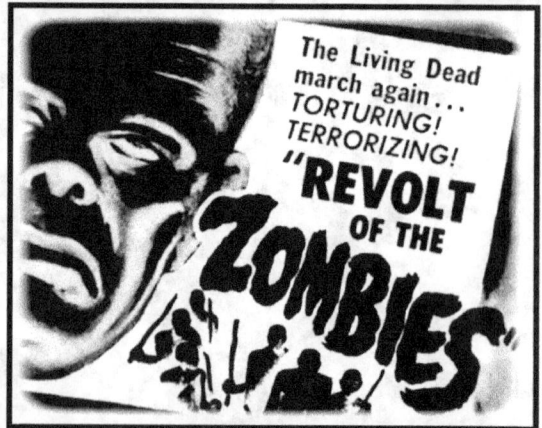

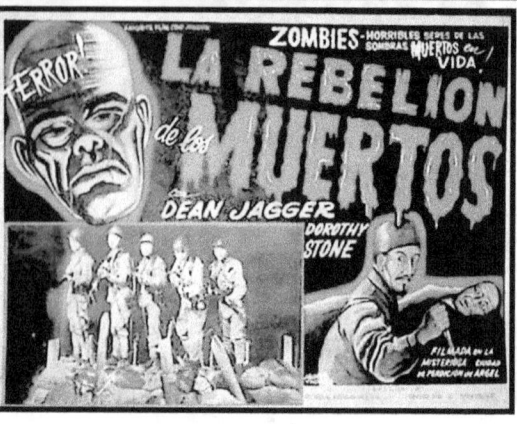

LOEW'S STATE—The Moon's Our Home: Margaret Sullavan, Henry Fonda.†
MUSIC HALL—The King Steps Out*; Private Number, opens Thursday.
PALACE—The Law in Her Hands and Sons o' Guns.†
PARAMOUNT—The Princess Comes Across: Carole Lombard, Fred MacMurray.
RIALTO—Revolt of the Zombies: Dorothy Stone.
RIVOLI—The Ex-Mrs. Bradford: William Powell, Jean Arthur*
ROXY—Little Miss Nobody: Jane Withers, Jane Darwell.
STRAND—Bullets or Ballots*; Hearts Divided, starts Friday.

ZOMBIES
TERROR!
LA REBELION de los MUERTOS
DEAN JAGGER
DOROTHY STONE

THE WEIRDEST STORY OF ALL TIME!

Camera Crew Sent To Mystic Cambodia

An entire camera crew was sent to Cambodia by the Halperin Brothers to secure interesting native material and records of the architectural splendor of lost Angkor to be used in the making of "Revolt of the Zombies," outstanding adventure attraction which is current at the ———— Theatre and which stars Dorothy Stone and Dean Jagger.

Army of Zombies To Conquer World?

"Find the secret of the zombies destroy it!—then we will have contributed our share toward the saving of civilization!"

This alarming note is sounded in "Revolt of the Zombies," Favorite Films Corporation production, coming to the ———— Theatre next ————, which is acclaimed as one of the most daringly different and unusual films to come out of Hollywood in many a year.

Zombies! Human beings turned into automatons! Men without souls! Hordes of supermen capable of annihilating armies of soldiers! Whoever had the power to make men like these, could destroy the world, and the fanatical oriental priest, attached to the Cambodian contingent of the French army, held the secret of the creation of zombies!

Imagine an army of robots, human beings turned into things of stone, their minds and bodies mysteriously controlled through mental telepathy, through some mystic power, charging through the enemies' lines, mowing down numbers of men, hit by rifle and machine gun bullets, yet they kept coming, piercing the enemies' lines; then as one man, they halted, grounded arms, and stood listening as though for the next command.

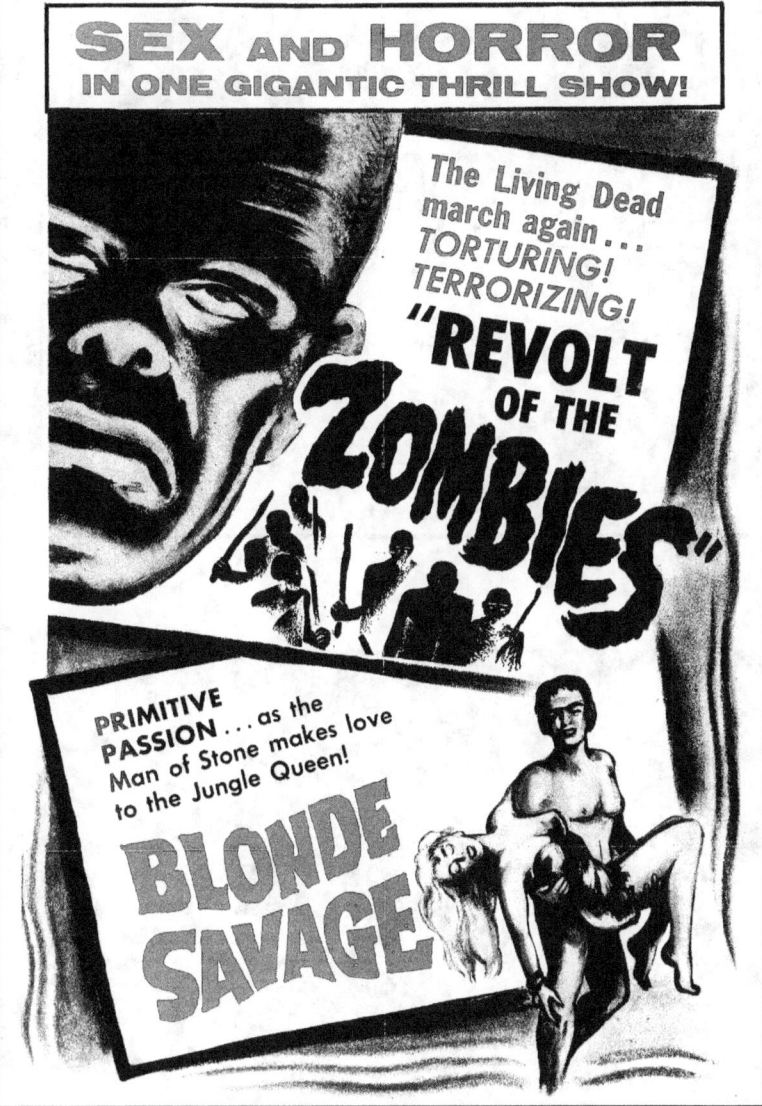

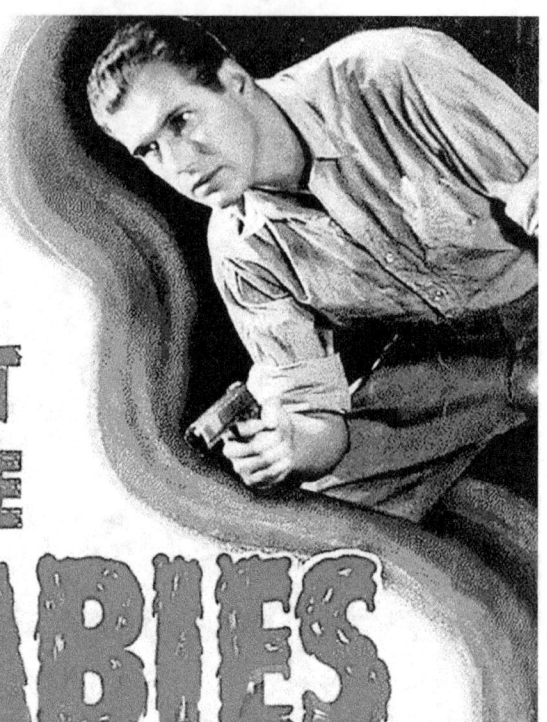

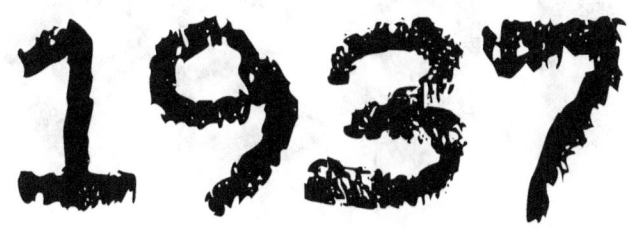

Genre films released in 1937
More mystery than horror!
(Will hopefully be covered in Vol. 2)
Night Must Fall
A Night of Terror
It's Never Too Late to Mend
The Thirteenth Chair
Sh! The Octopus

Genre films released in 1938
Again, more mystery than horror!!
(Will hopefully be covered in Vol. 2)

They Drive by Night
Charlie Chan in Honolulu
The Missing Guest
The Terror
The Black Doll

1939

Genre films released in 1939

Son of Frankenstein
The Gorilla (in Vol. 2)
The Man Who Changed His Mind (in Vol. 2)
Devil's Daughter (in Vol. 2)

Son of Frankenstein

Released U.S. Jan. 13, 1939

You've seen Frankenstein, Bride of Frankenstein, and now for horrible thrills we bring you "The Son of Frankenstein", with Basil Rathbone, Boris Karloff and Bela Lugosi. New weird characters in a new spine-chilling story. You will gasp in wonder at this half-man, half-demon monster. He looked... acted like a man... but the mania of the monster-maker... passing from father to son... raged in his mind. You might faint, so come with plenty of nerve when you come to see "Son of Frankenstein", Friday and Saturday at the Paramount.

—Friday-Saturday!—
BORIS KARLOFF   BASIL RATHBONE
Son Of Frankenstein

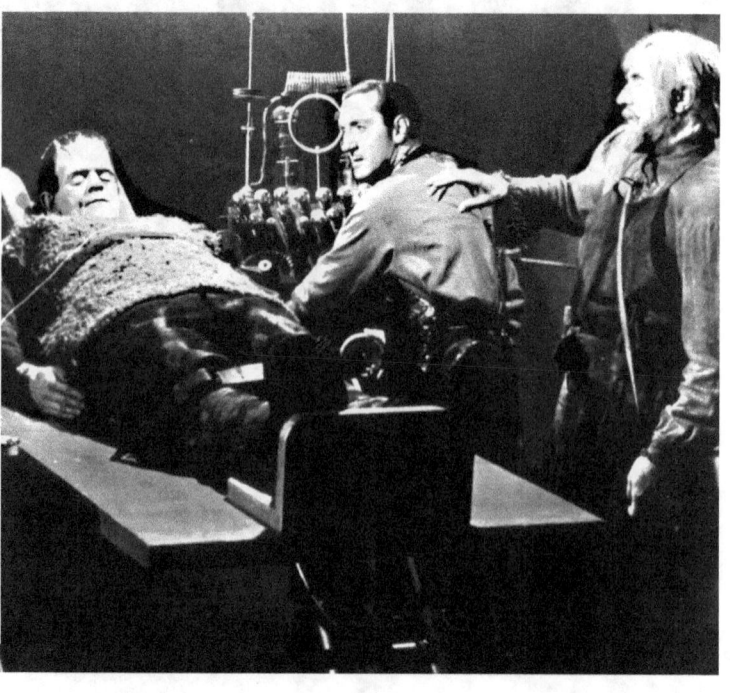

"Here's another thing. I read that the Egyptians used to bind some criminals hand and foot and bury them alive. When their blood turned to water after death, it flowed into their extremities, stretched their arms to gorilla length and swelled their hands, feet and faces to abnormal proportions. I thought this might make a nice touch for the monster, since he was supposed to be made from the corpses of executed felons. So I fixed Karloff up that way. Those lizard eyes of his are rubber, like his false head.

LINCOLN SUNDAY JOURNAL AND STAR, FEBRUARY 12, 1939.

D—SEVEN

Olivia De Haviland
George Brent
"WINGS of the NAVY"
Stuart

Boris Karloff
Bela Lugosi
"SON OF FRANKENSTEIN"
Lincoln

Carole Lombard
Jackie Taylor
James Stewart
"MADE FOR EACH OTHER"

George Brent
Kay Francis
"SECRETS OF AN ACTRESS"
Liberty

262

OH, YOU BEAUTIFUL MONSTER

MICHELANGELO had his "David," Auguste Rodin had his "Thinker" and Jack Pierce has profited by their example. He has his "Frankenstein Monster." If this be sculpture, Pierce is making the most of it. Using the unfortunate Boris Karloff again for a lay figure, he reconstructed the good gray monster for the third time in Universal's "The Son of Frankenstein," which is now showing at the Rivoli. And thereby hangs a tale, which is about the only thing Bela Lugosi does not wear in the picture.

Thirty years ago Jack Pierce was one of the best semi-pro shortstops in Chicago. Today he is one of Hollywood's ace makeup men. A gnarled little Nibelung gnome of a fellow, he is a perfect bit of type casting for his ten-year role of turning out ghouls, mummies, werewolves and vampires for the horror trade. The Frankenstein troll is his monsterpiece. Usually reticent about his black arts, Pierce, during the shooting of "The Son of Frankenstein," laid down his trowel and told for the first time how he constructs this popular, peripatetic cadaver. Pierce's technique is that of a surrealist sculptor. Out of a bucket of blue grease, a few bolts and rivets, a pair of asphalt spreader's boots, some black shoe polish and a suit of old clothes with two pairs of pants worn simultaneously he achieves his ghoul.

* * *

"If the monster looks like something I dreamt after something I ate, don't blame me," says Pierce. "Blame science! I made him the way textbooks said he should look. I didn't depend on imagination. In 1931, before I did a bit of designing I spent three months of research in anatomy, surgery, medicine, criminal history, criminology, ancient and modern burial customs and electrodynamics.

"My anatomical studies taught me that there are six ways a surgeon can cut the skull in order to take out or put in a brain. I figured that Frankenstein, who was a scientist but no practicing surgeon,

Billy Gilbert demonstrates the latest honking device for Franceska Gaal in "The Girl Downstairs," at the Criterion.

look longer by shortening the sleeves of his coat, stiffened his legs with two pairs of pants over steel struts and by means of asphalt-walker's boots gave him those Newfoundland dogs. I cover Karloff's face with blue-green greasepaint which photographs gray. I blacken his finger nails with shoe polish. It takes me four hours to build him up every morning and two hours to tear him down every night. I figure I've heaped some 5,400 pounds of makeup on him as the monster in the past seven years."

Bela Lugosi, not Karloff, was the lay figure originally intended to bear this white man's burden as the monster in 1931, following his success as "Dracula." He declined on the ground that he could not carry all that makeup in a hod, much less on his face. Now both men are in the same picture. Boris is the monster again. Bela, hitherto strictly a barefaced villain, is practically unrecognizable under a haystack wig, yak hair whiskers, a set of artificial fangs and an anatomically correct broken neck. Pierce smiles as he cites this instance of the futility of attempting to escape one's destiny in the hands of the makeup man.

Pierce's own career is a similar instance. He came to California from Chicago's fast Logan Square team to break into Coast League baseball, not into the movies, in 1908. He was good, but too light for that company, so he took a projectionist's job in a nickelodeon, later managed theatres for Harry Culver, founder of Culver City, then began making pictures with Young Deer, famous redskin producer for the K. B., independent outfit, and in 1914 joined Universal as actor and assistant camera man. He did makeup work for Jackie Coogan and Jesse Lasky and achieved his first grotesque transformation for Fox, making a monkey out of Jacques Lerner in "The Monkey Talks." That year, 1926, he rejoined Universal and since then has used his small muscular fingers (the right index and pinky fingers badly bent by baseball bumps) exclusively to make the human face more horrible and, in the case of feminine stars, more beautiful than nature ever intended.

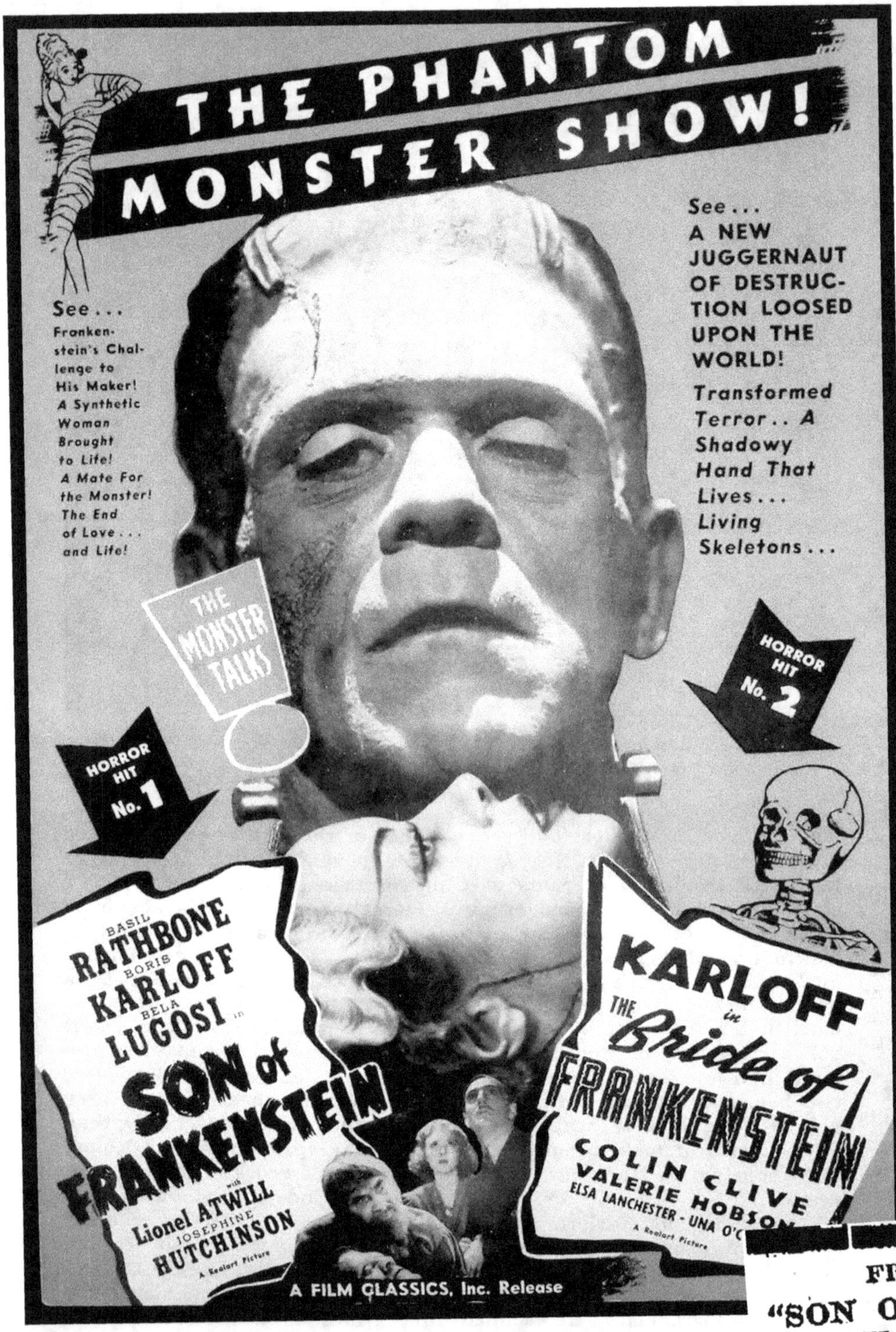
THE PHANTOM
MONSTER SHOW!
See . . .
Franken-
stein's Chal-
lenge to
His Maker!
A Synthetic
Woman
Brought
to Life!
A Mate For
the Monster!
The End
of Love . . .
and Life!
See . . .
A NEW
JUGGERNAUT
OF DESTRUC-
TION LOOSED
UPON THE
WORLD!
Transformed
Terror . . A
Shadowy
Hand That
Lives . . .
Living
Skeletons . . .
THE MONSTER TALKS
HORROR HIT No. 1
HORROR HIT No. 2
BASIL RATHBONE
BORIS KARLOFF
BELA LUGOSI in
SON of FRANKENSTEIN
with Lionel ATWILL
JOSEPHINE HUTCHINSON
A Realart Picture
KARLOFF in
THE Bride of FRANKENSTEIN
COLIN CLIVE
VALERIE HOBSON
ELSA LANCHESTER - UNA O'C
A Realart Picture
A FILM CLASSICS, Inc. Release

NOW - - - -
Can You Take It? . .
It's Spine-Chilling!
Weird! Horrific!
With the
Greatest
Fear
Figures
in
Screen
History!
BASIL
RATHBONE
BORIS
KARLOFF
Bela LUGOSI
IN
"SON OF
FRANKENSTEIN"
WITH
Lionel ATWILL
JOSEPHINE
HUTCHINSON
A UNIVERSAL PICTURE
PLUS!
It's Howlarious!
Franchot Tone
Franciska Gaal
IN
THE GIRL
Downstairs
Always a
Seat for
25c
LINCOLN
Lincoln's Greatest Show Value

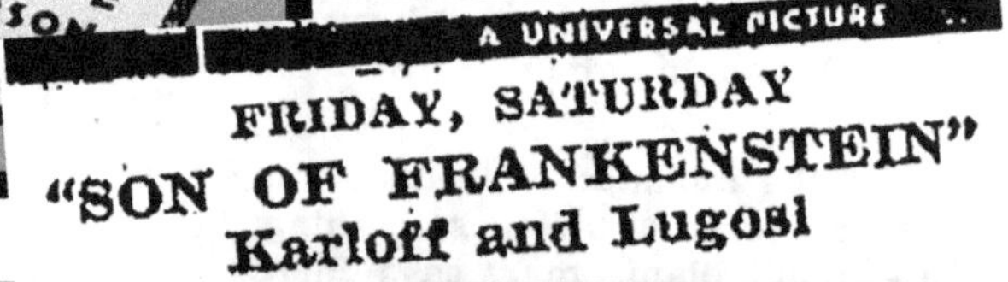
A UNIVERSAL PICTURE
FRIDAY, SATURDAY
"SON OF FRANKENSTEIN"
Karloff and Lugosi

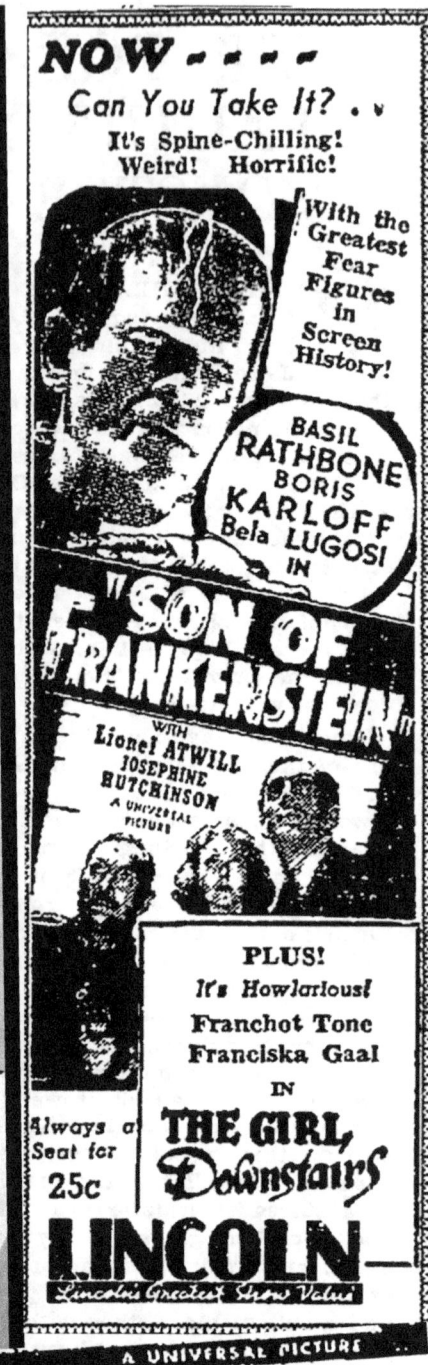

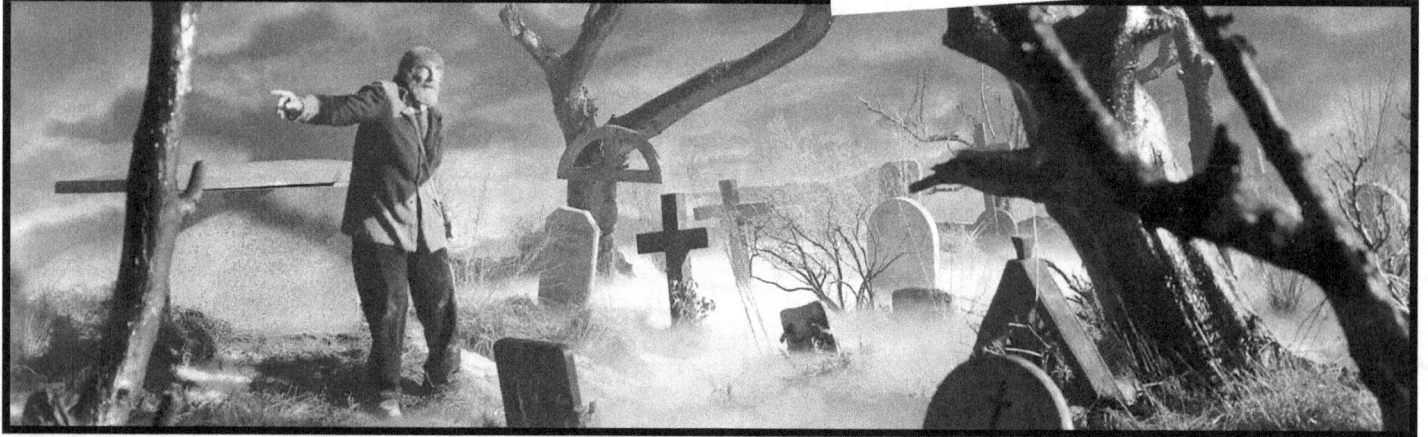

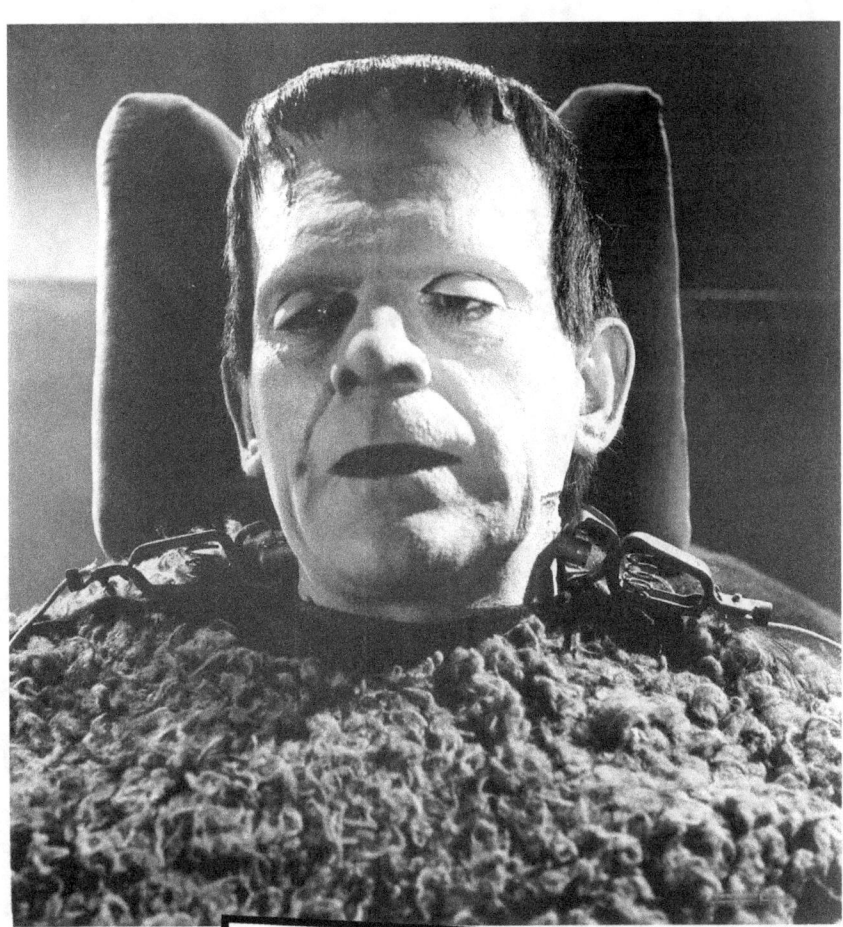

Deleted Scene!

THRILLER BEING OFFERED ON SCREEN AT SIGMA SATURDAY

"The Son Of Frankenstein" Has Great Cast; Gable And Shearer Starring In Hit Production At Ohio

Boris Karloff recreates the monster role which he first portrayed in "Frankenstein" in the new Sigma offering, "The Son of Frankenstein" which starts Saturday. Basil Rathbone is cast as the son of "Frankenstein" who carries on the work of his father who created the monster. Bela Lugosi of "Dracula" fame assumes another of his harrowing roles.

FRANKENSTEIN AT TIVOLI TODAY

Should a scientist who first creates human life be reviled as "playing with fire," or should he be acclaimed even though the result of his experiment proves a monstrous killer?

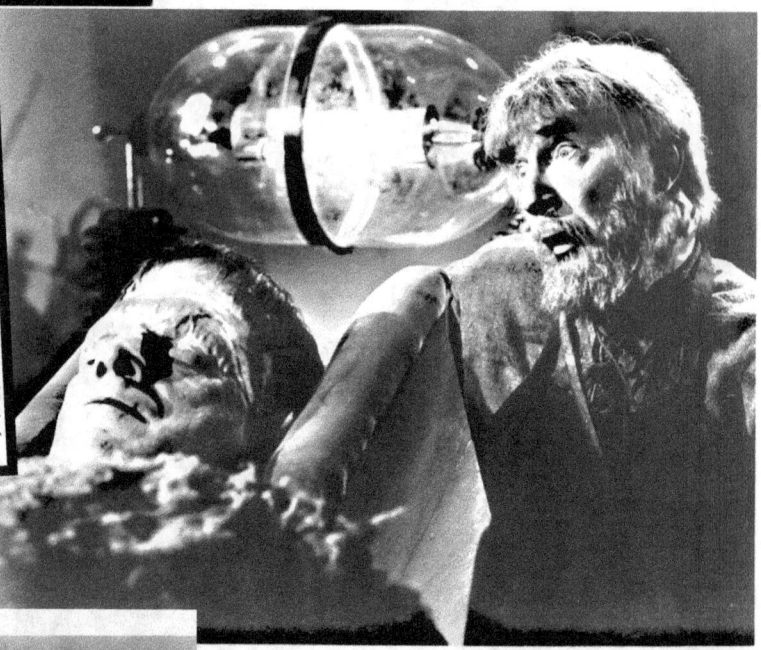

EASTWOOD
TONIGHT & TUESDAY
BIG HALLOWEEN PROGRAM!!!
"SON OF FRANKENSTEIN"
with KARLOFF & BELA LUGOSI
— Feature No. 2 —
"ICE FOLLIES OF 1939"
with JAMES STEWART
JOAN CRAWFORD
FREE PARKING

Creator of the haunting "Lights Out" radio show, Willis Cooper, supplied the screenplay for the streamlined shocker, "Son of Frankenstein," which presents Rathbone as heir to the Frankenstein life-creating experiments. Baron Wolf von Frankenstein brings the monster back to life, unwittingly paving the way for new and horrible murders and placing even his own wife and baby son in peril.

Lionel Atwill, Josephin Hutchinson, Emma Dunn and Donnie Dunagan have other roles in the picture, which was produced and directed by Rowland V. Lee.

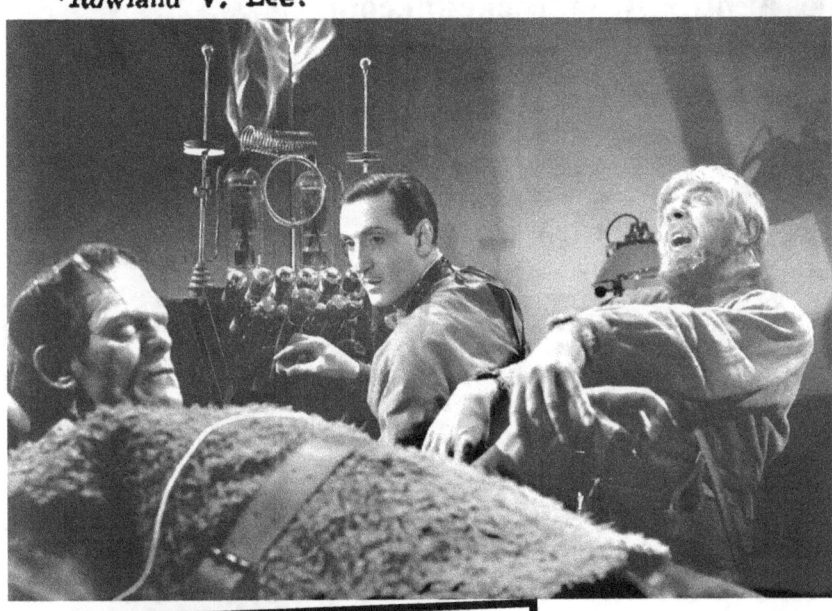

HORROR FILM IS BOOKED AT STATE

'Son of Frankenstein' to Play Four Days Beginning Monday.

You can research old movies for yourself at

NY Times: Times Machine at www.nytimes.com
Newspaper Archives at newspaperarchives.com
Variety at Variety.com

They do charge a yearly fee, although the NY Times Machine is free to subscribers.

For models and model kits some of the largest vendors are:
Monsters in Motion at https://www.monstersinmotion.com
Rocketfin Hobbies at http://www.rocketfin.com
Sideshow at https://www.sideshowtoy.com
ebay.com
amazon.com

Rare and B- (and Z-) movie titles
Alpha/Oldies at http://www.oldies.com or phone 1-800-336-4627
Sinister Cinema at http://www.sinistercinema.com or phone 1-541-773-6860

For a catalog of Midnight Marquee titles
visit our website at www.midmar.com
or send $2 for a catalog
(sorry it's not free, postage is killing us.)
Midnight Marquee Press, Inc.
9721 Baltimore, MD 21234
410-665-1198

www.ingramcontent.com/pod-product-compliance
Lightning Source LLC
Chambersburg PA
CBHW081718100526

44591CB00016B/2423